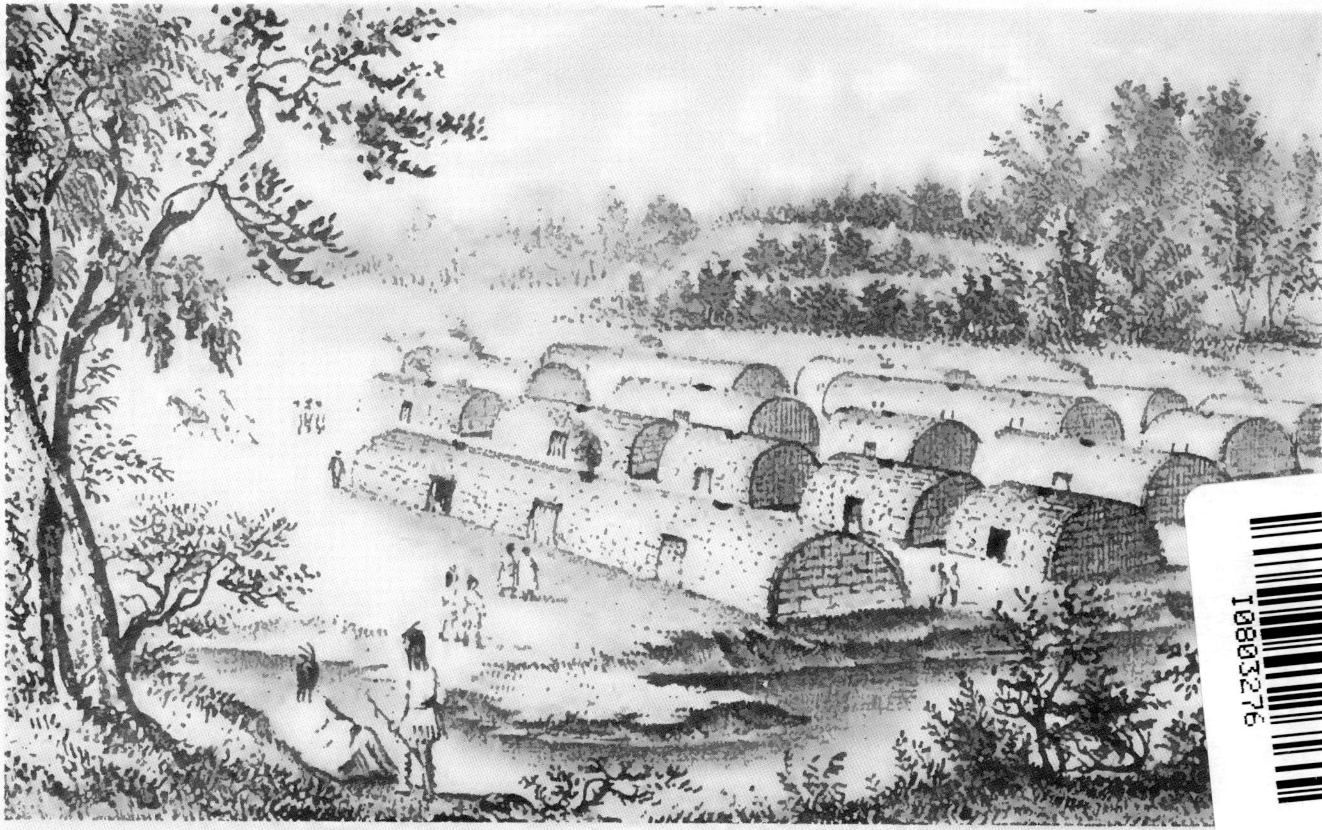

An Indian village on Manhattan Island. From an old print in Valentine's Manual for 1858.

Marula

An imprint of Arcadia Publishing

A Landmark History of New York
by Albert Ulmann

A Marula Historical Reprint
Originally published in 1901

Published by Arcadia Publishing
Charleston SC

ISBN 978-0-7385-9467-5

Printed in the United States of America

For all general information contact Arcadia Publishing at:
Telephone 843-853-2070
Fax 843-853-0044
E-mail sales@arcadiapublishing.com
For customer service and orders:
Toll-Free 1-888-313-2665

Visit us on the Internet at www.arcadiapublishing.com

A LANDMARK HISTORY OF NEW YORK

ALSO THE ORIGIN OF STREET NAMES AND A BIBLIOGRAPHY

BY

ALBERT ULMANN

MEMBER OF THE AMERICAN HISTORICAL SOCIETY

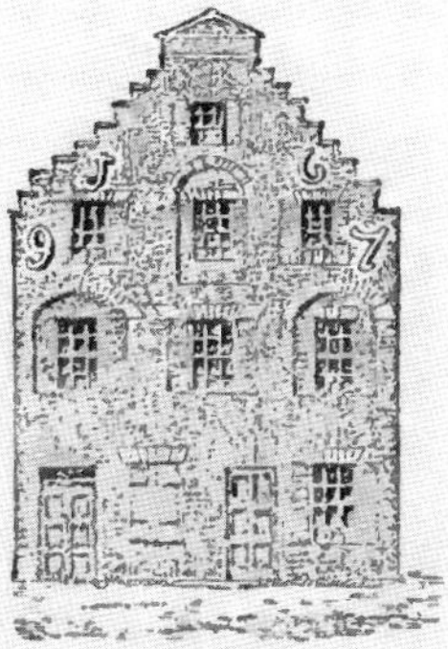

NEW YORK
D. APPLETON AND COMPANY
1901

PREFACE

In a city like New York, governed by a spirit of tearing down and rebuilding at short intervals of time, it is not surprising that landmarks have been destroyed and that old places have been in danger of losing their historical associations. Fortunately, of late, through the worthy efforts of certain patriotic societies, many of the more important historic sites have been determined and marked by suitably inscribed tablets. These memorials serve the double purpose of awakening attention and of investing with an air of reality the events they perpetuate. They are, however, but isolated mementos, bearing a suggestive phrase or two that have a meaning only to the student who has delved into the city's past. To make clear the full significance of these tablet-marked sites, to visit them in their chronological order, together with other landmarks worthy of consideration, and to weave around these relics and reminders of other days an interesting, graphic, and precise story, has been the object of this little work.

In order to lend additional value to the book and to emphasize how much the welfare and the progress of the city depend upon the efforts, the civic love, and the civic pride of the citizen, special pains have been taken to introduce as much information as space would permit, of the characteristics and the careers of those individuals that have figured prominently and worthily in the development, from a little Dutch town, of our great metropolis.

While the plan has been particularly to interest the young, it is believed that the careful reproduction of inscriptions, the exact location of historic sites, the explanation of the origin of street names, and the addition of a comprehensive bibliography and list of references, can not fail to prove of interest to the teacher and to the student of history.

For their generous assistance in this undertaking, thanks are due to Mr. Hugh Hastings, State Historian, at Albany; to Mr. Robert H. Kelby, Librarian of the New York Historical Society; to Henry P. Johnston, Professor of History at the College of the City of New York; to the librarians of the Mercantile, Astor, and Lenox Libraries; to Dr. Frank B. Kelley, of the City History Club; to Dr. Henry S. Leipziger; to the Holland Society; and to the Society of the Sons of the Revolution.

A. U.

NEW YORK, *January, 1901.*

LIST OF ILLUSTRATIONS

PAGE
An Indian village on Manhattan Island . . *Frontispiece*
Stuyvesant's town house, erected in 1658 15
First City Hall. Erected 1642, taken down in 1700 . . . 17
View of the Wall and Water Gate, at the foot of Wall Street . 18
Broad Street, 1659 20
Peter Stuyvesant 24
Stuyvesant's country house 26
Peter Stuyvesant's tombstone, St. Mark's church 28
Milestone on Kingsbridge road 31
Stuyvesant's pear tree 33
Map of New York in 1642 35
The earliest view taken of New Amsterdam 37
Section of Jewish cemetery established during Stuyvesant's time. 39
New York in 1664 43
New York as it appeared about the year 1667 45
The city's seal 47
New York in 1695 53
Map of New York in 1728 66
View of the fort about the year 1750 70
New York Historical Society 76
Site of Fort Amsterdam, directly south of Bowling Green . . 79
Marinus Willett tablet, corner Broad and Beaver Streets . . 94
Tearing down the statue of George III on Bowling Green . . 99
The old Post Office, originally the Middle Dutch church . . 101
Harlem Heights battlefield looking north from One Hundred and Sixteenth Street, west of Broadway 116
Statue of Nathan Hale in City Hall Park 119
Tablet to commemorate the battle of Harlem Heights . . . 121
Library, Columbia University 122
Point of Rocks, One Hundred and Twenty-seventh Street and Convent Avenue 125
The Grange, as it appeared in Hamilton's time 126
The thirteen trees planted by Alexander Hamilton at One Hundred and Forty-third Street, east of Amsterdam Avenue . 127

PAGE

The Jumel Mansion 131
Rhinelander sugar house, prison during the Revolutionary War . 136
The old prison ship Jersey 138
Washington's house in Cherry Street 149
Wall Street in 1789, showing Federal Hall 151
Tammany Hall, 1830; present site of the New York Sun Building. 155
View of old buildings on William Street in 1800 159
Statue of Alexander Hamilton in Central Park 161
Collect Pond, 1800 164
First boat propelled by steam 166
Cooper Union and Peter Cooper's statue 171
New York Free School No. 2, Chatham Street, 1808 173
Modern schoolhouse, West End Avenue and Eighty-second Street 174
New Hall of the Board of Education 175
Map of McGowan's Pass and Forts Fish and Clinton 177
Fortifications at McGowan's Pass, 1814 179
Site of Fort Clinton in Central Park 181
Blockhouse, One Hundred and Twenty-third Street 183
Canal boat village, Coenties Slip 185
View of St. Paul's church and the Broadway stages, 1831 . . 188
Departure of the Seventh Regiment 199
Grant's tomb, Riverside Drive 201
Astor Place Riot, 1849 204
Style of engine used in 1812 206
Scene at a fire, 1800 207
Theological Seminary, Twentieth Street and Ninth Avenue . 213
A glimpse of Hudson Park, Leroy and Hudson Streets . . . 216
St. John's chapel, Varick Street 220
Montgomery's tomb, St. Paul's church 224
Trinity church 226
Hamilton's tomb 227
Trinity churchyard 228
Bowling Green, 1830 234
Old mansion in State Street 236
Statue of Liberty 238
Fraunces's Tavern 240
Statue of Washington, Subtreasury Building 243
Statue of Washington, Eighty-ninth Street and Riverside Drive. 245
Washington Arch 248
Columbus Column, Fifty-ninth Street and Eighth Avenue . . 250
City Hall and Printing House Square 254

It is only fair to say that the red men met the whites in a friendly spirit. They greeted Hudson with every sign of welcome and brought him food, for which he gave them axes, knives, shoes, and stockings. Not knowing the purposes of these articles, they surprised Hudson by hanging the axes and shoes around their necks as ornaments, and used the stockings as tobacco pouches. It was only when the whites injured them that the Indians turned against the Dutch. The Indians were exceedingly revengeful—revenge was a part of their religion—and they never rested until they had shed blood to atone for that of any relative that had been killed."

"Christopher Street!" shouted the guard.

"We are now in old Greenwich village," said the professor.

"Where is it?" asked Tom in his impulsive way, looking out of the window, as if he expected to see some of the ancient farmhouses.

"The village has long ago disappeared," explained the professor; "in fact, excepting the neighborhood of the Battery, this is probably the oldest settlement of white men on the island of New York. Originally, it was an Indian village called *Sappokanican*, and Indian huts stood near the shore where you can see the red funnels of that French steamer. A little stream, called Manetta Creek, emptied into the river near by, and though it can no longer be seen, it still flows through its ancient channel underground. It rises somewhere east of Fifth Avenue near Twentieth Street, touches Union Square, and then turns westward. Builders putting up new buildings discover, to their cost, that the old stream is still there, as it means expensive pile driving. I shall tell you more of Greenwich village at the proper time; meanwhile we are traveling along the old Greenwich road, which was one of the principal and most popular roads of colonial New York."

"How is it that the streets in these parts are so mixed up?" asked George.

"We shall get to that later," responded the professor. "It will be necessary, in order to avoid confusion, to take one period at a time. First, we shall inspect the old Dutch town, passing over a number of English landmarks that belong to a later period. In this way we shall follow the historical order of events, even if we have to pay a second visit to some of the localities. I suppose you have noticed that Manhattan Island is like a long stocking, having its toes at the Battery and its heel at the eastern terminus of Grand Street. It was at the toe end that the earliest settlement was located."

"Rector Street!" called out the guard.

"Ah, here we are in the old Dutch town at last," said the professor, rising and leading the way out.

As we passed up Rector Street toward Broadway, Tom, who had been casting disapproving glances around him, remarked: "Why did the Dutch have such narrow streets?"

"They never thought that their little lanes would some day become the thoroughfares of a great metropolis. In their time such a street as this was nothing more than a country pathway, and the old Dutch burghers found it wide enough. The wonder is that, as the city grew, no attempt was ever made to improve the old paths."

"Hello," said Tom suddenly, "here's a graveyard. I never knew they buried people downtown."

"That's Trinity," said the professor. "The churchyard is over two hundred years old, but it belongs to the English period, and so we shall pass it for the present."

"I wonder what the Dutch would say if they were to come back now and see these high houses," remarked George as he raised his eyes to the top of the American Surety building, three hundred and six feet above the ground and twenty-two feet above the top of Trinity steeple.

No one attempted to solve this problem, and so we turned into Broadway, walking down the west side.

"I don't see," remarked Tom, "why they ever called this *Broad*way."

"Others have made the same comment," said the professor. "At first it was nothing more than an Indian trail, running along the ridge of a hill that formed the backbone of the island. The original settlers did not consider it a choice locality, preferring Pearl and Broad Streets, as we shall presently learn. In fact, for some years the houses, especially on the east side, were little better than hovels, consisting of a single room with a fireplace. But here we have Tablet No 1."

Pointing to a bronze plate near the downtown edge of Aldrich Court, 41 Broadway, the professor asked George to read the legend. George thereupon read the inscription, which was as follows:

> THIS TABLET MARKS THE SITE OF THE
> FIRST HABITATIONS OF WHITE MEN
> ON THE ISLAND OF MANHATTAN.
> ADRIAN BLOCK
> COMMANDER OF THE TIGER
> ERECTED HERE FOUR HOUSES OR HUTS
> NOVEMBER 1613.
> HE BUILT THE RESTLESS THE FIRST VESSEL
> MADE BY EUROPEANS IN THIS COUNTRY.
> THE RESTLESS WAS LAUNCHED
> IN THE SPRING OF 1614.
> THIS TABLET IS PLACED HERE BY
> THE HOLLAND SOCIETY OF NEW YORK
> SEPTEMBER 1890.

"What's the Holland Society?" queried Tom.

"It is an association," answered the professor, "of descendants of those who can trace their ancestry back, through the male line, to the colonists from Holland prior to 1675. That little text," continued the professor, referring to the tablet, "furnishes us with a good starting point, and will give us a clew to the manner in which the first attempt at anything like a settlement was made. I have already told you that the first vessel to reach Manhattan after the Half Moon, was fitted up by private individuals. Its voyage proving a success, other merchants followed the example of the pioneers, and in this way the fur trade was fairly established. One of the pioneers in this traffic was Adrian Block, whose name appears there on the tablet. His vessel, the Tiger, took fire just as he was about to sail for home. Nothing daunted, he set about building a new ship, aided by the Indians, who helped him drag trees to the shore, and supplied him with food. While engaged in constructing the first boat ever launched in the waters of Manhattan, he erected the houses or huts to which reference is made. Block was thus the first *house* as well as *boat* builder in this vicinity."

"Was the Restless a good boat?" asked George.

"Oh, yes. Block sailed it up through the East River into the Sound and discovered Block Island, which still bears his name."

"Why is it called the East River?" queried Tom.

"Because," said the professor, "the current from the *heel* of the stocking to the *toe*—that is, the section first settled by the Dutch—flows east and west. North River was so called to distinguish it from the South or Delaware River, where the Dutch had also planted a colony. Now, let us go down to Bowling Green."

A short walk brought us to this miniature park.

"Let us pass right through," said our guide, "ignore the statue, and examine yonder tablet on the Cunard Company's building." *

---

* This and the neighboring buildings have recently been removed to make room for the new Customhouse, to which, no doubt, the tablet will be affixed.

We crossed the street, mounted the stoop, and George read the inscription which is here copied:

THE SITE OF FORT AMSTERDAM BUILT IN 1626. WITHIN THE FORTIFICATIONS WAS ERECTED THE FIRST SUBSTANTIAL CHURCH EDIFICE ON THE ISLAND OF MANHATTAN. IN 1787 THE FORT WAS DEMOLISHED AND THE GOVERNMENT HOUSE BUILT UPON THIS SITE. THIS TABLET IS PLACED HERE BY THE HOLLAND SOCIETY OF NEW YORK. SEPTEMBER, 1890.

"You will notice that this date is thirteen years later than that of Tablet No. 1. Some very important events took place during this period. At first no attempt was made to establish a colony—that is, to have people come over and make their homes here, but soon the English began to lay claim to the territory, asserting that, owing to the discoveries of Cabot, they had a right to the whole coast. The Dutch quickly saw that to hold their possessions they would have to found a permanent settlement on Manhattan Island, whereupon, in 1624, a number of families crossed the ocean, followed shortly after by a director general, whose name you no doubt remember, George."

"I think it was Minuit."

"Quite right; Peter Minuit. He began his administration by purchasing the island. The Indian chiefs met him, probably in this neighborhood, under some spreading trees, and concluded the bargain. As they looked with contempt on European money, considering it worth nothing, they accepted a quantity of beads and other showy trifles, amounting to twenty-four dollars. For this they gave up all title to Manhattan Island, containing some twenty-two thousand acres. This was the first real estate transaction in the history of New York. Have you any idea what its real estate is worth to-day?"

As none of us could answer this question, the professor informed us that the latest valuation fixed by the tax commissioners was over two thousand three hundred millions of dollars.

"Having now become lawful owners of the land, the settlers made plans to provide for their personal safety. A fort was at once staked out, consisting of a blockhouse surrounded by cedar palisades and called Fort Amsterdam. This rude structure did not last long, and a few years later a larger fort was erected, three hundred feet in length by two hundred and fifty in breadth, consisting of stone and earth. One side of it covered the ground where these six steamship buildings now stand. Inside, three windmills, a guardhouse and barracks, a stone church, and a house for the director were set up. Above them all waved the Dutch flag."

"What was it like?" asked Emily.

"Red, white, and blue, in horizontal stripes, thus

curiously supplying Manhattan with a red, white, and blue ensign two hundred and fifty years ago.

"The settlement," continued the professor, "comprising about thirty simple huts, was strung along the shore of the East River, close to the fort. Every settler had his own house, kept his cows, tilled his land, or traded with the natives—no one was idle. Opposite the fort a space was kept open, and there it is to-day," added our guide, pointing to the Bowling Green through which we had just passed. "It was the heart of the old Dutch town. There the children played, there the youths and maidens danced around the May pole, there the soldiers paraded, and on Sundays the country wagons were gathered while the people were at church. There, too, after a bloody war with the Indians, a great assembly of chiefs took place, the pipe of peace was smoked, and the tomahawk buried as a sign of peace. Later on it was used as a market place and for an annual cattle show. Still later, during the English period, it was the scene of many stirring events of which we shall learn at the proper time."

"Let's go over again and look at it," suggested Tom.

"Not now," said the professor; "I want to take you next to the oldest street of the old city."

Following our guide, we turned into State Street and walked southward, having on our right hand Battery Park.

"Looks just like a part of Central Park," remarked Tom, "only the water, and the ships, and the Statue of Liberty are more interesting."

"All but the little corner right opposite us," said the professor, "was originally under water. A number of rocks jutted out here and there, and not until the city was about seventy-five years old were they covered over and a battery of guns put in place. But here we are at Pearl Street."

"Is Pearl Street the oldest street in the city?" asked Emily.

"Yes," answered the professor; "it is the oldest and twists about more than any other."

"Why was it called Pearl Street?" queried Tom.

"Because of the quantity of pearly shells found there. The city, you know, was considerably narrower in the old days, Pearl Street being right at the water front."

"And why is it so twisted?" asked George.

"Perhaps it wound round the foot of a hill. This will explain the existence of other crooked streets. The hills are gone, but to this day we keep walking around them. Then, too, it must be remembered that the original town grew up in a haphazard sort of a way. People placed their houses where they pleased at first, and so when it came to the laying out of roads the latter were more likely to be crooked than straight. You must try to imagine," continued the professor, as we turned the corner into Pearl Street, "that instead of those buildings opposite, you have the line of the shore before you, and here, on this side, a straggling row of quaint Dutch houses with their gable ends toward the road, topped with crowstep roofs."

"Why were the roofs made that way?"

"To enable the chimney sweeps to climb up easily and reach the chimneys from the outside."

A short walk brought us to Whitehall Street.

"In the old days," said the professor, pointing toward the river, "you could have seen there a white

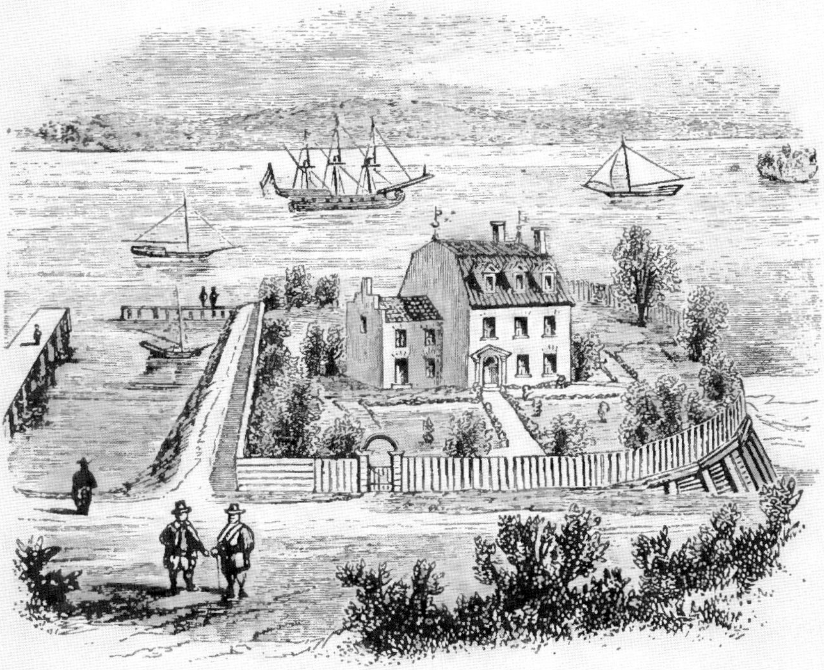

Stuyvesant's town house, erected in 1658. Afterward called the White Hall. From an old print in Valentine's Manual for 1862.

residence of no mean appearance, surrounded by a garden and stately trees. This was Stuyvesant's official town house, known as the 'White Hall' which has left its name to the street it used to adorn."

"Here's another tablet," said Tom, looking up at No. 73 Pearl Street.

George being now recognized as the official reader, at once began to decipher the inscription, but not without difficulty, as it is high up.

THE SITE OF THE
FIRST DUTCH HOUSE OF ENTERTAINMENT
ON THE ISLAND OF MANHATTAN.
LATER THE SITE OF THE OLD "STADT HUYS"
OR CITY HALL.
THIS TABLET IS PLACED HERE BY
THE HOLLAND SOCIETY OF NEW YORK.
SEPTEMBER 1890.

"This," said the professor, "is one of the most interesting sites of New Amsterdam. As the fort was the center of military life this was the center of all the great political discussions. Originally, as you see, it was a tavern to entertain traders and visitors who stopped on their way from New England to Virginia. Being five stories high it could be seen from the decks of ships a long distance off. Later on it was turned into the City Hall and Stuyvesant and his council took possession, the council listening and Stuyvesant laying down the law. He regulated everything, from fixing the taxes to the hour when people ought to go to bed. Here, in 1653, the official announcement was made that converted the settlement into a city with a court of burgomasters and *schepens*, and an officer called a *schout*, who was a mayor, a sheriff, a district attorney, and a chief of police all in one."

"He must have been the most important man in the town," remarked Tom.

"Oh, no," answered the professor, "Stuyvesant was still supreme. It was intended, you must know, that all these officers should be *elected*, but Stuy-

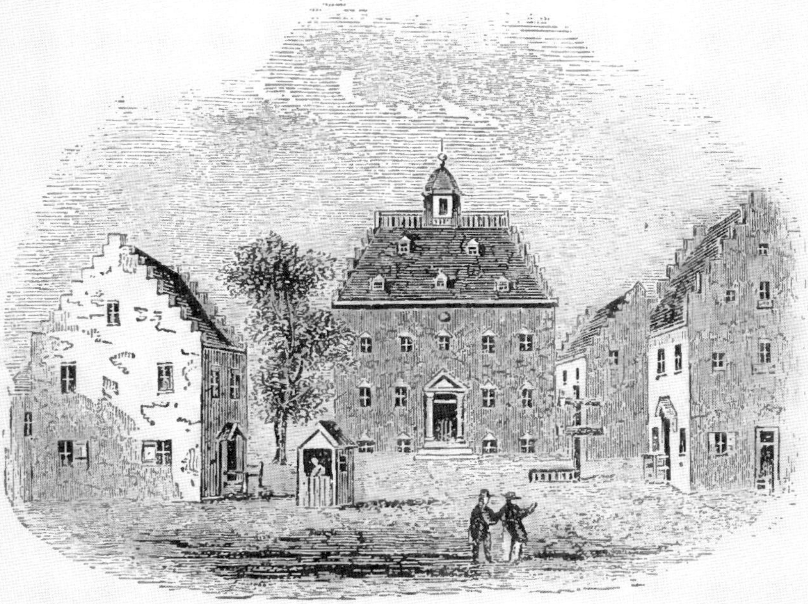

First City Hall. Erected 1642, taken down in 1700. From an old print in Valentine's Manual for 1852.

vesant thought this altogether too much responsibility to rest on the people. So he took the burden on his own shoulders and *appointed* whom he pleased."

Continuing along Pearl Street we soon reached Wall Street.

"We have now practically walked around the old

town," remarked the professor, "as from this point over to the North River there was a wooden wall.

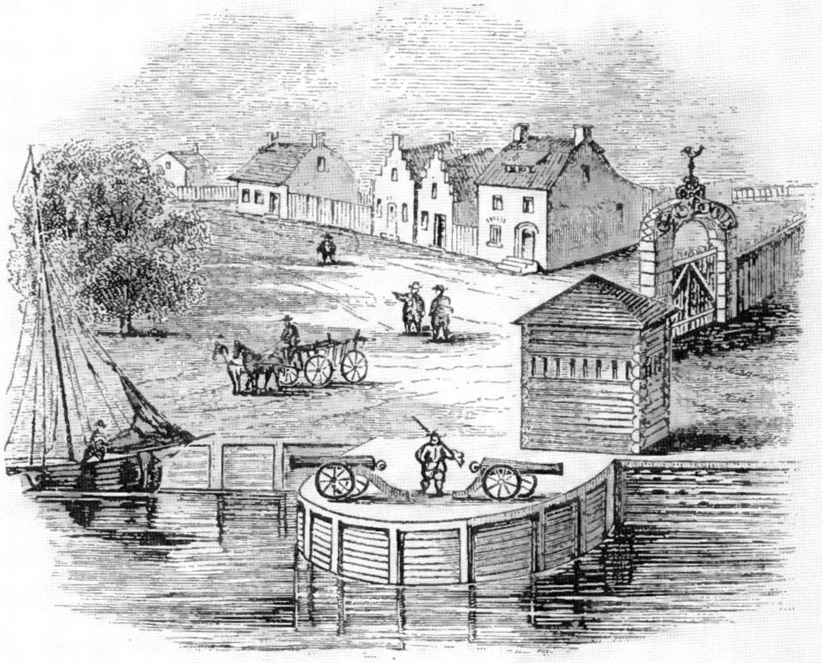

View of the Wall and Water Gate, at the foot of Wall Street. From an old print in Valentine's Manual for 1862.

Right here there was a gate, called the Water Gate; at Broadway there was another, called the Land Gate. A little battery extended into the river near this spot, guarded by a Dutch soldier.

"Why did they have a wall?" asked George.

"In 1653 news came of a threatened invasion of New Englanders. They were considered a slippery and pushing people, and regarded with a mixture of contempt and fear. Great excitement followed, the fort was repaired, a night watch established, and a resolution passed to build a wall. The New Englanders never came, but the wall was erected and it did more harm than good, as for nearly half a century it kept the town from growing beyond this unnecessary barrier.

"Let us now go back," suggested the professor, "and take a look at Stone Street, which has an interesting history."

"Hello, there isn't room even for the lamp posts," remarked Tom, pointing to a lamp bracketed to the side of a building.

"This was the first street to be paved," said the professor, "and it owed this honor to the energy of a woman. Among the earliest colonists were the Van Cortlandts. They lived in this road, Herr Van Cortlandt having a brewery near by. The wife, like all true Hollanders, abhorred dust and dirt, and complained over and over again that she could not keep her house clean because of the condition of the road. She protested so persistently that at length the authorities, to quiet her, put down a rough stone pavement. This was regarded as a wonderful piece of work, and people came from all parts to look at it, calling it, in joke, the *stone* street, which name has ever since clung to it."

The professor had just finished his story, when Tom, using his favorite expression, exclaimed, "Hello, here is a real big, broad street once more."

"Quite right," said the professor, "it is Broad Street. In the old days it was the most picturesque and truly Dutch thoroughfare of the town. The water entered here from the river and formed a ditch which the burghers turned into a water street with bridges and a walk along the banks. This reminded them of similar streets in their beloved Amsterdam, and it became their favorite promenade. Here they built some of their best houses, with wide stoops and benches, where the whole family could sit during the

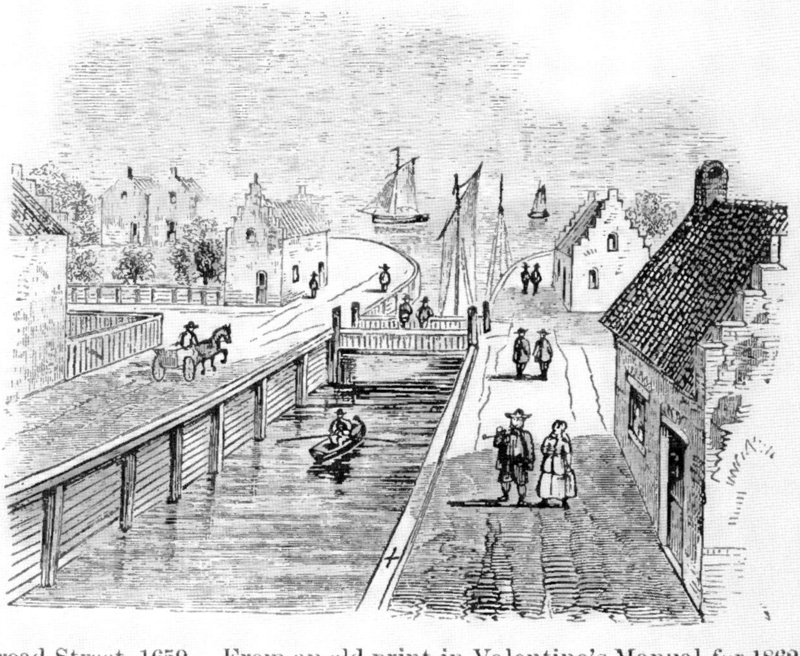

Broad Street, 1659. From an old print in Valentine's Manual for 1862.

pleasant summer evenings, the father smoking his long pipe, the mother knitting, as long as the light would permit, and the children romping about. The neighbor or friend who happened to come along was invited to sit down and discuss some topic of the day, such as Stuyvesant's quarrels with the burgomasters, or the likelihood of trouble with the Indians.

"Just below us," continued the professor, "is Bridge Street, so called because a bridge crossed the creek at that point; near it is Moore Street, where the first dock was located and ships were *moored*, while just above us is Beaver Street. Beavers, you know, played an important part in the traffic of the colony, their skins being eagerly sought. It is said, by some, that Beaver Street was the original fur center of the town; hence its name. But now let us get back to Broadway, and I'll point out to you the statues of Hudson and Stuyvesant."

We walked up Beaver Street to Broadway, crossed to the west side, and going northward a short distance came in sight of the new Exchange Court building on the corner of Exchange Place.

"Notice the figures over the southern portico," said the professor. "The first is that of Hudson—simple in outline but very picturesque in its general effect. In the case of Stuyvesant, observe how cleverly the wooden leg has been managed. The long cloak forms an attractive background, while the cane, leaning outward and supporting the strong arm, forms an angle that carries the eye away from the inartistic wooden peg. Fine statues, are they not?"

We all assented, took a last look at the two noble bronze figures, and, heartily thanking our guide, made our way uptown, feeling that we had spent a profitable and memorable afternoon.

CHAPTER II

"I THINK," said the professor the next time we met, "that it will be well to have a talk before we take our second walk, so as to learn a little more of the founders of New York.

"The Dutch never did things by halves. So, having made up their minds to establish a colony, they went about it vigorously, fully determined to make it a success.

"Of course, in order to manage the people who now lived on Manhattan Island, some sort of government had to be provided. Accordingly, a director-general was appointed to take charge, and a council of five wise men was selected to give him advice. The first director, as you know, was Peter Minuit, who ruled from 1626 to 1632. He seems to have been a good man, but after a time he was accused of favoring the patroons and was recalled."

"Who were the patroons?" asked Tom.

"Owners of great estates outside of Manhattan Island. Land was granted to the patroons in order to encourage farming, as nearly everybody wanted to go into fur trading. The patroons agreed to transport fifty settlers at their own expense, to provide each with a farm and cattle, and to employ a schoolmaster and a minister. In return each settler was bound to his patroon for ten years. Thus the latter was not only a rich but a powerful individual. The first of the patroons was Killian Van Rensselaer, to whom was granted a tract of seven hundred thousand acres, near the site of our present city of Albany.

"The second director was Wouter Van Twiller, a young man who turned out to be a very poor official. He was stout, stupid, and stubborn, but was clever enough to look out for his own interests. In fact, if he had not been called home he would, in all likelihood, have seized the whole island. But his blunders in public matters were so ridiculous that the people quickly lost all respect for him, and they were glad to see him leave the colony. He ruled from 1632 to 1637.

"The West India Company, now thinking it necessary to send a strong, energetic director, selected William Kieft, who soon showed that he was an out-and-out autocrat, and, unfortunately, not a wise one. He was of a quarrelsome disposition, and plunged the colony into a war with the Indians, in the course of which the little settlement was almost entirely destroyed. Luckily, David De Vries, a worthy patroon, had won the confidence of the natives, and through his efforts peace was restored. Shortly after, Kieft was ordered home. He sailed in August, 1647, but never reached his native land, the vessel going down in a storm off the coast of Wales.

"The fourth and last director, Peter Stuyvesant,

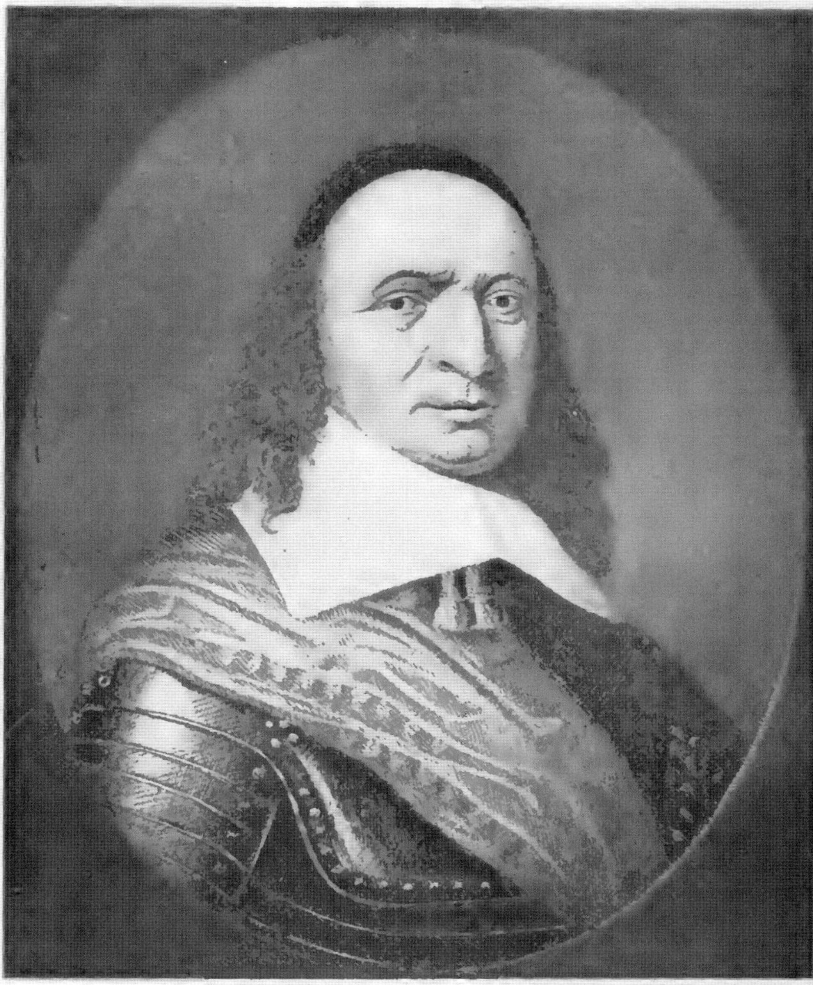

Peter Stuyvesant. From an oil painting in the possession of the New York Historical Society.

sometimes called Peter the Stiff-necked, now appeared on the scene. He governed for seventeen years, from 1647 to 1664, and was easily the most interesting and picturesque of the Dutch rulers. A wooden leg supplied the place of one of his limbs, which he lost while fighting for his country in southern seas. Like Kieft he was an autocrat, but he was wise and earnest, and honestly sought to promote the welfare of the colony. When he arrived it was almost in a state of ruin, the population having dwindled from three thousand to one thousand, owing to the Indian wars, and the people were badly discouraged. Stuyvesant issued a number of strict laws, many of which we would not accept nowadays, but at the time they were necessary. By steadily enforcing them he introduced order, cleanliness, and improvements of all kinds, and presently New Amsterdam began to look something like the thrifty towns of Old Holland.

"Stuyvesant, as you know, had a town house at the foot of Whitehall Street; he also had a country residence in the neighborhood of Fourteenth Street. The place was known as the Great Bouwerie, or farm, and covered many acres of ground, extending from Fourth Avenue over to the East River.

"Quick of temper was Stuyvesant and quarrelsome, and often he brought his wooden leg down on the floor with an angry thump when people disagreed with him. But he was full of energy, never shirked what he considered his duty, and, soldierlike, was at the front whenever there was danger. So when, in

1664, Captain Nicolls, in the name of the Duke of York, sailed up the bay at the head of a fleet of English war vessels, Stuyvesant stood at an angle of the fort, next to a gunner, ready to die in the defense of the town. Nicolls, knowing that he could easily capture the almost defenseless island, sent a haughty

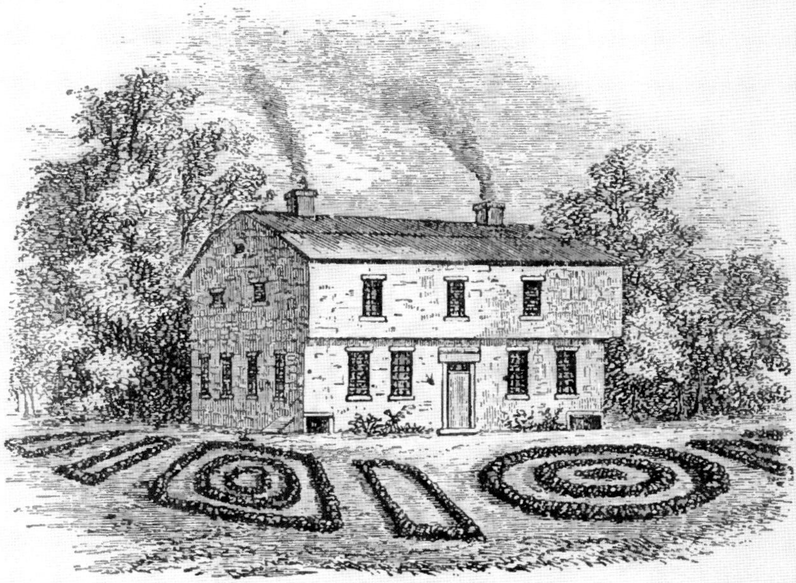

Stuyvesant's country house. From an old print.

message demanding surrender. 'I had rather be carried a corpse to my grave than to surrender the city,' replied Stuyvesant. Such was his courageous nature, but to have opposed the guns of the English would not only have meant terrible destruction of property, but the slaughter of many innocent women and children. Thus the dominie and the leading burghers argued with the determined fighter, and at last he gave in, his proud spirit broken at the idea of hoisting the white flag. With bent head he stumped out of the fort at the head of his soldiers, never more to govern or to regulate the laws.

"Stuyvesant now retired to his Bouwerie. His orchards and gardens, kept in perfect order by a number of negro slaves, were the finest on Manhattan Island. Shortly after the surrender, the authorities in Holland, wishing to throw the blame of losing the city on somebody, summoned their faithful servant before them and calmly charged him with cowardice. Of course Stuyvesant easily proved that this was a mean and baseless accusation, and he did not hesitate to say that had the company sent him a sufficient number of soldiers and weapons he might have had some chance of defending the town. After such treatment he had no wish to remain in Holland, and as soon as possible he came back to his beloved Bouwerie, where peacefully he passed his days, often inviting the English governor to dine with him. At the ripe old age of eighty, in the year 1672, he died, and was buried in the family vault within the walls of a church that he had built at his own expense near his country seat. The church is now gone, and in its place, at the corner of Tenth Street and Second Avenue, stands St. Mark's. This, as you will, no doubt, be interested to know, is the oldest church site in New York now occupied by a house of worship."

"Older than Trinity?" asked George.

"Yes, the latter was not founded until thirty years after Stuyvesant built his church."

"When Stuyvesant was laid to rest, a tablet was

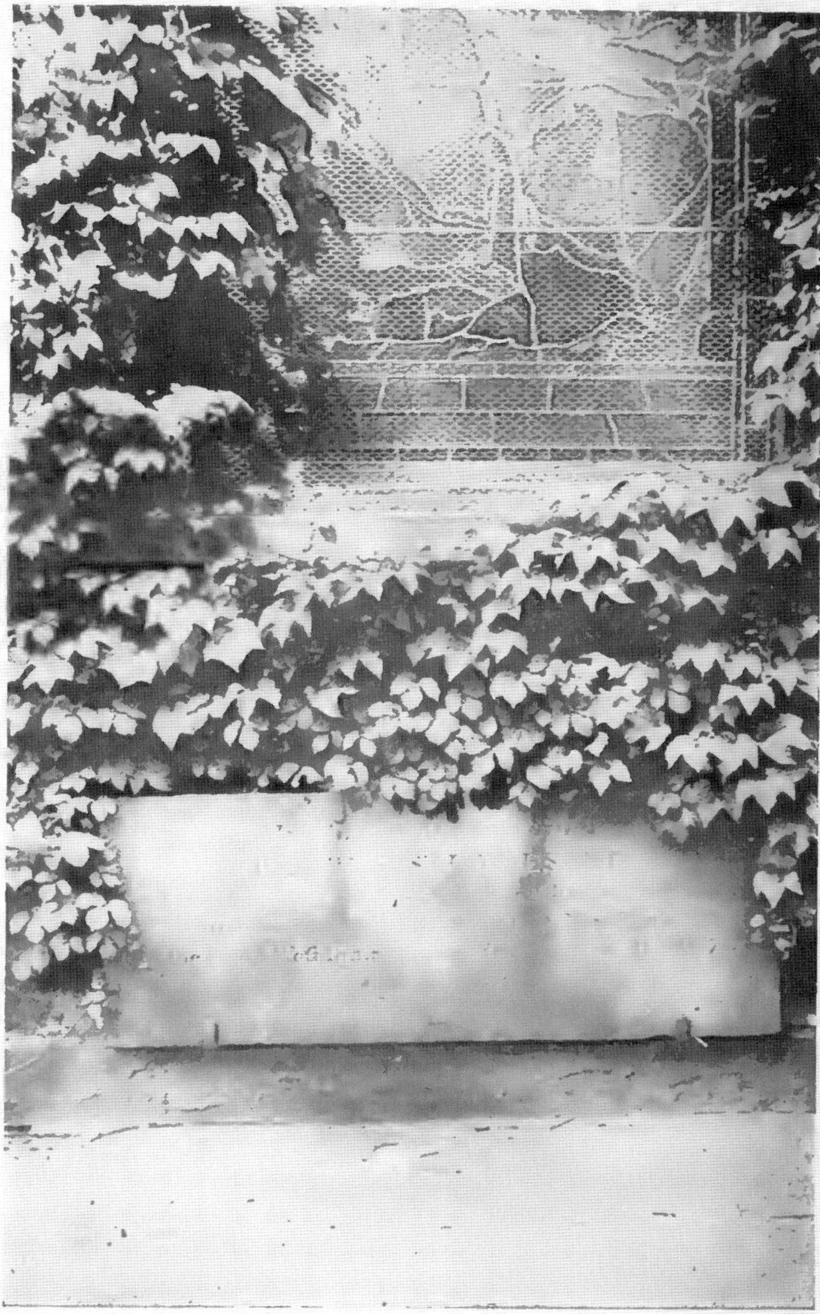

Peter Stuyvesant's tombstone, St. Mark's church.
Photographed 1900.

placed above his grave. This has been preserved, and has been affixed to the eastern wall of St. Mark's. The inscription," added the professor, referring to his memorandum book, "is as follows:

IN THIS VAULT LIES BURIED
PETRUS STUYVESANT,
LATE CAPTAIN GENERAL AND GOVERNOR IN CHIEF OF AMSTERDAM
IN NEW NETHERLAND NOW CALLED NEW YORK,
AND THE DUTCH WEST INDIA ISLANDS, DIED IN A.D. 167½,
AGED 80 YEARS.

"The date 167½ indicates that he died between the first of January and the 25th of March, 1672."

"Is Bouwerie the same as the Bowery?" asked George.

"Yes," answered the professor. "Originally it was called Bowery Lane. While Stuyvesant was director an Indian outbreak took place, and the people living beyond the city wall, being in great danger, were at once ordered either to move into the town or to collect in villages for common protection. Thus a village was formed in the neighborhood of Stuyvesant farm. A country path connected this hamlet with the city, and later on it was made into a carriage road and extended to Harlem. Its starting point was about where the post office now stands, whence it followed Park Row and the Bowery up to Fifteenth Street, where it again met Broadway. Along this route the first postman, armed with pistols, made his way on horseback once a month to

Boston. It was a risky trip in those days, as there was danger from Indians and wild beasts. Bowery Lane gradually developed into one of the most important and popular highways of Manhattan Island. It became a favorite drive for the fashionable people at all times of the year, being especially lively in winter, when merry sleigh bells made the crisp air resound with lively sounds of merriment. But now its old-time glory is gone, and only a few relics remain to remind us of its past history. Opposite Rivington Street is a milestone, which, if free from posters, shows the inscription:

I MILE TO CITY HALL.

"A famous inn stood here in the old days, and it was a custom to accompany a friend starting on the long journey to Boston, as far as this tavern, drink a parting glass of wine with him, and wish him Godspeed."

"Are there any other old milestones?" asked George.

"Yes; the two-mile stone is in Third Avenue near Sixteenth Street, the four-mile near Fifty-seventh Street, the five-mile near Seventy-seventh Street, the nine-mile at One Hundred and Fifty-second Street and Amsterdam Avenue, and the twelve-mile on the Kingsbridge road, near Inwood.

"The Governor's room in the City Hall contains

an odd and interesting memento of the Bowery. It is a branch of a pear tree that was originally planted in Stuyvesant's orchard. Long after the orchard had been covered by modern houses, this tree, encircled by an iron railing, stood at the corner of

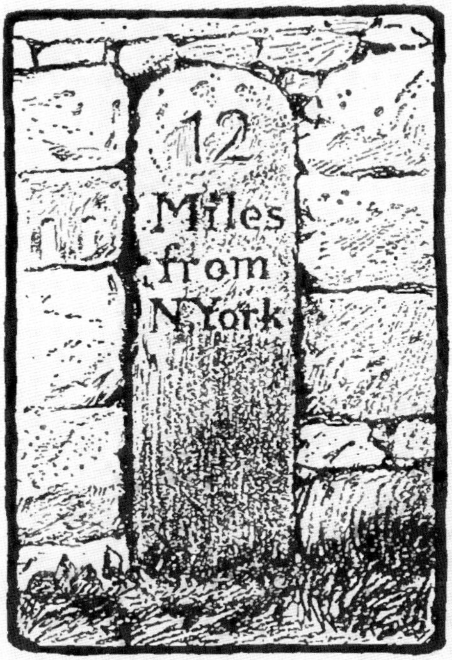

Milestone on Kingsbridge road.

Thirteenth Street and Third Avenue. Many a time have I seen it there, covered with blossoms, just as it used to appear, no doubt, when Stuyvesant looked upon it. One day, in 1867, fully two hundred years after it was planted, a careless truckman drove his heavy wagon against it and crushed it to the ground, thus ruthlessly ending its existence as a landmark. At the corner where it stood so long, a bronze plate has been placed bearing the following inscription:

> ON THIS CORNER GREW
> PETRUS STUYVESANT'S PEAR TREE.
>
> RECALLED TO HOLLAND IN 1664,
> ON HIS RETURN
> HE BROUGHT THE PEAR TREE
> AND PLANTED IT
> AS HIS MEMORIAL,
> "BY WHICH," SAID HE, "MY NAME
> MAY BE REMEMBERED."
> THE PEAR TREE FLOURISHED
> AND BORE FRUIT FOR OVER
> TWO HUNDRED YEARS.
>
> THIS TABLET IS PLACED HERE BY
> THE HOLLAND SOCIETY
> OF NEW YORK
> SEPTEMBER 1890.

"You said last week you would tell us something about the Indians," said Tom, who had just finished reading The Last of the Mohicans, by Cooper.

"Yes," answered the professor, "and this is probably as good a time as any to keep my promise.

"When the natives first saw Hudson's boat in the distance they were greatly puzzled. They thought it was a monster canoe with wings whiter than those of a swan, and much wider than those of many eagles. Some imagined it was the Great Spirit coming to visit them from the land of the Rising Sun, and they prepared to give him a proper reception. Presently they ventured out in their little birch canoes, offered tobacco and food, and showed by signs that they were glad to see the palefaced strangers.

"The Europeans soon discovered the skill with which the Indians handled their bows and arrows,

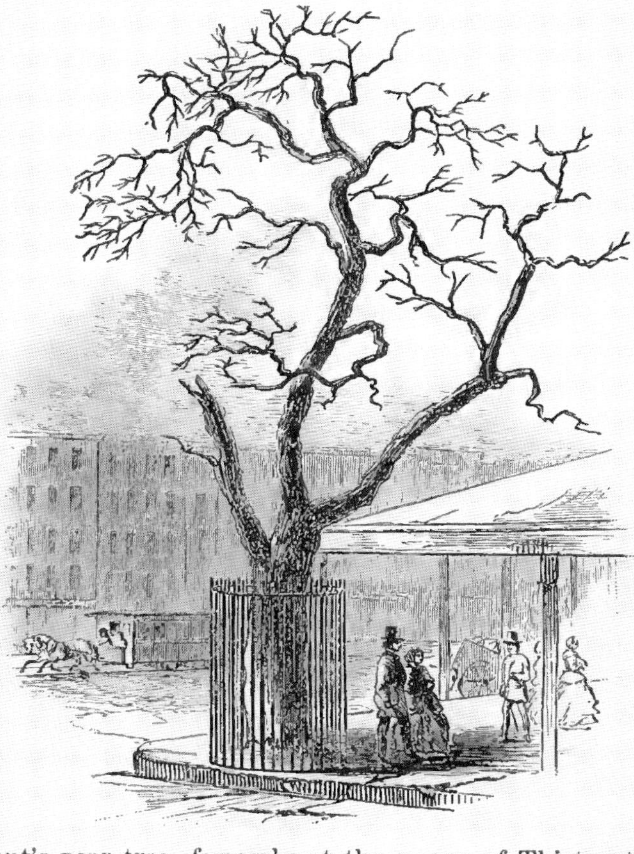

Stuyvesant's pear tree, formerly at the corner of Thirteenth Street and Third Avenue. From Mary L. Booth's History of the City of New York.

and greatly admired the manner in which they could hit the swiftest animals. Oftentimes the visitors arranged shooting contests among the boys. A small coin placed at a distance of fifty feet the young redskins would generally hit five times out of ten.

"As far as we can judge, the Europeans might have lived at peace with the Indians, but the former soon aroused angry feelings in the breasts of the natives. One day an Indian and his nephew came down toward the town to sell some furs. In the vicinity of Collect Pond, a body of water near the site of the old Tombs prison (Center and Franklin Streets), three of Minuit's farm servants attacked the pair, robbed them of their furs, and killed the older man. The younger, a mere boy, escaped, and, according to the custom of his people, vowed to avenge the death of his uncle. Twenty years later, during the time of Kieft, he deliberately set out one afternoon to do what he considered his religious duty. He visited the house of a harmless old wheelwright who lived some distance out of town and pretended that he wanted to trade some beaver skins for blankets. While the old man was bending over his box, the Indian struck him a cowardly blow on the head with his axe and killed him. This act led to a terrible war, during which men, women, and children were murdered, their houses burned, and their farms laid waste. The horrors of this time are too awful to repeat, for the Indians, when enraged, inflict the most cruel tortures on their unfortunate victims."

Emily shuddered, while the boys were strangely silent.

"Another serious outbreak occurred in Stuyvesant's time," continued the professor. "Near the present site of Trinity church, one Van Dyck had a fine orchard of peach trees. This fruit was new to the Indians, and not being able to resist the tempta-

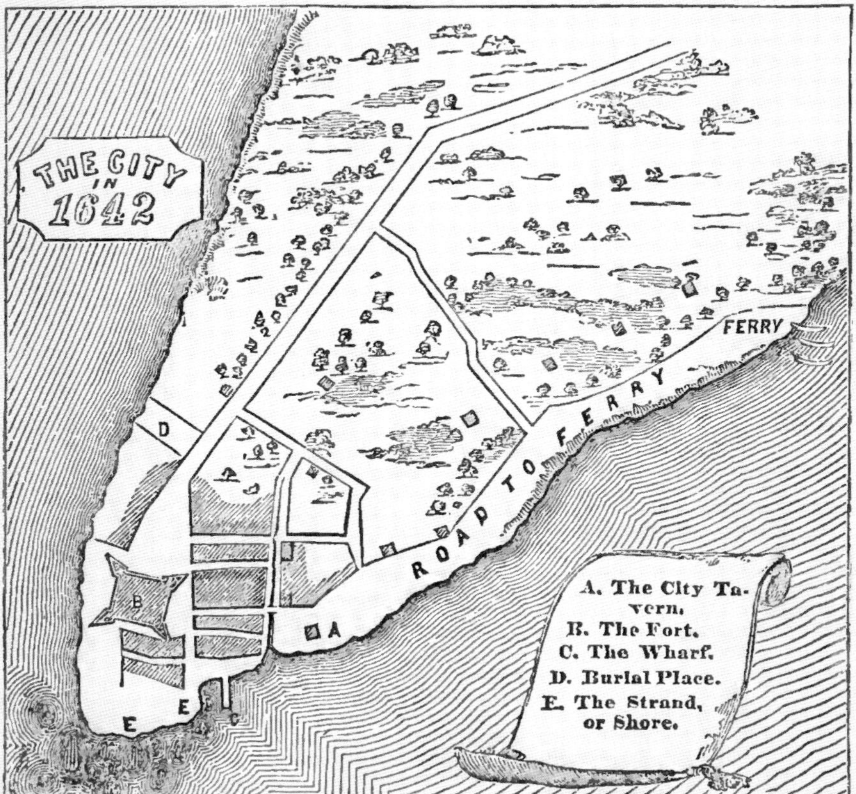

Map of New York in 1642, drawn "from the best data in his possession" by D. T. Valentine, compiler of the city's Manuals.

tion of tasting it, they often slipped into the orchard at night and stole a few peaches. This practice so vexed Mrs. Van Dyck that she made her husband load his gun and watch for intruders. He had not long to wait. All too soon a slim form crept up to one of the trees and began shaking a limb. Van

Dyck, without uttering a word of warning, raised his piece, aimed and fired. The form dropped and never stirred again. When Van Dyck rushed up to see the result of his shot, he found at his feet the lifeless form of a young Indian girl. Dearly the colony had to pay for this hasty action. Over one hundred settlers were killed, one hundred and fifty taken prisoners, and eighty thousand dollars' worth of property destroyed."

"That was an awful price to give for a few peaches," said George impressively.

"Yes, indeed," answered the professor. "Many fond mothers and innocent babies were included in that payment of blood."

"And it all happened right here in New York?" said Emily, in an incredulous tone.

"Here, and in the immediate neighborhood. But let us change the subject to one of peace. I mentioned a few minutes ago, as you know, a pond where the Tombs used to be. This was a beautiful spot originally. Wooded hills surrounded a placid body of water that was thought to be without bottom. Near it was a point of land which, when first seen by the Dutch, was covered with shells, left there by the Indians, who used them for making wampum, as they designated their money. The Dutch called it *Kloch*, meaning shell point, which gradually was changed to Collect, and, finally, applied to the little lake itself. In the old days there was a tradition that at midnight, at certain periods, the spirit of an Indian chief crossed the pond, the splash of his paddle being easily heard. Of course, this was an idle

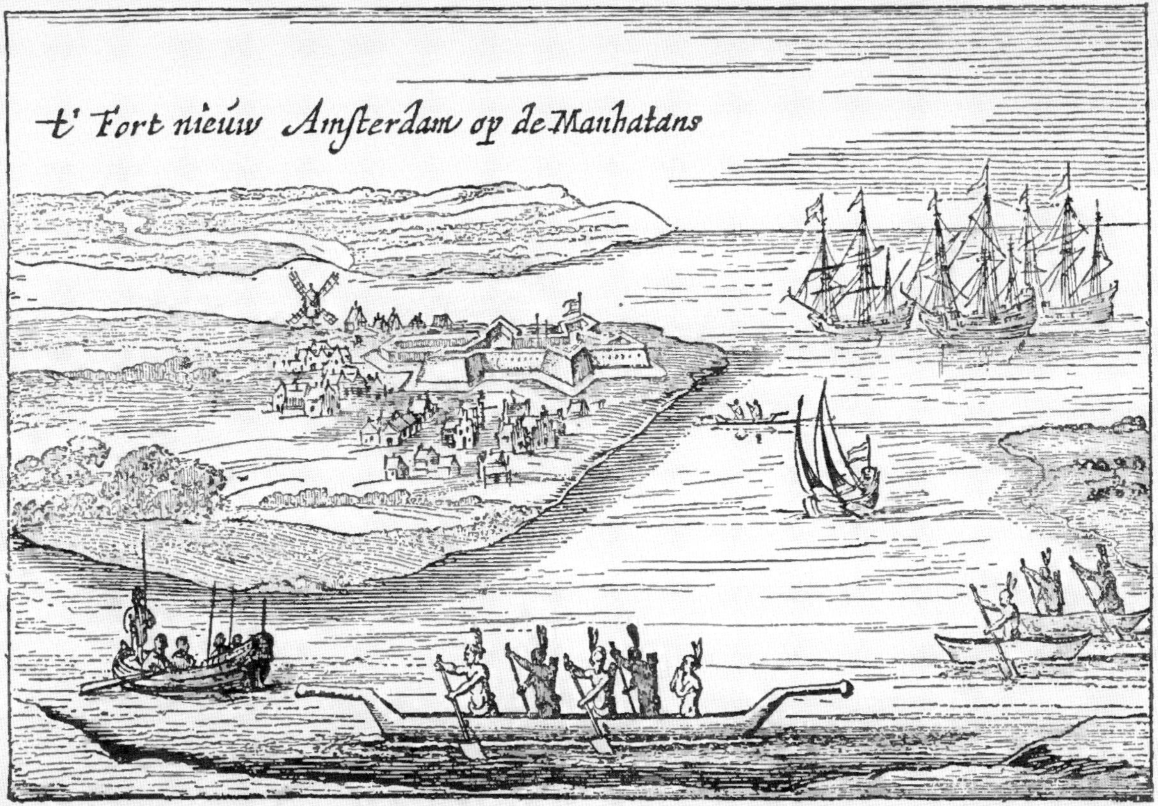

The above cut represents, beyond question, the earliest view taken of New Amsterdam. It appears in Joost Hartger's description of Virginia, New Netherland, New England, and the islands Bermudas, Barbadoes, and St. Christopher, published at Amsterdam, 1651.

tale, but many a child believed it firmly. Collect Pond remained a feature of the island for many years, and I shall have occasion to mention it again."

"How did the Indians make wampum?" asked George.

"The women were the money-makers. With great patience they dug out the blue parts of clam shells, broke them into small pieces, polished them, drilled them, and then strung them on grass or hemp. These strings were then braided into belts and used as we use dollar bills. Sometimes white shells were employed, but these were not considered as valuable as the blue. The Manahatas, living near the sea, had, so to speak, an unlimited money supply, and became one of the wealthiest tribes.

"A collection of Indian relics found in this neighborhood can be seen in the Museum of Natural History, at Seventy-seventh Street, west of Central Park. Go there the first opportunity you have, and you will find an interesting exhibit.

"But let us return to the little Dutch town of New Amsterdam. It nestled below Wall Street, and, although it lacked many conveniences we enjoy to-day, it was a merry place in its way. Stoves, carpets, and rocking chairs were unknown, but house-warmings were arranged without them, and were hugely enjoyed. Not a fork was to be seen in the entire settlement, but the people managed very well with spoons and knives. Watches and clocks were rarities, but the hourglass kept track of time in their stead. A few silver watches were introduced after a while, but they presently got out of order, and, as

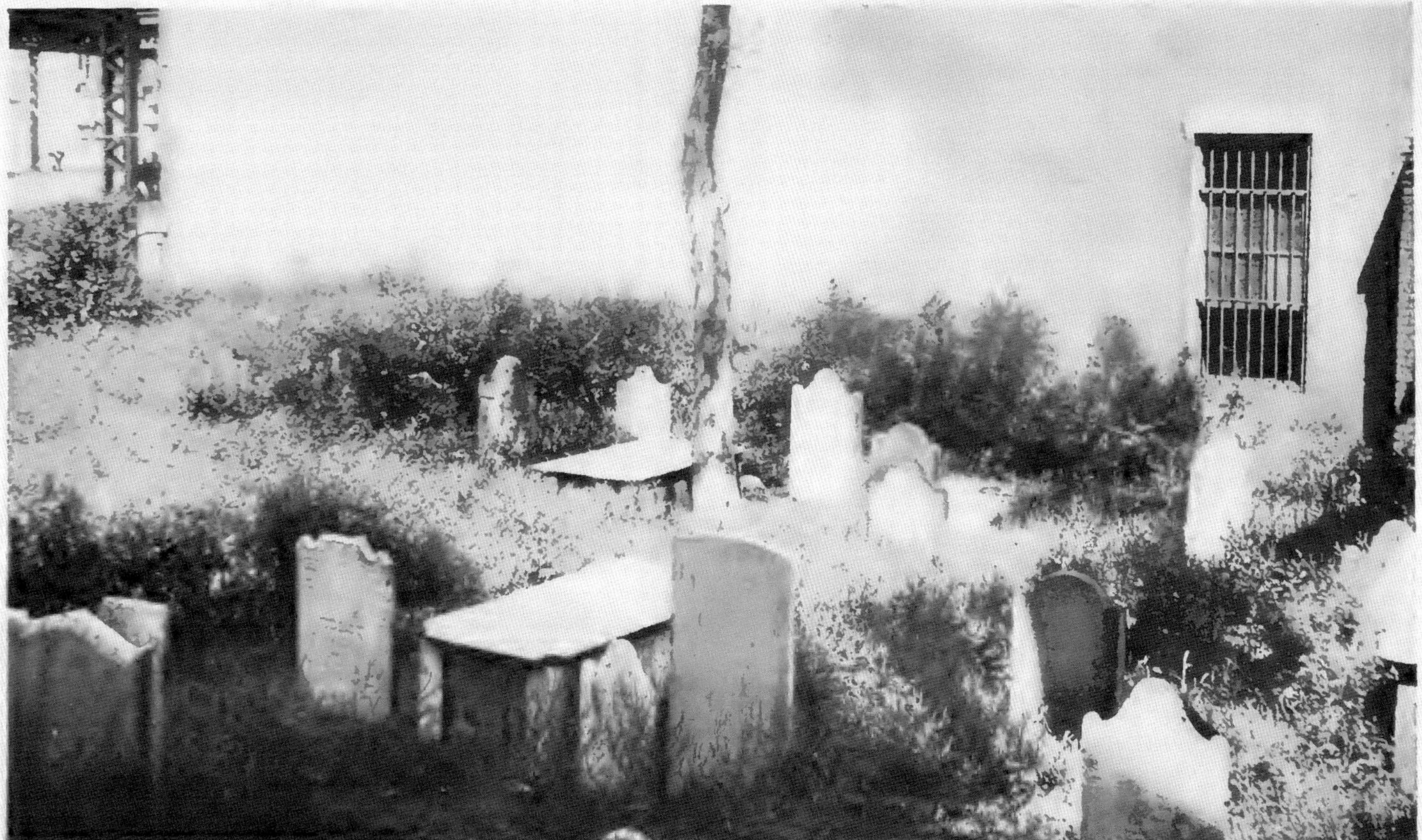

Section of old Jewish cemetery established during Stuyvesant's time, located on New Bowery near Oliver Street. Photographed 1900.

there were no watch repairers in the town, these timepieces were soon rendered useless. Excepting the director's coach, there was no conveyance in New Amsterdam. People traveled on horseback, and, as there were no sidesaddles in those days, cushions were used for the ladies, who rode behind the gentlemen and held on to them for support."

"Must have been a funny sight," said Tom, smiling.

"The Dutch were very hospitable," continued the professor; "strangers were always welcome and were well entertained. Quilting bees, apple bees, and husking bees were popular, and dancing was a favorite amusement. Every autumn there was a Kermess that lasted six weeks, during which time cattle were exhibited, farm tools were sold, and all sorts of needlework and fabrics displayed, while athletic sports, dances, and other amusements served to entertain the young people. You may be surprised to learn that golf was one of the favorite pastimes, and it is recorded that people were arrested for playing it in the streets.

"There were several great festivals: Christmas, New Year's day, Paas or Passover, and Santa Claus, or Christ-Kinkle day.

"Christmas day was observed by wishing everybody 'A Merry Christmas,' after which the young men went out to one of the frozen swamps beyond the town to shoot at turkeys.

"On New Year's day everybody visited everybody else. Every one, including the stranger within the gates, was welcome, and cake and wine were freely offered. This hospitable custom was kept up in New York until a few years ago.

"On Paas, or Easter Monday, the children cracked colored eggs, and the fancy egg of the present day is, no doubt, a memento of this once popular holiday.

"Of all the festive occasions the most popular, however, especially among the children, was Santa Claus, or St. Nicholas day, which was celebrated on December 6th. St. Nicholas was the town's patron saint, and he was believed to take special care of his favorite city. He was supposed to be a jolly, rosy-cheeked little old man, with a low-crowned hat, who came in a well-laden sleigh drawn by reindeer. Stockings were hung up and a hymn was sung, the last four lines of which were:

> "'Saint Nicholas, my dear good friend,
> To serve you ever was my end;
> If you me now something will give,
> Serve you I will as long as I live.'

"Gradually, Santa Claus and Christmas time became associated, and the visit of the former was not expected until December 25th. Then there was a merry celebration, which good old Dutch custom the people of New York have kept up ever since."

CHAPTER III

"GENERALLY," said the professor, "when a city is captured the people feel a strong sense of resentment against the conquerors, but such was not the case when the English took New Amsterdam in 1664. The Dutch burghers felt that the West India Company had neglected them and treated them badly; the English inhabitants, of whom there were quite a number, were pleased to see their own flag aloft; and the French, who formed the next most important part of the population, were indifferent. Already, as you will notice, there was a decidedly mixed population, and it would have been as difficult then as now to say who was a typical Manhattanese."

"Did the English have any real right to take New Amsterdam?" asked George.

"Yes, and no," answered the professor. "They claimed that because the Cabots had sailed along the coast, they (the English) were entitled to the land by right of discovery. On the other hand, the Dutch were the first settlers, and there is no dispute about the fact that they bought the land from the Indians, who certainly were the original owners."

"It seems to me, then, that the Dutch had a right to it," remarked Tom.

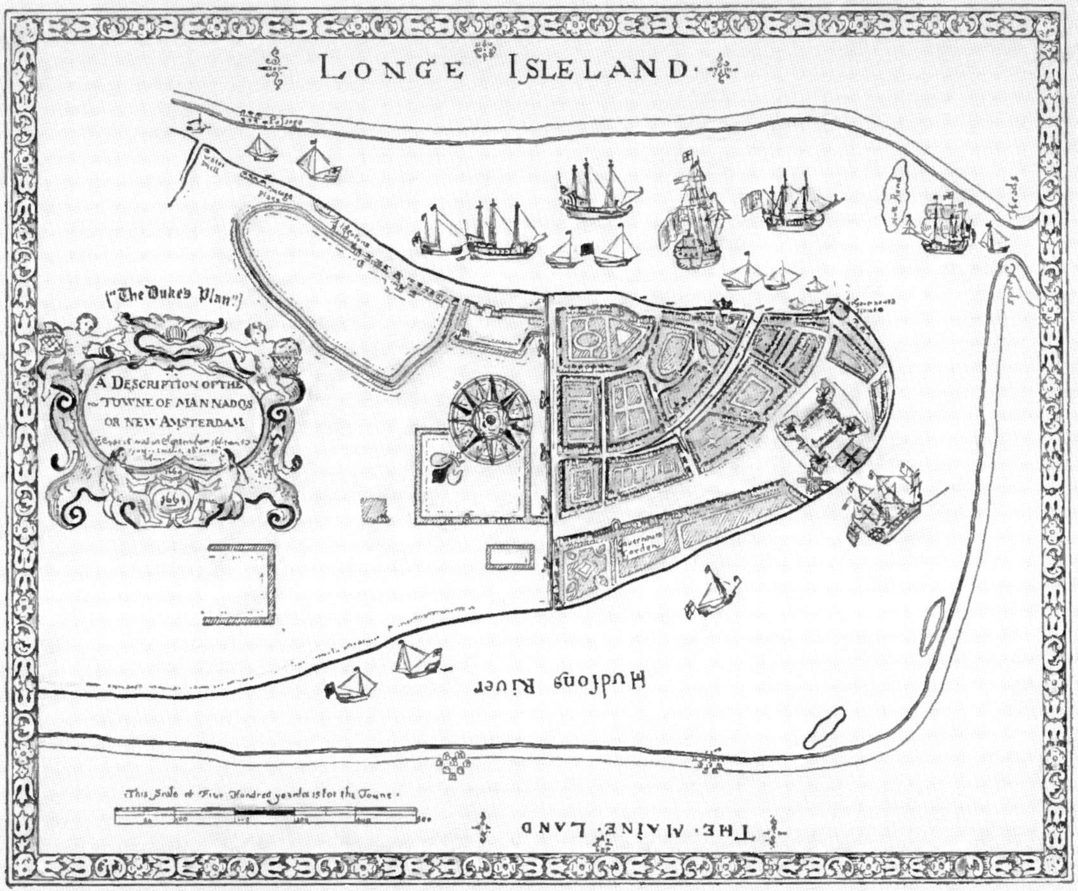

New York in 1664. The original of this map, known as "The Duke's Plan," is in the British Museum.

"Such is my view of the case," said the professor; "but in those days might was generally considered right, and so the English remained in possession.

"Nicolls, the new governor, was a gentle conqueror and a pleasant gentleman, and tried in every possible way to make his rule popular. The Dutch and the French, as well as the English, were allowed to use the church in the fort, and no effort was made to disturb any of the customs of the old burghers. After a while English was declared to be the official language, and a mayor, a sheriff, and aldermen took the places of the Dutch officials. About the same time the name of the city was changed from New Amsterdam to New York, in honor of the duke. I have always felt sorry that this change was made, because the city was in reality a *New* Amsterdam, but never a *New* York. Fortunately, the good old Dutch name of Harlem was not disturbed, and still serves as a reminder of its true origin.

"The second governor was Francis Lovelace, who, like Nicolls, had pleasing ways, and treated the people well. Still, as far as real liberty was concerned, they enjoyed little more than when they were under the control of the West India Company.

"There is one of Lovelace's acts, however, that deserves special mention, and renders his name worthy of remembrance. In 1672 he established a postal service between New York and Boston. In January of that year the first letter carrier mounted his horse and began his journey up the Bowery road toward the village of Harlem. Here his arrival caused great excitement, and he was treated to some

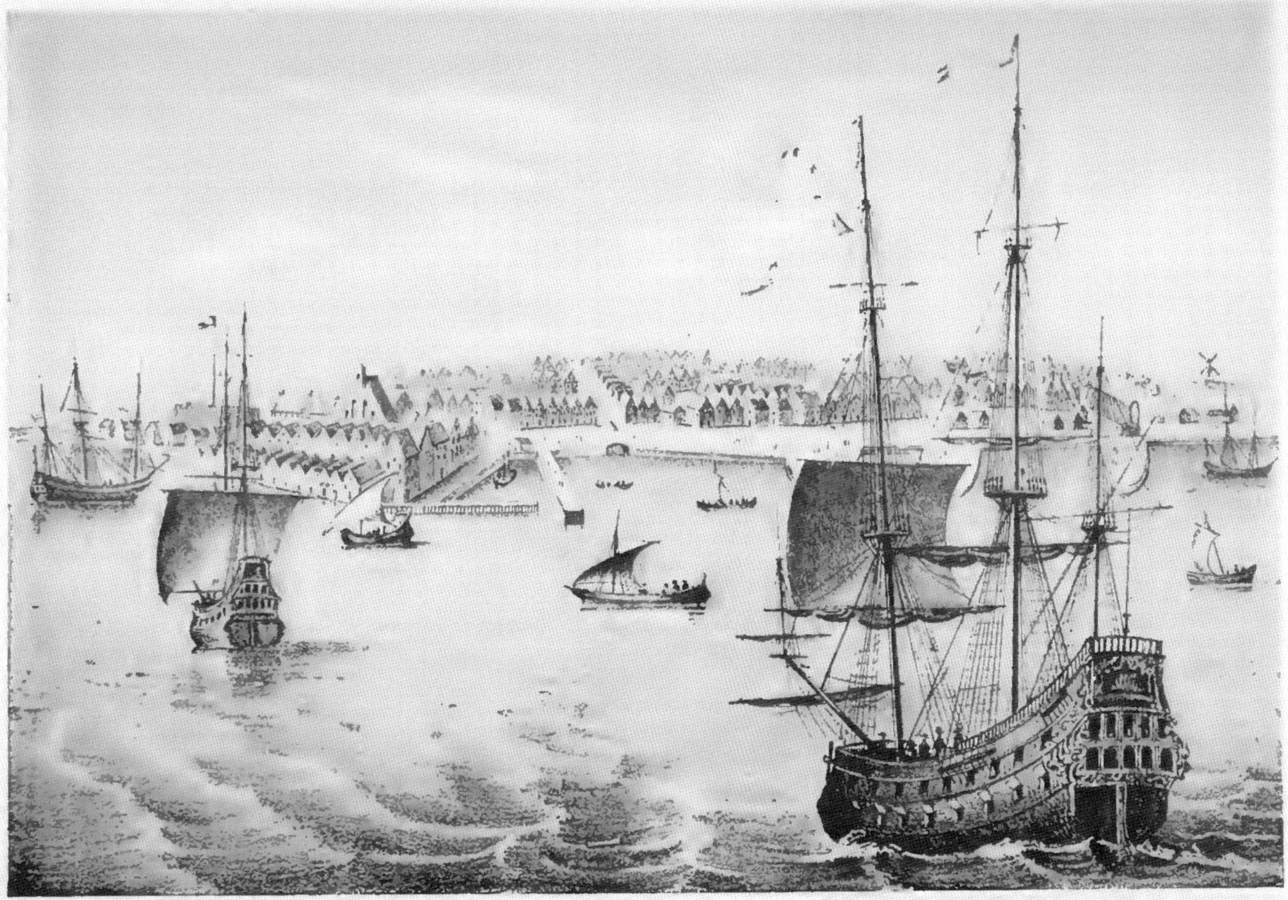

New York as it appeared about the year 1667. Reproduced from an old print in Valentine's Manual for 1851.

home-brewed beer. As he passed on through the woods of Connecticut he marked the trees so as to be able to find his way back. At Hartford he changed horses, and after a tedious trip reached Boston. In the meantime a locked box was kept at a convenient place in the town to receive letters and parcels for the next month's mail. Such was New York's earliest post office. Have you any idea to what extent it has now grown?"

None of us could answer this question.

"In 1898," said the professor, "it sold over three hundred millions of stamps and seventy-five millions of postal cards, and instead of a delivery once a month, there are now nine mails a day each way between New York and Boston. It was through Lovelace's postman that the first communication was established between the colonies, and this gradually developed into a bond so firm that, in after years, all England's strength could not break it.

"In 1672 war broke out between England and Holland, and one fine day two fierce Dutch captains, Colve and Evertsen, sailed into New York Harbor and ordered the town to surrender, in very much the same manner as Nicolls had done in 1664, the difference being that the Dutch came openly in a period of war, while the English stole in during an era of peace. The latter proved to be no better defenders than the Hollanders, and the two captains were soon in possession of the city, which they quickly converted once more into a Dutch town, calling it by its original name of New Amsterdam. This lasted for little more than a year, when peace was declared, and the city was yielded to the English, the Dutch taking Surinam in Guiana instead. Strange to say, both the English and the Dutch believed, after the bargain had been made, that Surinam was the more desirable possession.

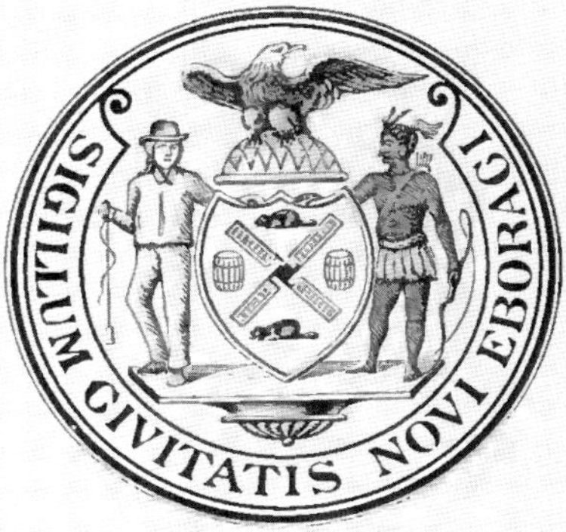

The city's seal.

"A privilege was granted the city in 1678 that helped it along prodigiously, and has been remembered ever since by symbolizing it in the city's seal. By the way, can you describe the seal?"

"There's a sailor and an Indian," said George.

"Correct; and what else?"

"An eagle, I think," suggested Tom.

"Yes, and several other objects that you have probably never noticed. Here is a copy of the seal," said the professor, taking a paper from his pocket. "Let us examine it carefully. The presence of the beavers you will, no doubt, understand; but what is the meaning of the windmill arms and two barrels?"

We did not answer, and awaited an explanation.

"In 1678 New York was granted the exclusive right to bolt flour—that is, to sift the coarser from the finer particles—and to pack it for export. This monopoly brought great prosperity to the people, and helped immensely to build up the city. Several hundred new houses were erected in a short time, and many new ships were built. Thus the flour barrels and the windmill arms, together with the beavers, were chosen as symbols to represent the earliest causes of the city's prosperity."

"What do the Latin words mean?" asked Tom.

"Seal of the City of New *Eboracum*, the Latin name given by the Romans to the town of York in England."

"How old is the seal?" asked George.

"It was granted in 1686, and then had a crown where now the eagle appears.

"The Bolting Act went into force during the rule of Sir Edmund Andros, who governed from 1674 to 1682. He was a hot-tempered individual, and became known as 'the Tyrant.' This was hardly fair, as he was no more of an autocrat than those who had preceded him, but it seems that the people expected much greater liberties than the duke was willing to grant. Andros was followed by Thomas Dongan, who remained in office for six years from 1682. Like his master, the duke, he was a Catholic, and for this reason was at first regarded with suspicion, nearly all the citizens of New York being of the Protestant faith. Gradually, however, his pleasing ways, his justness, and his integrity won the good will of most of the people—a feeling that was strengthened when he announced that he was authorized to grant the colony a liberal charter. This important grant—since known as the Dongan Charter—forms the basis of our rights as citizens to-day, and it was the first real taste of liberty given to the people. It provided trial by jury, freedom of religion, and taxation only by the consent of those taxed. A copy of the charter, bearing the date of April 22, 1686, is preserved in a tin box in the City Hall, where it can be seen by all those who care to look at it.

"In 1685 the Duke of York succeeded his brother and became King of England, under the title of James II. After being sure of his place, he threw off the mask of liberality he had worn as duke and showed himself in his true light. He began a series of religious persecutions of the cruelest kind, and treated those who opposed his political views with the utmost barbarity. Men were shot or hung without trial, and women were burned at the stake. Presently he revoked the charter he had granted New York, and actually wiped the province out of existence by making it a part of New England. In order to make this very plain to the people, he ordered the city's seal to be publicly broken and that of New England to be adopted in its place. His reign was a prolonged period of awful cruelties and oppression, and finally, in 1689, the English drove him from the throne."

"I am sorry New York was ever named after him," said Emily.

"He surely did not deserve any such honor, but there is one satisfaction connected with the name. It suggests York of England, where the civilization of Europe began, and where to-day flourish many splendid institutions of learning and fine arts.

"The dethronement of James caused great excitement in England and stirred up an extraordinary commotion in New York. 'If the king has fled,' said the people, 'then the officials he appointed have no further power over us; furthermore, we do not trust any one that is a Catholic or has been appointed by a Catholic.' All sorts of rumors were soon afloat regarding plots to burn the city and to kill the Protestants. Two parties arose, one eager to discharge the old officials without delay, the other desirous of awaiting new instructions from England. In the meantime, Mary, daughter of James II, and her husband, William of Orange, a prince of Holland, both Protestants, were invited to occupy the throne of England. This piece of news was joyfully received in New York, but the excitement continued. At length a Committe of Safety was organized, and Jacob Leisler, a respected citizen and captain of one of the militia companies of the city, was chosen to be commander pending the arrival of a new governor. The opposition party rebelled against this act and caused Leisler no end of trouble. Thus the community was in a constant turmoil, and once Leisler was almost killed. Finally, toward the end of 1690, Henry Sloughter, a broken-down English adventurer, was appointed governor, and Richard Ingoldsby lieutenant governor. They set sail for America, but on the way the ships parted company, and Ingoldsby arrived first. He at once ordered Leisler to give up the fort and submit to him. This, Leisler very promptly refused to do, as Ingoldsby had no papers with him to show that he had any authority. The situation now grew worse than ever, and the strain became so great that bloodshed was feared. It took Sloughter nearly two months to find New York, and not until the middle of March, 1691, did his ship enter the harbor. Leisler then resigned his position, but was at once arrested and charged with treason. He was found guilty, but Sloughter, whose conscience, no doubt, troubled him, would not sign the death warrant. Leisler's enemies, however, were active, and they knew how to manage Sloughter. One evening they invited him to a banquet, filled him with wine, and obtained his signature. A few days later, Leisler and his son-in-law were led to the gallows, erected, it is believed, where the building of the New York Sun now stands. Here, in a drizzling rain, the two men were executed. It was a terrible scene; men wept, women fainted, and many carried away pieces of Leisler's garments, looking upon him as a martyr."

"Poor man!" said Emily, with tears in her eyes.

"Poor in one sense, but great in another," remarked the professor. "Leisler gave up his life that others might enjoy more happiness. During his rule the people were given greater liberty than they had ever enjoyed before, and the seeds thus sown bore fruit in later years. His name deserves a lasting tribute, and it is to be hoped that some day New York will erect a fitting memorial to his memory. I must not omit to say that, after a time, Parliament was just enough to remove the stain of treason from his record."

"That did not do him much good," said Tom dryly.

"No, but it benefited his widow and children, removed the blot from his reputation, and restored to them his property, which had been confiscated. As for Sloughter, he did not live long to exert his pernicious power. In July, 1691, he died—whether from remorse or drink is not known."

"Who was the next governor?" asked George.

"Benjamin Fletcher, who arrived in August, 1692. The people were glad to get rid of their old ruler, and welcomed the new one, hoping that he would be better than his predecessor. Fletcher received a particularly fine welcome, the extravagant sum of one hundred dollars being voted by the city for a banquet in his honor. The French and their allies, the Huron Indians, became troublesome during his time and attacked the Iroquois, who were friends of the English. The invaders' first move was against Schenectady, after which they intended to capture Albany and New York. Fletcher quickly organized a force, sailed up the Hudson, marched against the French and Indians, and won a decisive victory. The Iroquois, admiring his promptness, called him 'The Lord of the Swift Arrow,' the people of Albany voted him an address of congratulations, and New York presented him with a beautiful gold cup."

"Good!" exclaimed Tom.

"A period of improvement now began, and the city showed signs of growth. Fortunately, we have an interesting old map, drawn in 1695, that illustrates how the town commenced to spread. Here is a copy of this relic," said the professor, laying the map before us, "and it is well worthy of a little study. New York at this time contained about five

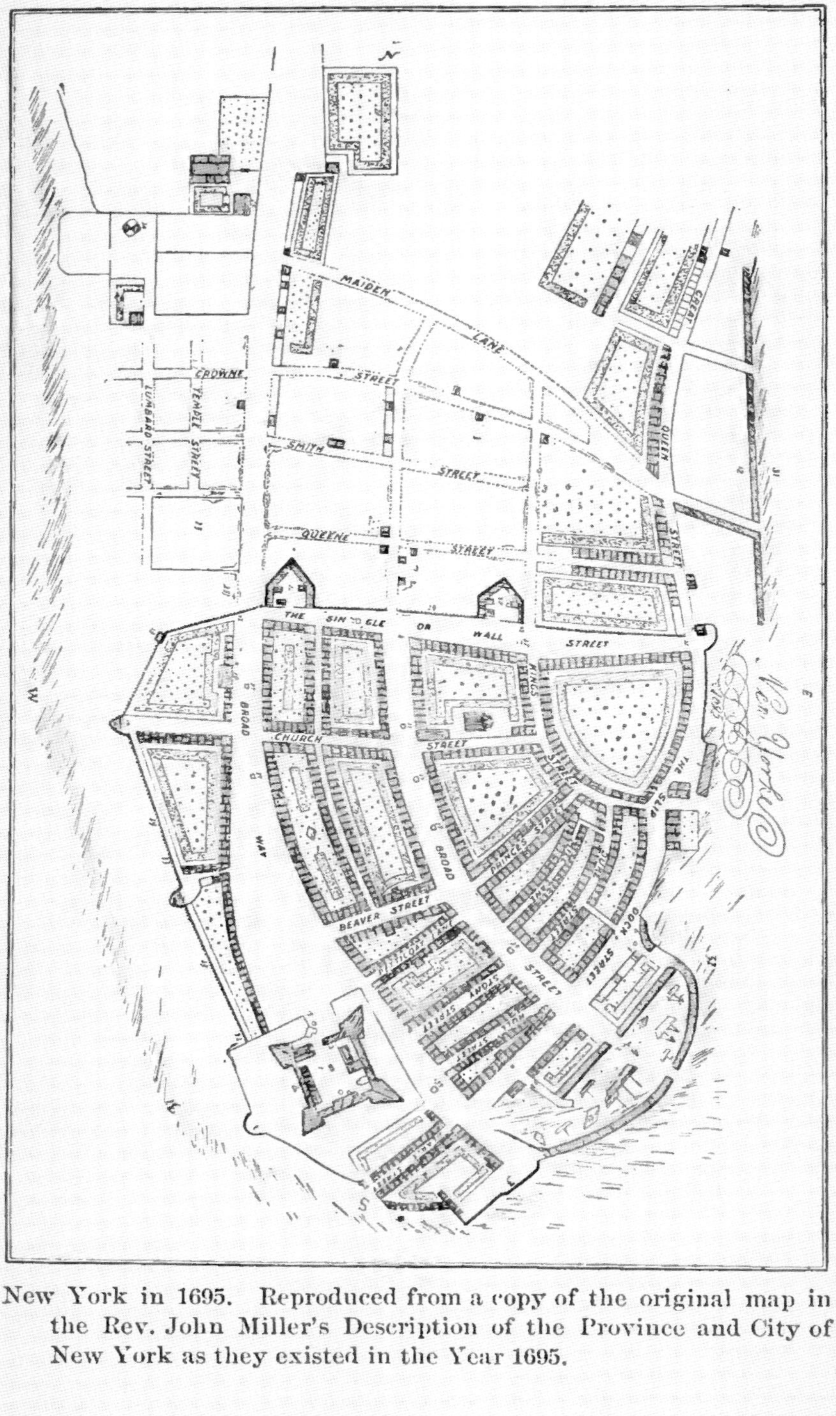

New York in 1695. Reproduced from a copy of the original map in the Rev. John Miller's Description of the Province and City of New York as they existed in the Year 1695.

thousand people and some seven hundred and fifty houses. The wall, as you see, is clearly indicated, extends over to the North River and all the way down to the fort, almost surrounding the old Dutch town. You will notice also that an uptown movement had begun, and four new streets appear east of Broadway, the most northern being Maiden Lane. The other three streets—Crown, Smith, and Queen—are now known as Liberty, Cedar, and Pine. Broadway was not yet considered important, and the two little streets west of it did not amount to much. The favorite thoroughfare was Great Queen Street, the road along the river, which at present is called Pearl Street. As you can see, it stretches up beyond Maiden Lane, and in fact it led up to a primitive ferry that ran between Peck Slip and Fulton Street, Brooklyn. If the ferryman happened not to be at hand, people were expected to blow a horn that hung on a tree near by, whereupon the master of the boat would leave his plow or his cow, hurry down to the bank, and row his passengers across the river."

"How did they chance to call a street Maiden Lane?" asked Emily.

"Because in the early days it was, in all likelihood, a lovers' lane," said the professor; "being a natural path marked by a gentle stream and overhanging trees. Here, according to some historians, the Dutch maidens washed their linens; according to others, they and their swains wandered up and down on pleasant afternoons and evenings, never dreaming, it is safe to say, that this road outside of the town's wall would ever become a busy street in a great city. The Dutch called it the Maiden's Path; later it was changed by the English to Maiden Lane. Here are some verses that present a pretty picture of this interesting locality:

"'Down Maiden Lane, where clover grew,
  Sweet-scented in the early air,
Where sparkling rills went shining through
  Their grassy banks, so green, so fair,
Blithe little maids from Holland land
  Went tripping, laughing each to each,
To bathe the flax, or spread a band
  Of linen in the sun to bleach.

"'More than two centuries ago
  They wore this path—a maiden's lane—
Where now such waves of commerce flow
  As never dazed a burgher's brain.
Two hundred years ago and more
  Those thrifty damsels, one by one,
With plump, round arms their linen bore
  To dry in Mana-ha-ta's sun.

"'But now! Behold the altered view:
  No tender sward, no bubbling stream,
No laughter—was it really true,
  Or but the fancy of a dream?
Were these harsh walls a byway sweet,
  This floor of stone a grassy plain?
Oh! vanish, modern city street,
  And let us stroll down Maiden Lane!'

"The city at the time under consideration was about seventy-five years old, and for twenty-one years had been under the control of the English. Several important changes were now made that are of interest and that are noticeable to this day. I have already told you that the old church in the fort served three congregations—the Dutch, the English, and the French. This arrangement was no longer considered satisfactory, and each began to look about for a place of its own. As early as 1688 the French Huguenots built a small church where the Produce Exchange now stands, opposite Bowling Green. The Dutch erected their first house of worship in Garden Street, now Exchange Place, in 1693. A great silver baptismal bowl was made for it in Holland, and this can be seen at the present day in the church at Fifth Avenue and Twenty-ninth Street, which is the direct descendant of the old congregation in Garden Street. In 1696 the members of the Church of England decided to move uptown and selected the present site of Trinity. In February, 1697, the dedication sermon was preached by the Rev. William Vesey, whose name has been bestowed on a street that formed a part of the original church property. A special pew was set aside for the mayor and the Council, and every election day a sermon was preached for their special benefit.

"During this period a wave of enterprise swept over the little city. Not a single printing press had up to this time been established in New York, in which respect both Philadelphia and Boston were in advance of Manhattan. Early in 1693 William Bradford, Philadelphia's printer, got into a quarrel with the Quakers, and New York invited him to transfer his plant. He did so, set up his press at 81 Pearl Street, and printed the laws, almanacs, and many curious pamphlets, all of which are now eagerly sought by collectors of old books. A tablet, which we shall see later, marks the site of Bradford's first office.

"The second undertaking was the lighting of the streets. Except when the moon was good enough to shed her beams upon the town, New York was a city of darkness. Now, an order was issued providing that every seventh householder 'in the dark time of the moon' hang a lantern containing a candle on a pole, the charge to be equally divided by the tenants of the seven houses.

"The third step was the formation of a night watch, consisting of four good and honest inhabitants, whose duty it was to watch from nine in the evening until the break of day, to go around the city each hour of the night with a bell, and to call out the hour and the condition of the weather.

"Rumors of one of the many wars between France and England having reached New York about this time, the governor ordered a platform to be built on the rocks that jutted out of the water near the fort, to support a battery that would command both rivers. Thus the name Battery came to be applied to this section. The rocks, it is believed, are now under the made ground at Battery Park. The French, fortunately, did not cross the ocean to disturb the peace of New York, and all fear of such an occurrence having passed, the old stockade along Wall Street, being in a dilapidated condition, was pulled down.

"Having made these various improvements in the interest of the city, the authorities began to think of their own dignity and comfort. As the old City Hall in Pearl Street was showing signs of decay, they proposed erecting a fine new building at the corner of Wall and Broad Streets, where the Subtreasury stands to-day. In 1699 the corner stone was laid with considerable ceremony, and for more than a century this new hall served the purposes of the city. After the Revolution, Congress met within its walls, and on its balcony, in the presence of a great assemblage of people, the presidential oath was administered to Washington. But, of course, in the year 1699 no one thought of a President or a republic, or even of a great city whose population would be counted by the million."

CHAPTER IV

"PIRATES, smugglers, and slave dealers," announced the professor the next time we met, as if he were giving out a text.

"I do not wonder," he added, "that you appear surprised, but it is a fact that in the early years of 1700 New York not only permitted but actually welcomed men engaged in all three of the vocations I have mentioned. It was no unusual sight to see fierce, sun-browned individuals, swaggering through the streets, wearing a broad crimson sash across the left shoulder, a laced cap, a fancy jacket, white knickerbockers, a heavy gold chain, and no less than three or four richly mounted pistols in a gaudy belt. These men, just returned, perhaps, from a cruise in the Indian Ocean, felt quite at home in New York, and were entertained, it is said, in some of its best houses."

"How did it all come about?" asked George.

"In those days there was very little manufacturing in the colonies, and New York, being a seaport town, was dependent on ocean industries. The merchants engaged in river traffic, sent vessels up and down the coast, and traded with England, Africa, the East and West Indies. Now, every few years the European nations became involved in war, whereupon the seas were scoured by war ships and privateers, privateering being considered legitimate and perfectly honest. It meant that any man could get a commission to fill a ship with armed men and prey on the merchant vessels of the enemy. But men engaged in this sort of traffic were not overscrupulous, and the temptation to attack any vessel, no matter what flag it happened to fly, was sometimes too strong to be resisted; so the step from privateering to piracy was a short and an easy one. Of course, everybody posed as a good, honest privateer, and few questions were asked as to just how the rich silks and other costly products of the Orient were obtained. Furthermore, it was an open secret that some of the most prominent men in the city were interested in these enterprises."

"You don't say!" exclaimed Tom.

"Yes," said the professor, "but at length matters became so bad that no vessel was safe on the high seas, whereupon King William called a meeting of prominent lords, including Lord Bellomont, who later became Governor of New York, and, pointing out the audacity with which the pirates roamed the seas, announced that he had formed a company to exterminate these pests of the ocean. The plan was to wage war against the pirates and divide the spoils with which their ships were laden. In other words, the king entered into a partnership to prey upon dishonest privateers, and keep the booty instead of returning it to its rightful owners. This extraordinary scheme was devised, it is said, because the king was very short of money. A man was now wanted to head the expedition, and Bellomont recommended Captain William Kidd, of New York, a seaman of 'tried courage and integrity,' who happened to be in London at the time."

The name of Kidd caused the faces of the boys to light up with unusual interest.

"Without delay, the 'true and well-beloved Captain Kidd,' as the king called him, was made commander of the fine ship Adventure, in which he sailed from England in May, 1696, carrying thirty guns and a crew of eighty men. He arrived in New York in due time, increased his crew to one hundred and fifty-five, said good-bye to his wife and children, and sailed forth. Time passed, and after a while strange rumors began to circulate. It was whispered that Captain Kidd, instead of hunting pirates, had turned pirate himself; in fact, had become a very king of pirates, striking terror into the hearts of many a New York shipowner. In the meantime Bellomont had been appointed Governor of New York. Naturally he was greatly exasperated at Kidd's treachery and hoped for the time when he could catch the false captain. Three years passed, and then, one day, Kidd slipped into Long Island Sound, stopped at one or two places, buried some of his treasure, it is said, and then went on to Boston. He had learned that Bellomont was there, and believed that his old friend would protect him. In this he was mistaken. He was arrested, sent to England and hanged."

"And how about his treasure?" asked Tom.

"I can not say," said the professor. "Perhaps a little was found, and this was enough to excite any number of people to search in all manner of out-of-the-way places for more. Thus Kidd became an object of great interest, his deeds were magnified, and many ballads were written recounting his exploits.

"Smuggling, as I have already mentioned, was another evil of the times. There was a law that almost every article brought into the colonies must come from England. This was a loss and a hardship to the merchants, and tempted them to smuggle. Thus many a piece of French silk, Italian lace, and Indian finery was secretly slipped into New York. Fletcher made no serious efforts to stop smuggling, partly, perhaps, because he thought England was too severe on the colonists, but principally, it is said, because the smugglers bribed him to keep quiet. Fletcher's behavior in reference to these matters caused his recall in 1698, and then came Bellomont."

"He was a better governor, was he not?" asked George.

"Yes, he was a man of high character and pure motives—a far nobler type than the average governor. He sided with the Leisler party—that is, with the common people—as against the aristocrats, who wanted to run affairs entirely for their own benefit. One of his first acts was to have the bodies of Leisler and his son-in-law disinterred and buried with honor. Then he began a war against all bribe-takers, pirates, and smugglers. Unfortunately, he died after ruling only three years."

"How about the slave dealers?" asked Tom.

"Oh, yes," said the professor, "I must not forget to tell you about them. The business of stealing negroes from their native land was considered perfectly proper and honorable. Ships bearing such pious names as the Good Prophet sailed out of New York and returned with a cargo of human unfortunates that were sold like so many beasts of burden at a market near the foot of Wall Street. It was a common thing to find advertisements in the papers describing likely negroes, men and women, just imported from the coast of Africa. Often the slaves ran away, whereupon other advertisements appeared offering rewards for the return of the negroes. The number of such servants a family owned was regarded as a sign of wealth and social position. Of course, these negroes were a wild and savage lot when they arrived, and the treatment they received did not improve their character. In 1712 some discontented slaves met in an orchard near Maiden Lane and set fire to an outhouse. When the citizens ran to put out the flames, the blacks fired upon them, killing nine and wounding six. Great excitement ensued, the soldiers were called out, a pursuit organized, and twenty-one slaves captured. All of them were executed—some were hanged, some burned at the stake, and others, suspended in chains, were left to starve."

Emily shuddered, while Tom and George looked horrified.

"Those were cruel times," continued the professor, reading their thoughts, "but it must be remembered that there was no such protection then as there is now, and as all sorts of rumors were heard of a terrible plot to murder the citizens, it was deemed necessary to make a telling example of the ringleaders. Twenty-nine years later, in 1741, there was another scare. Several suspicious fires occurred in quick succession, a robbery was committed, and some of the stolen articles were found in a low tavern owned by whites where negroes used to congregate. The whole family, including servants, was arrested, and, according to the law of the day, sentenced to death. An offer of pardon was made to any of them who would tell the truth. Thereupon, Mary Burton, a wicked white servant, told of a plot on the part of the negroes, who then numbered only two thousand in a total population of twelve thousand, to destroy the town and kill all the people. This was an out-and-out falsehood; the evil character of Mary was well known, but the citizens were quickly excited, memories of the old plot of 1712 were revived, all sorts of stories were believed, and, before the inhabitants came to their senses, fourteen negroes were burned alive, eighteen were hanged, and seventy-one transported to various places. Two white persons were also executed—John Hughson, the owner of the tavern, and John Ury, a clergyman. He was supposed to be a Catholic priest who was in league with the blacks and was inciting them to murder the Protestants. It was proved that he was not a Catholic, and no connection between him and the blacks was established, but false testimony sent him to the gallows. Such was the fearful result of this foolish scare, and a day of thanksgiving was actually appointed to celebrate the city's escape from a horrible fate."

"Weren't Catholic priests allowed in New York at that time?" asked George.

"No; there was a law that all Catholic priests found in the colony should be condemned to death."

"How narrow-minded!" said Emily with feeling.

"True," agreed the professor; "but in those days there was great intolerance. Catholic governments persecuted and executed Protestants, and the latter, I suppose, thought they were justified in retaliating. Of course, it was all wrong—religion should teach men to love one another as brothers, even though they have different ways of worshiping their Almighty Father."

"Did you not say something about advertisements and newspapers?" asked George. "When was the first newspaper published?"

"A very proper question," remarked the professor. "The first New York newspaper appeared in 1725, and was issued by William Bradford, who was then over sixty years old. It was called The New York Gazette, published once a week, and was supposed to contain all the news. The print, as you can imagine, was not what we see to-day, and in fact the whole paper was a very crude affair, but it paved the way for the great feats of journalism that have since been accomplished by the New York press.

"Nine years later, a new paper, called The Weekly Journal, made its appearance, the editor being John Peter Zenger, who had served as an ap-

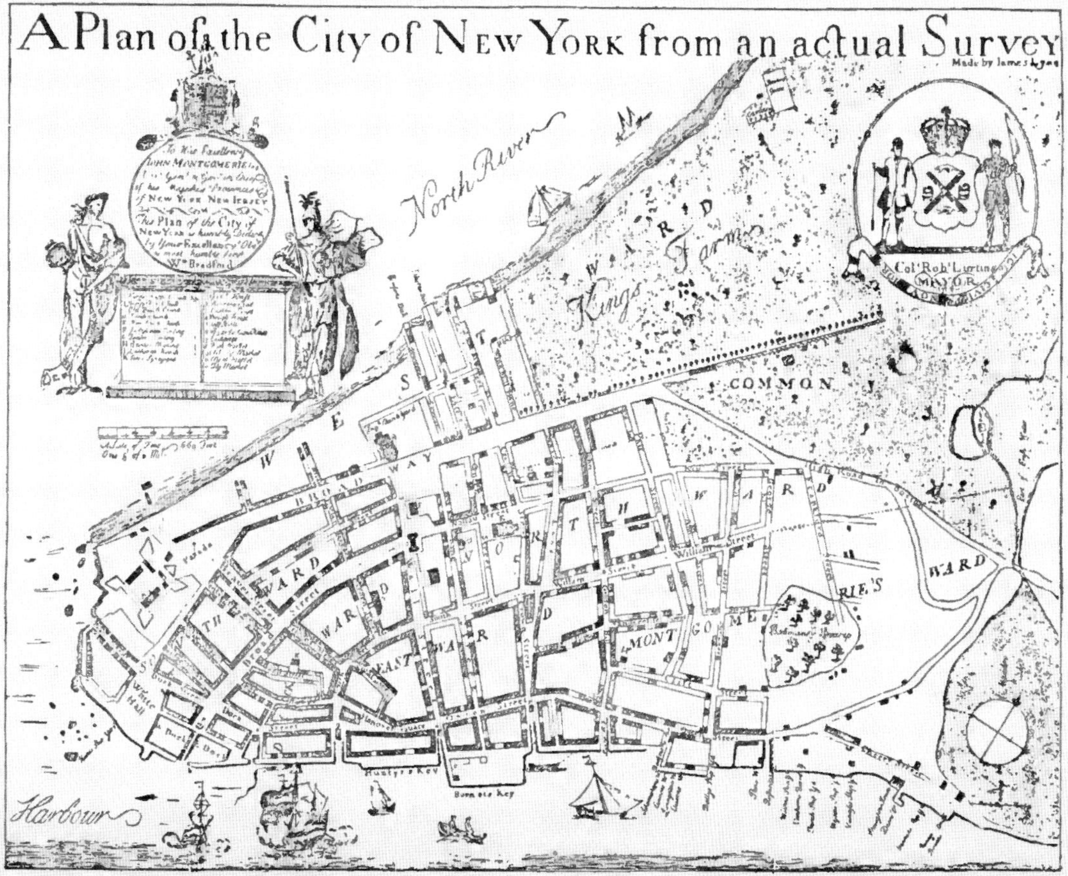

Map of New York in 1728, from a survey by James Lyne. Printed by William Bradford. Seal in upper right-hand corner.

prentice under Bradford. Zenger was led to undertake this enterprise against his old master because there was need of a paper to favor the cause of the people, Bradford's Gazette being pledged to the aristocrats and the governor.

"The governor, William Cosby, was a despot who sought to deprive the people of some of their dearest privileges. This stirred up a great deal of feeling, and the Journal, among whose writers were some of the cleverest men of the day, began to publish articles that attracted widespread attention. Squibs, ballads, and witty items appeared that hit the governor and his friends very hard. These paper bullets at last irritated Cosby to such an extent that he had Zenger thrown into prison on a charge of printing false, scandalous, and seditious matter, and at the same time he ordered the city's hangman publicly to burn certain copies of the paper. The judge of the court was a strong friend of Cosby, and could be depended on to treat the prisoner with the utmost severity. Zenger had the best two lawyers in the town to defend him, but by a trick they were declared in contempt and forbidden to act. There being no other New York lawyer that could be hired, the enemies of Zenger thought they had him completely at their mercy.

"The trial took place in August, 1735. A great crowd filled the court room, and listened eagerly to the charge made by the attorney-general. When he had finished there was a stir among the people, which was followed by a murmur of surprise when a fine-looking, white-haired man arose and said he was there to defend the prisoner. He was instantly recognized as Andrew Hamilton, of Philadelphia, who, though eighty years of age, was acknowledged to be one of the ablest lawyers of the country."

"Good!" said Tom, who loved fair play.

"Hamilton asked to have a chance to prove the truth of all that had been published. This was the last thing in the world the other side wanted, and the judge refused the request. Hamilton cleverly turned this refusal to his own advantage in speaking to the jury. A long argument now followed between the attorney-general and Hamilton, in the course of which the latter claimed, in a fine speech, that every freeman had a right to complain against abuses of power and to preserve the blessings of liberty. He pointed out that this was not the case merely of a poor printer, nor of New York alone, but one that would affect every citizen that lived under the British Government in America. In conclusion, he explained to the members of the jury that their verdict would decide whether men had the right to oppose the acts of tyrants by speaking and writing the truth!

"The speech of the venerable lawyer was listened to with the closest attention. The jury, after a few words from the judge, then withdrew, and in a short time returned with a verdict of *not guilty!*"

"Hurrah!" shouted the boys, while Emily clapped her hands.

"That's the way the verdict was received in the court," said the professor, smiling. "The judge tried to stop the shouting, but nobody paid any attention to him. As to Hamilton, the grand old man who had thus established the liberty of the press, he was cheered, banqueted, and presented with the freedom of the city, the certificate being inclosed in a beautiful gold box. When, a day or two later, he departed for Philadelphia, nearly the whole population turned out to do him honor."

"What do you mean by the freedom of the city?" asked George.

"It is a special mark of appreciation conferred on a non-resident for public services, and entitles him to all the rights and privileges of a citizen.

"You have, no doubt, noticed," continued the professor, "that some of the governors sent over by England were not very desirable persons. In fact, with the exception of a few, they were unsucessful men who expected to repair their broken fortunes in the colonies. Naturally, they thought less of the welfare of the people than of their own affairs. One, Cornbury, indulged in the silly habit of wearing women's clothes; while another, Osborne, having lost his wife, imagined that a change of scene would benefit him. This sort of treatment on the part of England, of course, was felt by the colonists, but, for a time, matters of greater importance absorbed their attention.

"The French, having established flourishing settlements in Canada, and having made friends with the Indians, were pushing westward and southward, and were actually planning to take New York. Montcalm, the French general, was quick, shrewd, and successful; the English generals were slow, conceited, and unsuccessful. At Ticonderoga, in 1758, not heeding the advice of American soldiers, whom he looked upon with contempt, Abercrombie sacrificed two thousand brave men. At length a new

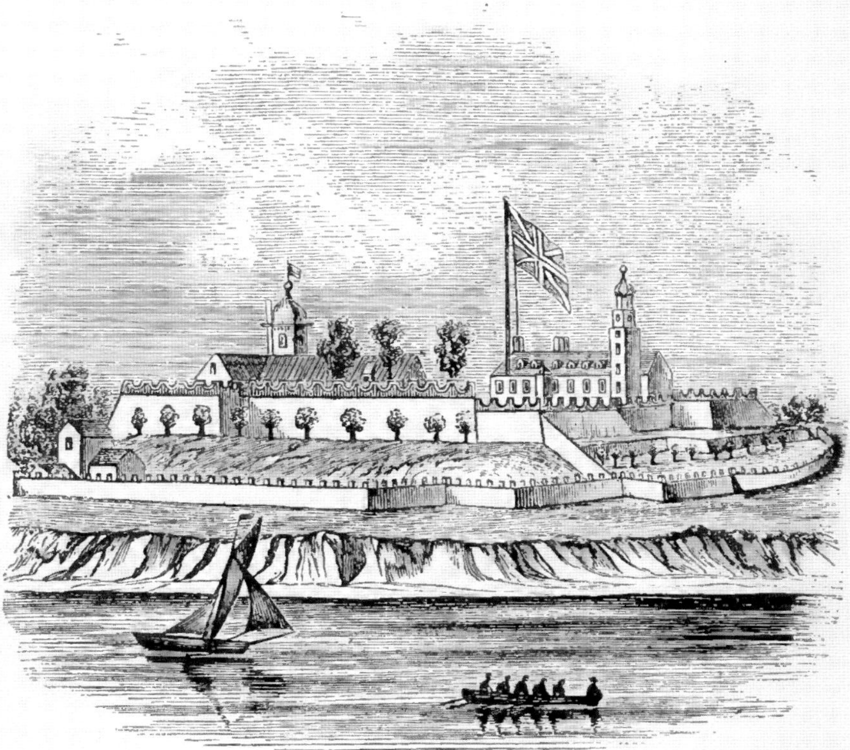

View of the fort about the year 1750. From an old print in Valentine's Manual for 1862.

commander, Wolfe, was sent over, and he turned the tide of affairs. Under his able leadership, Quebec, situated on its high rock and considered impregnable, was captured in 1759. Both commanders fell in this attack, and both were deeply mourned, for they were gallant and able generals. Thus Canada came into the hands of the English, the Indians for the time being were cowed, and New York was safe.

"In its small way, New York was now quite a fine town. True, its entire population was less than the attendance at any popular football match of to-day, and one did not need to walk very far along Broadway, north of Trinity, to reach the country; but there was plenty of spirit and enterprise, and the people felt that they ought to have the best in the way of education. Accordingly, a college was suggested. Trinity church helped along the project from the beginning, and as early as 1754 a class met in a schoolhouse belonging to the church. Then Trinity presented the trustees with some land forming part of a large tract west of Broadway, that had been granted to it by Queen Anne. The college tract lay between Barclay and Murray Streets, and extended to the Hudson River, 'in the skirts of the city,' as an old paper puts it. In 1756 the corner stone was laid, and in 1760 the buildings began to be used. This was the beginning of Columbia College, originally called King's College."

"Why did they change the name?" asked George.

"Because, after the Revolution the people hated everything that suggested royalty so much that they would not tolerate a King's College, or a Queen, a Crown, or a Duke Street.

"Just before the meddling and blundering acts devised by young King George III, and his short-sighted advisers brought matters to a crisis, New

York was a sort of little London. The governor represented the king, and with his officers made up a petty court, where the aristocrats loved to assemble. The governor's coach was a magnificent affair, drawn by four or six horses, his lackeys wore fine liveries, and the harness used for state occasions was remarkably elegant. Without doubt the town was putting on lots of airs.

"The fashionable promenade was the Mall in the neighborhood of Trinity church. Here, on fine afternoons, while one of the military bands played, the young ladies of the town, accompanied by officers in scarlet coats and gold lace, or by gayly dressed young men, walked leisurely up and down, the young ladies being followed by their negro waiting maids. It was generally understood that the 'common people' were not to use this particular promenade."

"What a piece of impertinence!" said Emily.

"The common people at that time—that is, the mechanics and such like—wore big leather aprons, while the upper classes dressed in what we would now call fancy costumes.

"There was a little theater in Nassau Street that was patronized by the fashionables. The play began at half past six, but long before that hour the place was filled, not by those who were to see the performance, but by their negro slaves, who were sent early to secure good seats. Thus for hours this curious assemblage sat silent in semi-darkness, disappearing just before the time the curtain was about to rise.

"Up to 1765, I venture to say, young King George had no more loyal subjects in all his kingdom than right here in New York. The men were faithful, and many of the women thought no higher honor could befall them than to marry an English officer. But in those days an idea prevailed that a colonist was not so good as a man who lived on English soil, and did not have the same rights. Taxes had been levied from time to time, but not regularly or offensively. Now, a tax was proposed that was to be vigorously collected—a stamp to be affixed to all sorts of paper, even to a marriage license. It was as if the mother country were about to put her hand in the colonists' pockets and spend their money without asking them. Englishmen at home would not stand such treatment, and English subjects in America saw no reason why they were not entitled to the same privileges. The Stamp Act was presently repealed, as were other obnoxious laws, but not until the mischief had been done and the breach irretrievably made."

CHAPTER V

"We are now ready," said the professor at our next meeting, "to take a look at New York as it appeared just before the Revolution, when it was still an English town, but when the spirit of irritation and discontent had become decidedly noticeable."

Accordingly, we boarded an elevated train and rode down to Battery Park. Here the professor called our attention to the big flag pole near the new Barge Office, and asked us to bear it in mind in connection with the evacuation of the city by the English after the Revolutionary War.

"Let us now cross to the Third Avenue road," he suggested, "and ride over to Hanover Square."

"Why was it called Hanover Square?" asked Emily.

"In honor of King George I, who was of the house of Hanover."

Having entered the train, we soon were made aware of the crookedness of the city's old streets by a series of sudden twistings and turnings.

Just as we rounded the second curve the professor called our attention to "Canal-boat village," consisting of a flotilla of flat-topped boats moored to one of the long piers of Coenties Slip, near the site of the old Dutch City Hall.

"Those boats come all the way from Buffalo," said our guide. "They each carry, besides a load of some eight thousand bushels of wheat, or its equivalent, the captain of the boat, his family, three helpers, three horses, and a dog. They are comfortable floating houses and well worth a visit. Try to remember about these boats when we come to the interesting story of the Erie Canal."

"What park was that near the boats?" asked Emily.

"Jeanette Park, named after the ship sent to the arctic regions by the New York Herald."

A few minutes later we arrived at Hanover Square.

"This," said the professor, "was the business center of the city about the year 1765—the shopping district where ladies came in search of bargains, if such attractions existed at that time. In its way, it was a bustling quarter and, without doubt, presented a more varied and striking scene than our streets offer to-day, the ornamental sedan chair adding its old-world picturesqueness to the surroundings. It was also the first Printing House Square, where news a week or more old was made public."

"What's that fine building?" asked George.

"That is the Cotton Exchange. New York's first newspaper was issued where it stands, as you can see by consulting the tablet."

We crossed over to the spot indicated and George read the inscription, which is as follows:

ON THIS SITE
WILLIAM BRADFORD,
APPOINTED PUBLIC PRINTER, APRIL 10TH, A. D. 1693,
ISSUED, NOVEMBER 8TH, A. D. 1725,
THE NEW YORK GAZETTE,
THE FIRST NEWSPAPER PRINTED IN NEW YORK.
ERECTED BY THE
NEW YORK HISTORICAL SOCIETY,
APRIL 10TH, A. D. 1893,
IN COMMEMORATION OF THE 200TH ANNIVERSARY OF
THE INTRODUCTION OF PRINTING IN NEW YORK.

"What's the Historical Society?" queried Tom.

"A society founded in 1804 for preserving historical material. The principal organizer was John Pintard, who as early as 1790 established an American Museum. A highly interesting and valuable collection can be seen at the society's house, corner of Second Avenue and Eleventh Street."

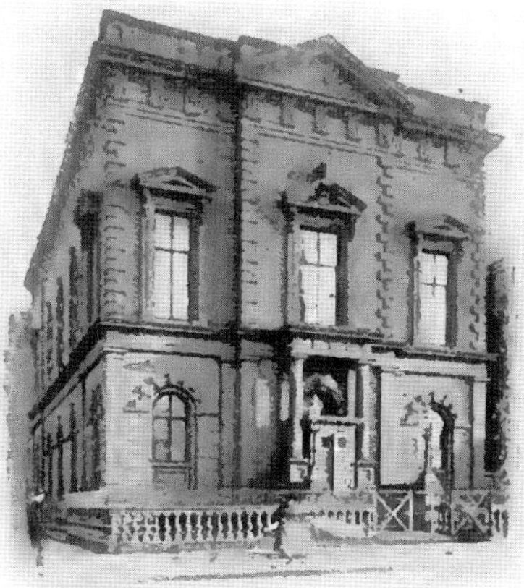

New York Historical Society,
Eleventh St. and Second Ave.

While we were talking, our guide led us southward along Pearl Street, the narrowness of which is very suggestive of the days when New York was a small town. At No. 81 we found a tablet, fastened to the jamb of the doorway, containing the following legend:

ON THIS SITE
WILLIAM BRADFORD,
APPOINTED
PUBLIC PRINTER
APRIL 10TH, A. D. 1693,
ESTABLISHED THE FIRST
PRINTING PRESS
IN THE
COLONY OF NEW YORK.
ERECTED BY THE
NEW YORK
HISTORICAL SOCIETY,
APRIL 10TH, A. D. 1893,
IN COMMEMORATION OF
THE 200TH ANNIVERSARY
OF THE INTRODUCTION
OF PRINTING IN
NEW YORK.

"These two plates," remarked the professor, "commemorate, as you see, the establishment of printing in the colony and the issue of the first newspaper—two very important events. Other journals were subsequently launched, and they all played a more or less important part during the time of unrest that preceded the Revolution.

"We are now about ready to turn our attention to that exciting and momentous period, but before doing so let us go over to Bowling Green," suggested the professor, "and see what changes have occurred since our previous visit."

Following Stone Street, we soon reached the Green, and, seating ourselves within the little park, listened to the professor's remarks.

"In 1765 the fort was still over yonder where the steamship offices used to be, but red-coated sentries paced up and down instead of Stuyvesant's old Dutch defenders. This space was no longer open ground, but was a veritable bowling green, with an iron railing around it, which remains to this day with the exception of the top balls. The latter were broken off and used by the Americans during the Revolution. As to the bowling, permission had been granted as early as 1732 to certain residents of Broadway to use the plot for that purpose. Some of the old Dutch houses were gone, and at No. 1, where now that tall office building towers up, a broad, spacious mansion, known as the Kennedy House, was located, a house of many historic associations, as you will learn."

"Whose statue is that?" asked George, pointing to the bronze figure that now adorns Bowling Green.

"Abraham de Peyster, son of a leading Dutch merchant of New Amsterdam. He was one of Leisler's supporters, was appointed mayor in 1691, and afterward became one of the judges of the Supreme Court.

"It is now high time," said the professor, changing the subject, "to introduce you to the Sons of Liberty."

"Who were they?" asked Tom.

"Just about what their name implies; but, curiously enough, the expression came from England. One day, while the Stamp Act was being debated in the House of Commons, Barré, friend and companion of Wolfe, the hero of Quebec, in a rousing speech,

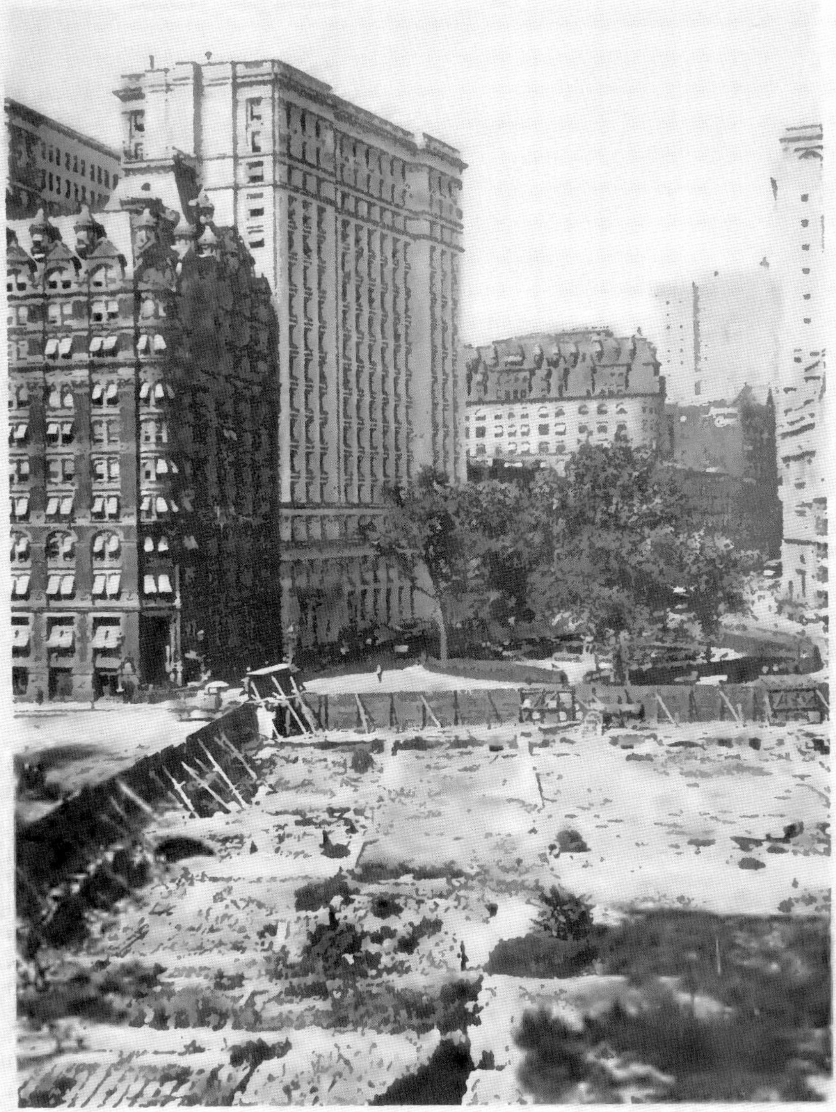

Site of Fort Amsterdam, directly south of Bowling Green. Cleared to make room for the new Customhouse. The building to the left is No. 1 Broadway. Photographed 1900.

justified the Sons of Liberty, as he called the Americans, in feeling aggrieved at the treatment they had received. The name was caught up as if it were a magic term. It spread through the colonies and was adopted by a secret order, composed of men who were determined not to yield the rights they had won, and to which they felt they were entitled.

"Had you lived in New York in the autumn of 1765 you would have seen exciting times. The thought that the Stamp Act was to be enforced was in everybody's mind, and had you joined any group of citizens you would, no doubt, have heard them protesting that they were just as good and just as loyal as the subjects of the crown who lived in England. You would also, I believe, have heard them say that the constitution of England provided that its people could be taxed only with their consent, but that the colonists had never been consulted about this tax, and that, therefore, it was unconstitutional and ought to be resisted."

"That's right," remarked Tom.

"You must remember," continued the professor, "in order to understand the situation clearly, that at this time there were four classes of people in New York: First, the king's officials, officers, and soldiers; second, a large number of Americans, known as Tories or Loyalists, who sided with the king and Parliament; third, the Moderates, who were opposed to all unjust measures, but were very conservative in their ideas; and, fourth, the Hot-heads, who wanted to do all sorts of wild deeds."

"To which class did the Sons of Liberty belong?" asked Tom.

"To the Hot-heads, most assuredly," answered the professor; "but, to be perfectly fair, I must say that the Liberty Boys meant well, even if they were impulsive. Among them, too, were many irresponsible fellows who were always ready to take part in any demonstration *for* or *against* the king, and help on any mischief that was afoot.

"The month of October was an exciting period, especially after a vessel had been sighted off Sandy Hook, which was known to contain a shipment of the hated stamps. Colden, the lieutenant governor, had his hands full, and Gage, the military commander, had to be very diplomatic.

"Mysterious posters now suddenly appeared threatening any one found using the stamps, and lively ballads were sung in the streets. Here's a verse from one," continued the professor, drawing out a little memorandum book from his pocket:

"'With the beasts of the wood we'll ramble for food
 And lodge in wild deserts and caves,
And live, poor as Job, on the skirts of the globe
Before we'll submit to be slaves, brave boys,
 Before we'll submit to be slaves!'"

"That's a good one," remarked Tom.

"The next important step was a meeting of merchants at a popular place on Broadway known as Burns's Tavern, where a resolution was passed called the 'Non-Importation Agreement,' which provided that no more goods were to be purchased from England. Orders were immediately canceled, and a host of English merchants suddenly found a large portion of their business gone. In the meantime, men and women wore simple home-made clothes, and denied themselves many luxuries that they had been in the habit of getting from the mother country.

"If you will now take a short walk with me," continued the professor, "I shall point out to you the memorial that commemorates the beginning of the Stamp Act troubles."

We arrived presently at No. 115 Broadway, and here George performed his usual duty, reading the following inscription:

THE SITE OF THE OLD HISTORIC DE LANCEY HOUSE,
AFTERWARD THE "CITY HOTEL."
THE TAVERN LOCATED HERE HAD VARIOUS PROPRIETORS
BY WHOSE NAMES IT WAS SUCCESSIVELY CALLED,
BEING AMONG OTHERS KNOWN AS
"THE PROVINCE ARMS," "THE CITY ARMS"
AND "BURNS COFFEE HOUSE OR TAVERN."
IT WAS HERE THAT THE CELEBRATED
NON-IMPORTATION AGREEMENT IN OPPOSITION
TO THE "STAMP ACT" WAS SIGNED OCT. 31ST, 1765.
ERECTED BY THE HOLLAND SOCIETY OF
NEW YORK, MARCH, 1890.

"At last the fateful November 1st arrived, the date when the Stamp Act was to go into operation. The stamps had come, but Colden kept them locked up for the time being. That evening the Liberty Boys assembled on The Common, or The Fields, as City Hall Park was then called, and held a stormy meeting. The park at that time was a large open space where the people met on all sorts of occasions. To my mind, it is a spot that every American, and especially every New York man, woman, and child, ought to cherish and respect. I always think of it as Liberty Park, for it is closely associated with all the early struggles against oppression.

"Had you been in the crowd that autumn evening you would have seen through the glimmer of torchlights a gallows on which hung a stuffed figure of Colden, and another beside it to represent the devil. After a while a noisy procession was formed that marched down Broadway, carrying the gallows and the effigies past St. Paul's, Burns's Tavern, and Trinity. In front of the fort, not many blocks from this spot, it halted.

"Then you would have had a good chance to notice the leaders: Colonel John Lamb; hot-headed Isaac Sears, called King Sears; shrewd Alexander McDougall; lawyer John Morin Scott, and patriot Marinus Willett."

"What did they do next?" asked Tom, his eyes bright with excitement.

"They cheered and they jeered; they dared the commander to fire upon them; they placed the gallows against the fort gate and hammered the doors with clubs. Then they brought the stuffed figures forward, and with them the governor's coach, which they had taken from his stable near by, and set the whole afire."

"And what did the governor do?" asked George.

"He acted with great moderation," answered the professor; "so did General Gage, who had command of the fort. No one was punished, and a promise was given that no stamps should be issued until further instructions came from England. As a matter of fact, in March, 1766, a new ministry entered into power with Pitt at its head, and the obnoxious act was soon repealed. Everybody was happy, especially the Liberty Boys, who went wild with joy.

"On June 4th, the anniversary of the king's birthday, a great jubilee was held on the Commons, the English flag floated in the breeze, the band played 'God save the King,' and a pole bearing a shield with the words 'The King, Pitt, and Liberty' was erected. Any one with half an eye could have seen that the colonists thus celebrating, were loyal, and if there had been no more meddling there might have been no more trouble.

"The soldiers, however, were not disposed to remain quiet. They were supposed to be the protectors of the colony, but such were their feelings against the people that they looked upon the Liberty pole erected on the Common as a symbol of triumph not to be tolerated. Accordingly, one night in August they cut it down. Another pole was immediately set in its place, and this was also cut down. A third met with a similar fate. By this time the citizens were in a state of fury, and more determined than ever to have their pole. A fourth was thereupon erected and fastened with iron braces. This was unmolested until January, 1770, when, at midnight, it was pulled down by the redcoats and sawed into pieces."

"What a shame!" exclaimed Emily.

"The outrage was discovered the next morning, and the news spread like wildfire. Great excitement followed, especially when the following day (January 18th) Sears came upon three soldiers in the act of posting up some scurrilous placards abusing the Sons of Liberty. Sears and a companion arrested two of them and started to take them to the mayor's office. A re-enforcement of twenty soldiers with drawn swords and bayonets now rushed up to the rescue of their comrades, and a number of citizens flocked to the spot armed with stakes.

"The mayor then appeared on the scene and ordered the soldiers to their barracks. The latter retired to Golden Hill (John Street near William), and there, making a stand, charged the people, few of whom had weapons, and a bloody fight took place in which several individuals on both sides were wounded.

"The next day the soldiers began the conflict again by thrusting a bayonet through the dress of a woman who was returning from market. This cowardly act aroused the indignation of the citizens anew. Later, a party of sailors, who generally sided with the citizens, came into collision with some redcoats, and a sailor was run through the body. In the afternoon the soldiers insulted several citizens and more trouble followed, in the course of which the troops were driven back to their barracks. Thus ended the battle of Golden Hill, a fight for a principle, in which the first blood in the War of the Revolution was shed."

"Was that before the Boston massacre?" asked George.

"Nearly two months before, and it was a much more important affair."

"Hurrah for New York!" shouted Tom.

The professor smiled at Tom's enthusiasm, and continued by informing us that the Sons of Liberty now raised a fifth pole—a great high staff with a vane at the top bearing the simple but significant word—Liberty. It was not molested.

"Is there a tablet at Golden Hill?" asked George.

"Yes," answered the professor, "and it may be well to visit it at once. We shall have to retrace our steps several times to see the tablets of this period in their proper order; but, I presume, you will not mind a little additional walking?"

No objection was made. The professor turned into Maiden Lane on reaching that interesting street, and we took great pleasure in passing down the old Dutch path so suggestive of romantic associations. Entering William Street and going northward one block, we paused at John Street.

"This is Golden Hill," remarked the professor.

"Why was it so called?" asked Emily.

"Because originally it was a sloping field of grain that looked like gold in the sunshine. The hill is still here, and perhaps plenty of gold, but not the kind that gave the historic place its name."

At the northwest corner of the two streets we found a small plain tablet bearing these noteworthy words:

> GOLDEN HILL.
> HERE JANUARY 18, 1770,
> THE FIGHT TOOK PLACE BETWEEN THE
> "SONS OF LIBERTY"
> AND THE
> BRITISH REGULARS, 16TH FOOT.
> FIRST BLOOD IN THE
> WAR OF THE REVOLUTION.
> ERECTED BY THE SONS OF THE REVOLUTION.

"There ought to be a fine marble monument here," said Tom.

"There's not enough room, but one ought certainly to be placed in City Hall Park, in memory of the first liberty poles."

"Who are the Sons of the Revolution?" asked George.

"A society intended to keep alive the patriotic spirit of the men who in military, naval, or civil service, by act or counsel, achieved American independence. To become a member a man must be at least twenty-one years old and be descended from an ancestor who in one form of service or another assisted in establishing American independence.

"Suppose we now take a look at the place where the Sons of Liberty used to gather," added the professor.

The suggestion was enthusiastically received, and

walking up John Street, past the First Methodist Church, we turned into Broadway once more and soon reached the big post-office building, wherein we found a handsome bronze plate inscribed as follows:

> ON THE COMMON OF THE CITY OF NEW YORK
> NEAR WHERE THIS BUILDING NOW STANDS THERE
> STOOD FROM 1766 TO 1776 A LIBERTY POLE ERECTED
> TO COMMEMORATE THE REPEAL OF THE STAMP ACT
> IT WAS REPEATEDLY DESTROYED BY THE VIOLENCE OF
> THE TORIES AND AS REPEATEDLY REPLACED BY THE
> SONS OF LIBERTY WHO ORGANIZED A CONSTANT
> WATCH AND GUARD. IN ITS DEFENCE THE
> FIRST MARTYR BLOOD OF THE AMERICAN
> REVOLUTION WAS SHED ON JAN. 18, 1770.
>
> A. D. 1897 ERECTED BY THE MARY WASHINGTON COLONIAL CHAPTER,
> DAUGHTERS OF THE AMERICAN REVOLUTION.

"Who are the Daughters of the American Revolution?" asked Emily.

"Sisters, cousins, or aunts of the Sons, I imagine," answered the professor; "at any rate the rules of admission are the same, except that a Daughter can become a member at eighteen, while a Son must be twenty-one."

Emerging from the building at one of the uptown exits, we saw the park before us.

"This was the Common, a big open space, not as attractive as it is now, but none the less sacred ground. No tall structures surrounded it, no swiftly moving cars glided by, no fountain graced a well-kept lawn—it was blank and barren; soldiers' barracks occupied the upper end along Chambers Street, a workhouse and a powder magazine being near by. A new jail, called the Bridewell, was situated just to the west of the spot where the City Hall now stands, and to the northeast was the Provost or Debtors' Prison. There it still stands," said the professor, pointing to the Hall of Records. "We shall pay it a visit later.

"During the ten distressing years that intervened between the passage of the Stamp Act and the beginning of the Revolution many remarkable meetings took place on the Common, and at one of these, held in July, 1774, Alexander Hamilton, then but a youth of seventeen, made an address. His slight figure and boyish appearance at once aroused curiosity, but he was so startled at the sea of strange faces before him that at first he faltered. Gradually, however, gathering courage, he warmed up to his theme; thoughts of wrongs and oppression that had long been in his mind found expression in such strong, clear, and thrilling words, that when he finished, for a moment, there was breathless silence, and then exclamations of wonder at his youth and praise of his extraordinary eloquence were heard on all sides.

"In spite of various forms of oppression, the people continued loyal, and in 1770, as a token of their gratitude for the repeal of the Stamp Act, they erected in Bowling Green a leaden statue of King George on horseback, very much in appearance like that of Washington in Union Square. They also placed a marble figure of Pitt in Wall

Street near William, which bore these significant words:

> THIS STATUE
> OF THE
> RIGHT HONOURABLE
> WILLIAM PITT
> EARL OF CHATHAM,
> WAS ERECTED
> AS A PUBLICK TESTIMONY OF THE GRATEFUL
> SENSE THE COLONY OF NEW YORK
> RETAINS OF THE MANY EMINENT
> SERVICES HE RENDERED AMERICA,
> PARTICULARLY IN PROMOTING THE REPEAL
> OF THE STAMP ACT,
> ANNO DOM. MDCCLXX.

"What became of Pitt's statue?" asked Emily.

"It was mutilated, as you will learn before long, and finally, after a varied career, it found an honorable resting place in the hall of the New York Historical Society.

"Young King George had not forgotten his defeat in connection with the Stamp Act, and he now foolishly decided to get revenge. Accordingly, he had a new measure passed taxing tea, which was a sort of challenge to see what the colonies would do about it. They treated it as it deserved, and New York indulged in a little Tea Party."

"Was that before or after the Boston Tea Party?" asked George.

"After. It appears that the ship intended for New York, the Nancy, was driven out of her course, and did not reach here until April, 1774, four months after the Boston tea episode. The Nancy, according to an article in one of the papers of the day, was said to have something on board worse than a Jonah. A committee of the Sons of Liberty took her in charge and kept her down the bay. In the meantime another ship, the London, arrived. Her captain said he had no tea on board, but the Liberty Boys found eighteen chests. These they opened, poured the tea into the river, and, after two hours of quiet amusement of this sort, dispersed in good order."

"What became of the Nancy?" asked George.

"She was sent back to England with her whole cargo of tea, and the untruthful captain of the London was sent along. Here is a poetic sentiment of the time that may interest you," added the professor, referring to his note-book.

"'When a certain great king, whose initial is G.,
Forces STAMPS upon paper, and folks to drink TEA;
When these folks burn his tea and stampt paper like stub-
ble—
You may guess that this king is then coming to trouble.'

"And here is another:

"'At this time arose a certain King Sears,
Who made his study to banish our fears;
He was without doubt a person of merit,
Great knowledge, some wit, and abundance of spirit;
Could talk like a lawyer, and that without fee,
And threaten'd perdition to all who drank tea.'

"King George was now very angry at the Americans, and especially at the people of Boston, because he thought they were more disobedient than the citizens of other cities. Accordingly, he made up his mind to punish Boston, and at the same time show the other colonies that he was master. In April, 1774, he managed to get Parliament, not without considerable opposition, however, to pass an act shutting up Boston as a port and annulling the charter of Massachusetts. This meant the destruction of all shipping business for the city and the appointment of a governor with despotic power for the Commonwealth. When this piece of news became known a wave of indignation spread through the colonies, and a feeling of sympathy with unhappy Boston stirred every patriotic heart. There had been jealousies and quarrels among the colonies before, but now a bond of brotherhood was created that grew stronger from day to day.

"I need scarcely tell you, I presume," continued the professor, "what occurred on April 19, 1775?"

"The battle of Lexington," answered Emily, George, and Tom, in one breath.

"Correct," said the professor. "Four days later, on Sunday afternoon, a dust-stained horseman dashed furiously down Broadway with the news of that world-changing battle. You can imagine the effect of his information as it was repeated by one excited group to another. New York was still in the hands of the Tories, but the patriots were quick to act. Forgetting all about the Sabbath, a band of Liberty Boys marched down to the City Hall in Wall Street, forced open the doors and took six hundred muskets, which they distributed among the more active citizens, who formed themselves into a volunteer corps and assumed the government of the city.

"To find the next historic site of special interest," continued the professor, "we'll have to go back almost to the spot whence we started, but we shall be well repaid for our pilgrimage."

In passing along Nassau Street, which, as we were informed, was once known as Piewoman's Lane, our guide began describing to us a memorial of what he termed "one of the most extraordinary acts of daring patriotism on record."

He stopped us at the corner of Broad and Beaver Streets, before a handsome tablet, and George, without waiting, began to read:

TO COMMEMORATE THE GALLANT AND PATRIOTIC ACT OF MARINUS WILLETT IN HERE SEIZING, JUNE 6TH, 1775, FROM BRITISH FORCES THE MUSKETS WITH WHICH HE ARMED HIS TROOPS. THIS TABLET IS ERECTED BY THE SOCIETY OF THE SONS OF THE REVOLUTION. NEW YORK, NOV., 1892.

BORN, JULY, 1740. MARINUS WILLETT. DIED AUG., 1830.
OFFICER OF NEW YORK MILITIA 1775-78. SHERIFF OF NEW YORK 1784-92.
MAYOR OF NEW YORK 1807-8. PRESIDENT OF ELECTORAL COLLEGE 1824.

"Notice the fine medallion of Willett," said the professor, "and the surprisingly clear picture of the troops, the houses, and the view of the City Hall at the end of Broad Street."

"What is the story?" asked Tom.

"A committee of one hundred patriots was in charge of the city at the time. In the harbor lay the

British frigate Asia, ready to convey a regiment of soldiers from the fort to Boston. A curiously confused state of peace and war now existed. No opposition was to be made to the landing of British troops, but force was to be met with force. Meanwhile, permission was given to the regiment to depart, but with such arms only as the men carried on their persons. In other words, a New York committee was dictating to British troops what they should be allowed to do.

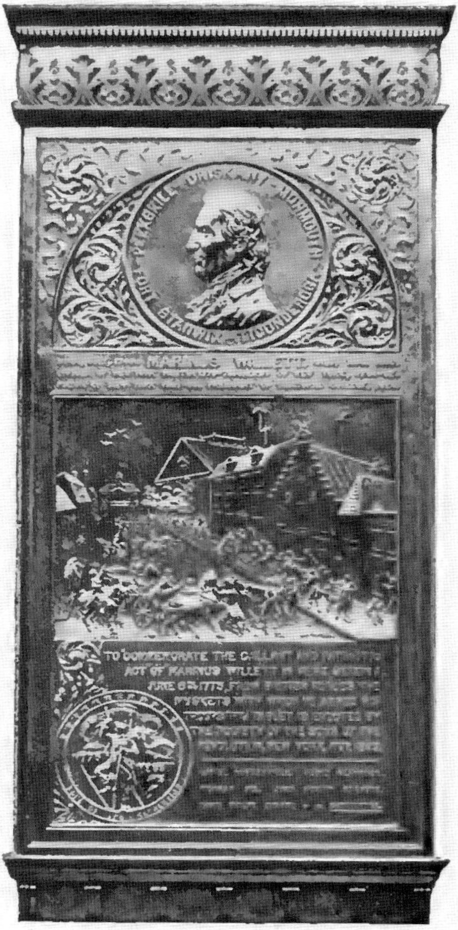

Marinus Willett tablet, corner Broad and Beaver Streets. Photographed 1900.

"On June 6, 1775, the soldiers marched along here on their way to the wharf, and many people were out to see them leave, saying in their hearts, 'Good riddance!' Suddenly the rumbling of carts was heard, and when they came into view it was seen that they contained stacks of arms. Noticing this, Marinus Willett stepped boldly forward and stopped the horse of the first cart. Immediately the major galloped up to see what was the matter, whereupon Willett told him that he had no authority to carry off the arms in the wagons.

"A discussion then took place, the upshot being that Willett jumped into the cart, turned it about, and, followed by the others, made his way up Broadway amid a constant accompaniment of cheers. The arms were safely put away, and afterward used by the first patriot troops raised in New York. The tablet tells you of Willett's subsequent honors, to which may be added the interesting item that two of our streets have been named after him—Willett and Sheriff Streets.

"The year 1775 continued to be a time of almost constant excitement and every one was restless and uneasy. Representatives of the different colonies were in session at Philadelphia, and all sorts of measures were being considered. At length a resolution was passed recommending each colony to organize companies of militia. A corps was formed in New York called The Hearts of Oak, the members of which wore green uniforms and leather caps bearing the significant inscription, *Freedom or Death.* Every day a drill took place and a crowd of enthusiastic citizens gathered to see the young men display their knowledge of military tactics.

"The Hearts of Oak soon had a taste of gunpowder. They had been ordered by the Committee of Safety to remove the cannons from the Battery, and while they were thus occupied a boat from the English man-of-war Asia approached, intending, it was supposed, to interfere with the work. Without stopping to think of consequences, some one fired at the boat, which immediately returned a broadside, killing one of the youthful militiamen.

"The result of this incident was a violent commotion, and crowds of Liberty Boys traversed the streets threatening every adherent of the crown with personal violence. One party made its way to King's College to seize the person of the president, Doctor Cooper, who was known to be a Tory. Alexander Hamilton and a few others, discovering the destination of the crowd, rushed forward and mounted the stoop. Young Hamilton, in order to give the president a chance to escape, began an earnest speech. He was progressing splendidly when the doctor, looking out of an upper window and thinking that the young orator was trying to incite the populace, cried out, 'Don't listen to him, gentlemen; he is crazy, he is crazy!' The effect may be imagined. Hamilton found it difficult to keep from laughing, but he managed in spite of the startling interruption to hold his audience long enough to permit the terrified doctor to make good his escape to a war vessel in the harbor.

"The situation kept growing worse and worse, reconciliation at length became an impossibility, and, as a last resort, it was solemnly and regretfully decided to sever the bond that united the colonies with the mother country and to proclaim independence.

"Five days later the stirring words of that immortal proclamation were read to the troops assembled near the Liberty pole on the Common.

"On the west wing of our present City Hall," continued the professor, "you can see a tablet referring to the great event, which bears this inscription;

NEAR THIS SPOT IN THE PRESENCE OF
GENERAL GEORGE WASHINGTON
THE DECLARATION OF INDEPENDENCE
WAS READ AND PUBLISHED
TO THE
AMERICAN ARMY
JULY 9, 1776.

"Of course, you know," said the professor, "that Thomas Jefferson's gifted pen wrote this wonderful Declaration, but as New-Yorkers you ought to bear in mind that one of the committee that assisted him in his work was Robert R. Livingston, of whose career his country and his State may well be proud. At this time, it is proper also to mention the name of Thomas Paine, an Englishman, who resided for many years in New York. In January, 1776, he issued a pamphlet called Common Sense, in which he advocated separation and independence. It immediately became popular, its circulation reached an astonishing figure, and it undoubtedly helped greatly to pave the way for the great step.

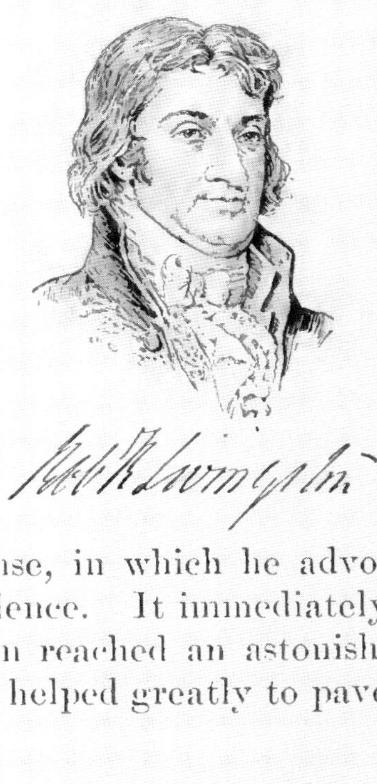

"The reading of the Declaration of Independence was an inspiring occasion. All the troops of the city were present, formed in a hollow square. Presently Washington and his staff rode into the center, and the immortal words were read. A burst of applause arose from the assemblage when the last sentence was uttered. Then the citizens, moved by a sudden impulse, rushed down to the City Hall in Wall Street, tore off the portrait of George III that was hanging there, and trampled upon it. Not to be outdone, the soldiers gathered at Bowling Green and pulled down the king's statue. Later, the British troops, in a spirit of revenge, mutilated the marble statue of Pitt. It was now evident that George the King was despised, and that a new George sat enthroned in the hearts of the people.

"At No. 1 Broadway, opposite Bowling Green, there is a tablet that refers to an incident I have just mentioned. Let us look at it."

We found it presently, and were much interested in the legend it contains, which is as follows:

HERE STOOD KENNEDY HOUSE
ONCE HEADQUARTERS OF
GENERALS WASHINGTON AND LEE.
ON THE BOWLING GREEN
OPPOSITE, THE LEADEN STATUE
OF KING GEORGE WAS
DESTROYED BY THE PEOPLE
JULY 9, 1776, AND LATER
MADE INTO BULLETS FOR THE
AMERICAN ARMY.

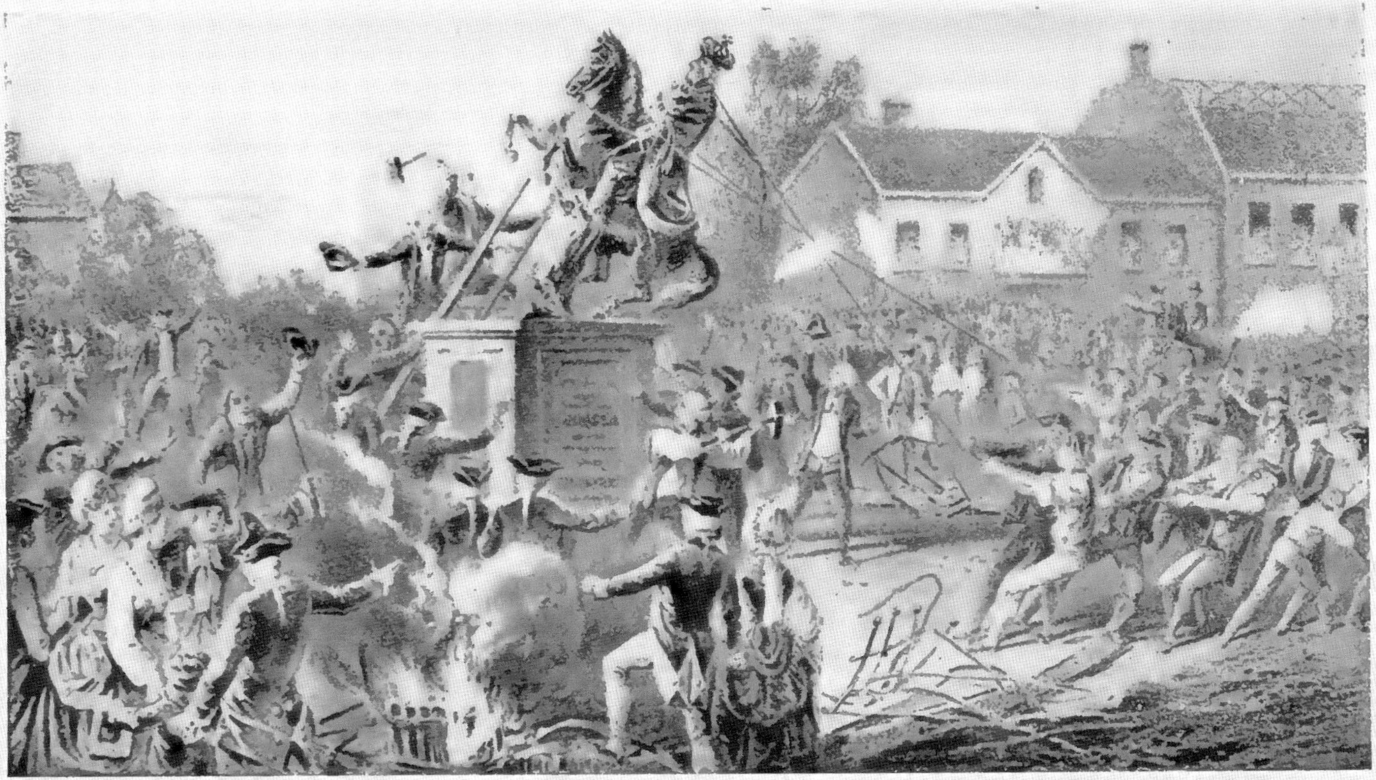

Tearing down the statue of George III on Bowling Green. From an old print.

"Served him right," commented Tom.

"'Twas lucky for the Americans that it was made of lead," suggested George.

"I am sorry, though," added Emily, "that Pitt's statue was mutilated."

After some further discussion of this interesting incident we were ready to proceed.

"Near by, on Nassau Street, is another interesting tablet," said our guide. "Let us pass through the arcade of yonder beautiful Equitable Building and we'll reach our destination in a few minutes."

We halted at Cedar Street, and glancing at the Mutual Life's great granite pile, easily found a lettered bronze plate, which George read aloud.

HERE STOOD
THE MIDDLE DUTCH CHURCH
DEDICATED A. D. 1729
MADE A BRITISH MILITARY PRISON 1776
RESTORED 1790
OCCUPIED AS THE UNITED STATES POST OFFICE
1845–1875
TAKEN DOWN 1882
THE MUTUAL LIFE INSURANCE CO.
OF NEW YORK.

"A church, a prison, and a post office!" repeated Emily.

"More, too, I believe," said the professor. "I have read that here New York's first theater was located, and it is recorded that during the Revolutionary War the English officers used the church as a riding academy."

"Because it was a Dutch church?" asked George.

"I don't know whether that influenced them. They probably thought it suited their purpose bet-

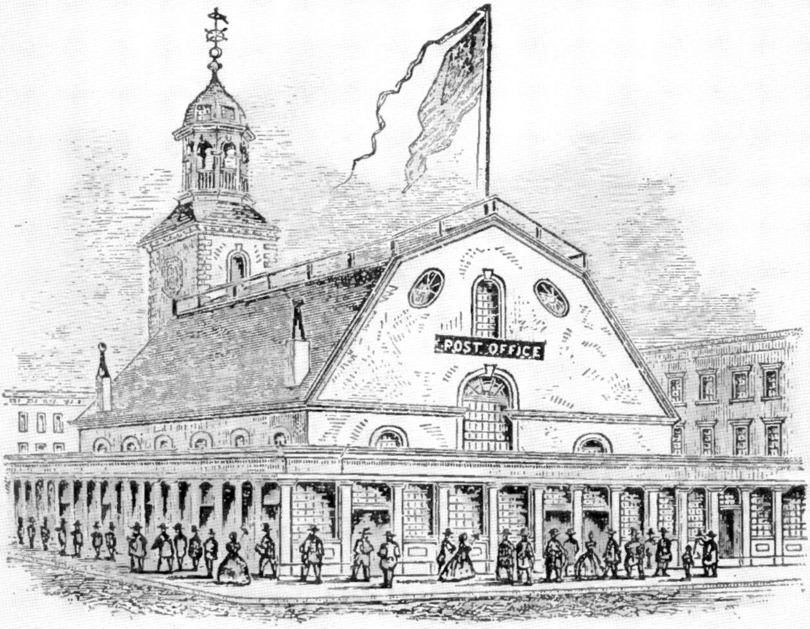

The old Post Office, originally the Middle Dutch church. Reproduced from Valentine's Manual for 1864.

ter than any other place. The point is, as the inscription indicates, that ere the close of the year 1776, New York had fallen into the hands of the British."

CHAPTER VI

"BEFORE we go on," said the professor, when we met again, "I think it necessary to mention what happened shortly before independence was declared, so that we may fully understand the steps that led up to that important event.

"The punishment of Boston began in June, 1774. That interference with the rights of one colony frightened all the others, and a Continental Congress, as it was called, met in Philadelphia in September, 1774, and drew up a Declaration of Rights, addressed to the *people* of Great Britain, and a second statement addressed to the *king*. The first was written by John Jay, a young New York lawyer.

"When these papers arrived in England they caused a decided sensation. Pitt, the great statesman, said that in all his reading he had never seen better reasoning or fairer demands expressed in firmer or wiser language, and he warned Parliament against trying to make slaves of men who thought and wrote in such a manner. But George and his ministers were obstinate and would not take warning.

"On April 19, 1775, the king's soldiers fired on

the farmers of Lexington and Concord; on June 17th the battle of Bunker Hill was fought, and the English, though victorious, acknowledged that the Yankees could fight, and that they had won a very dear victory.

"In the meantime the second Continental Congress, sitting at Philadelphia, had organized a Continental army and appointed George Washington commander in chief. On June 25th Washington passed through New York. The place where the patriots gathered to receive him—now West Street, near Laight—is marked by a tablet with this inscription:

TO MARK THE LANDING PLACE OF
GENERAL GEORGE WASHINGTON
JUNE 25, 1775,
ON HIS WAY TO CAMBRIDGE
TO COMMAND
THE AMERICAN ARMY.

"On July 2d he reached Cambridge, where, under the famous old elm, he assumed command of the assembled troops.

"Strange to say, on the same day that Washington came to New York, William Tryon, the king's governor, also arrived, and was received with becoming ceremonies. You can see from this what a confused state of affairs existed—a mixture of loyalty to the king and indignation at some of his tyrannical doings. In fact, Congress, after practically declaring war, still hoped to mend matters, and actually sent another petition to King George, but he would not look at it.

"In the meantime Washington was besieging General Howe in Boston, and, although the latter had a fine host of trained troops, they did not assert themselves against the Continentals, who were inexperienced, poorly equipped, and at one time almost out of powder. At last, in March, 1776, after nine months of dillydallying, the British were forced to evacuate the town.

"Washington now hastened to New York, expecting that this would be the next point of attack. Meanwhile a great battle of arguments had been going on in Congress; and, finally, on July 4, 1776, the motion that '*these United Colonies are and of right ought to be free and independent States*' was carried.

"The arrival of Washington in New York, and the preparations for defending the city, caused a general outburst of excitement and fear among the people. It was still, you must remember, a little town of four thousand houses and twenty-five thousand inhabitants, confined to the lower end of the island, the rest consisting of county estates and a few widely separated villages. A redoubt was cast up at Turtle Bay, on the East River above Forty-fourth Street; a breastwork at Fifty-fourth Street; a battery on a bluff at Seventy-fourth Street; another at the foot of Eighty-fifth Street; and a strong one, known as Thompson's Battery, on a jutting promontory at the foot of Eighty-ninth Street, then called Horn's Hook, which commanded the Harlem River and Hell Gate. A small work was also erected on Snake Hill, now Mount Morris, in the park of that name. In fact, the whole river front bristled with fortifications. A venerable New-Yorker, whom I used to meet occasionally," continued the professor, "often told me that he was in the habit of visiting these places and was able easily to trace the remains of the old works.

"Back of Trinity there was a strong redoubt; the fort, with six guns, and the Grand Battery, with twenty-three guns, protected the southern point of the island; other sections along the lower East River showed works and cannon, while Jones's Hill, near Broome Street, and Bunker Hill, on the Bayard Farm, where Grand and Mulberry Streets now cross, were crowned with powerful batteries. Barricades of logs, stones, boxes and barrels inclosed City Hall Park, stretched across Broadway opposite St. Paul's, covered the site of the present Tribune Building, and guarded other localities. Brooklyn Heights were also fortified, while Fort Washington on this side, and Fort Lee opposite, guarded the Hudson.

"With an anxious eye Washington watched the bay. On June 25, 1776, he noticed the first signs of the foreign fleet, and by July 2d fully one hundred and thirty vessels of various kinds were gathered in the neighborhood of Sandy Hook. Ere long a landing was made, and the hillsides of Staten Island were presently dotted with white tents.

"Here was a force of thirty-one thousand British and Hessian veterans, under Admiral Howe, his brother General Howe, and Generals Clinton, Cornwallis, and Percy—the best-officered and best-equipped force that Europe could furnish at that time.

"Against these trained fighters whom had we? Some twenty thousand raw troops, commanded by men who had seen but little service. Washington had taken part in some Indian skirmishes, but had never been at the head of a large body of men; Putnam—'Old Put,' as he was affectionately called—had seen about the same sort of warfare; Knox, a youth of twenty-six, knew more about selling books than handling a brigade; Greene, but little older than Knox, was more at home near an iron forge than near a cannon. Charles Lee had seen service abroad, but, it is safe to say, he hindered Washington more than he helped him, while Sullivan and Alexander (or, to call the latter by his title, Lord Stirling) were both young and had much to learn of the business of war.

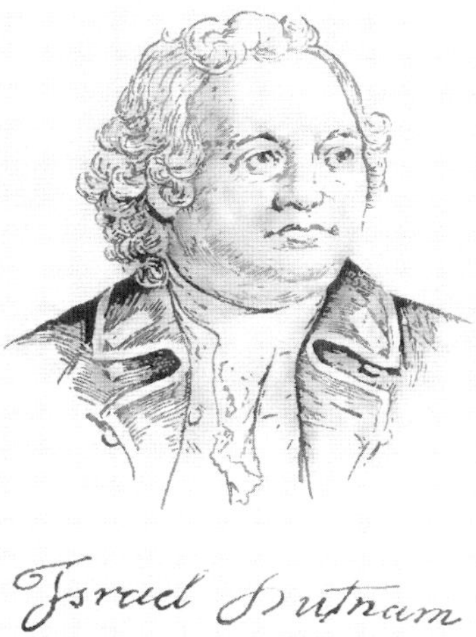

"Those were anxious days in New York, I can assure you," continued the professor earnestly, "and none had a more trying time than Washington and his officers. There was constant watching, drilling, and preparing. One day General Greene, while crossing the Common on his way to Washington's headquarters, noticed a company of artillery, and was struck with its able performance, as well as the tact of its youthful commander, who was but twenty years old. Greene, quick to appreciate military talent, spoke to the young man, saw in a moment that he was far above the ordinary, made a friend of him, and presently introduced him to Washington. The boy was Alexander Hamilton.

"Washington's headquarters were about two miles out of town, at Richmond Hill, a fine homestead in Greenwich village. You remember the location of the village, no doubt?"

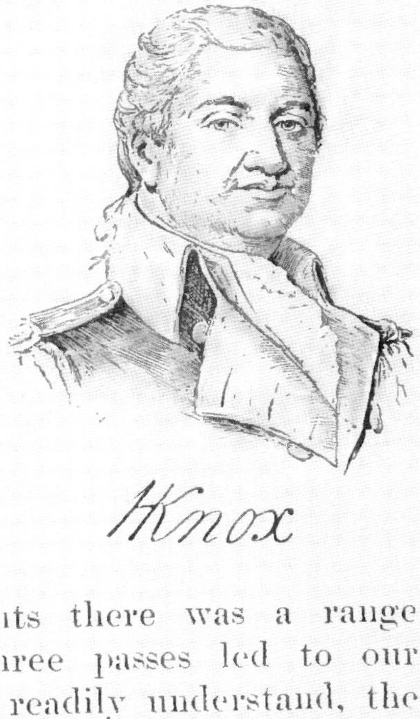

H Knox

"I know," said Tom, "where the ships start for Europe."

"General Howe never hurried matters, and so a month or more passed; but toward the end of August the British made a landing at Gravesend, Long Island. About two miles and a half in front of the American works on Brooklyn Heights there was a range of hills through which three passes led to our fortifications. As you can readily understand, the Americans sought to prevent the English from coming through these passes. Howe now put into execution a clever plan. Keeping passes No. 1 and No. 2 busy, he undertook during the night of August 26th a silent march in a roundabout way to pass No. 3, which was to his extreme right. Here, through somebody's blunder—no one knows to this day whom to blame—only a handful of troops was on guard. The pass was quickly taken, and thus the English were able to get to the rear of the Americans at passes Nos. 2 and 1. A signal gun announced to the British in front of these openings that Howe had turned the corner. Then the attack began in earnest, and the poor Continentals, many of whom had never been in battle before, were caught and slaughtered in as bad a trap as was ever laid. 'Good God!' cried Washington, when he realized the situation, 'what brave fellows I must this day lose!' Two thousand patriot soldiers were killed on that August 27th in the fatal battle of Long Island."

"How many did the English lose?" asked Tom sadly.

"Three hundred and eighty killed and wounded. Those of the Americans that were not captured or slain made their way as best they could back to the Heights, and, as you can readily imagine, they were a sad, dejected lot of men.

"The night following the battle was a weary, gloomy, and sleepless time for the Americans on Brooklyn Heights. At four in the morning Washington went the rounds to see that all was right, and to encourage, if possible, the dispirited soldiers. A dreary dawn showed large encampments of the enemy, who at once began to cannonade the American works, but, fortunately, a downpour of rain soon interfered. The next day a dense fog wrapped everything in its veil of uncertainty. Washington now decided upon a bold move, namely, to transfer his nine thousand men with all their trappings over to New York. Boats were quietly but quickly gathered from all parts of the river, and toward evening the great work was begun. To deceive the enemy, sentinels were kept on guard as usual. Thus, in the dead of night, surrounded by danger and uncertainty, the encampment melted away. Troops, artillery, ammunition, provisions, cattle, horses and carts, were safely embarked, and then Washington entered a boat and crossed the river with the last."

"When did the British discover the trick?" asked Tom, with lively interest.

"Just too late," answered the professor. "It was an extraordinary retreat, and was one of the most brilliant achievements of the war, adding greatly to the reputation of Washington, who for forty-eight hours scarcely closed an eye or left his saddle. It was a narrow escape, too, I can tell you, and came very near being spoiled. A Tory farmer's wife, it seems, discovered what was going on, and sent her slave to inform the English. It so happened that he fell into the hands of some Hessians, who, not being able to understand the negro, arrested him on suspicion, and held him long enough to let all the Yankees slip away."

"Ha, ha, ha!" laughed the young people; "that was a good one."

"Howe was now in control of Long Island and could easily have bombarded New York, but he was inclined to be lazy. In the meantime, 'Old Put' guarded the city—that is, the lower end of the island—his headquarters being at the Kennedy House, No. 1 Broadway, while at the foot of Grand Street, Twenty-third Street, Kip's Bay (Thirty-fourth Street), and along the Harlem, brigades were stationed. About the 10th of September, Washington moved his headquarters to the Morris mansion at One Hundred and Sixty-first Street, east of St. Nicholas Avenue. Day after day passed, and still no attack. Finally, on Sunday, September 15th, two divisions—one British, under Clinton, the other Hessian, under Donop—crossed the river and approached Kip's Bay. The sight of the redcoats and remembrances of the recent defeat unnerved the Americans, who, as soon as the English began to land, became panic-stricken and fled. At this moment Washington dashed in among the fugitives, who had reached the neighborhood of Park Avenue and Fortieth Street, and tried to rally them, but all in vain. Angered beyond endurance, he exclaimed, 'Are these the men with whom I am to defend America?' and whipping out his pistols, snapped them at some of the terror-stricken soldiers. He was so heedless of his own danger that, had not an aide-de-camp seized the bridle of his horse, he might have fallen into the hands of the enemy."

"Dear me!" said Emily, "I did not know that Washington ever lost his temper."

"Certainly he did," answered the professor; "but only on rare occasions, and under extraordinary provocation. He quickly regained his self-control, however, and immediately took measures to meet the general peril. In all haste he sent word to Putnam, and dispatched a messenger to Harlem to warn the forces there against a landing of the British in that section.

"Putnam was in a very dangerous position, and had the English moved quickly they might have caught him; but Howe, who was very fond of the good things of life, stopped a while at Inclenberg, now Murray Hill. Mrs. Murray, mother of the grammarian, Lindley Murray, a devoted patriot, entertained her visitors so well, and gave them so much wine and other refreshments, that they lingered, teased her about the way the Yankees had run, and thus gave 'Old Put' a chance to escape."

"Hurrah for Mrs. Murray!" shouted Tom.

"Meanwhile, Putnam's men, followed by a band of women and children, were struggling along toward Harlem. It was a hot, sweltering day, and they suffered terribly. Alexander Hamilton gallantly led on his company, while a young major—none other than Aaron Burr—acted as guide, riding back and forth, encouraging the soldiers, skillfully conducting them through woods and bypaths, and at last bringing them safely, toward evening, to Harlem Heights, where they were enthusiastically welcomed by the troops who had given them up as lost. Burr's extraordinary efforts during this march probably saved the entire retreating corps.

"Washington, as I need hardly tell you, was also on hand to lend assistance. His meeting with Putnam on this occasion has been commemorated by the Sons of the Revolution in the form of a tablet, which you can see on the west side of Broadway between

Forty-third and Forty-fourth Streets. It bears this inscription:

> GENERAL GEORGE WASHINGTON
> AND
> GENERAL ISRAEL PUTNAM
> MET NEAR THIS SPOT DURING
> THE MOVEMENT OF THE
> AMERICAN ARMY
> SEPTEMBER 15, 1776
> THE DAY BEFORE THE
> BATTLE OF HARLEM.

"Suppose we mount our wheels," suggested the professor at this point, "and visit some of the historic places that figured in the period we are now considering?"

The proposal was received with great favor, and presently we were speeding along the smooth roads of Central Park toward Mount St. Vincent.

"In Revolutionary times," said our guide, dismounting at the foot of the hill, "this was a very rough and rocky section, through which ran a road called McGowan's Pass, after Daniel McGowan, who owned a farm near by. The pass was an important avenue to Harlem. Here, on the memorable 15th of September, so the story goes, the last of the tired stragglers passed, and scarcely were they out of sight when a party of showily-uniformed British horsemen rode up, followed by a long line of troops, and demanded of a lad who happened to be there if he knew in which direction the rebels had gone. The lad was Andrew McGowan, a faithful little patriot, who had no intention of helping the enemy. Pressed into service, he guided the hated redcoats along a road that led them away from the weary Americans, and after taking them over a long roundabout path, he managed to slip away and get back to his home. In spite of this clever ruse the English met a few of the retreating patriots and a skirmish took place, in which one American was killed.

"The works in this vicinity were without delay occupied and strengthened by the British, and became a portion of their line of defense for the upper portion of the island. Again, in the War of 1812, as we shall see later, the high ground in this section bristled with the cannons of forts and blockhouses."

"Why was the hill we just left called Mount St. Vincent?" asked George.

"At one time St. Vincent's Convent was located there. Subsequently it was used as a soldiers' home."

Leaving the site once known as McGowan's Pass, we wheeled over to Claremont Hill, and here the professor described to us the battle of Harlem Heights.

"On the evening of September 15, 1776," said he, "the British forces extended in a diagonal line from the Beekman House, a fine mansion at Fifty-first Street near the East River, where General Howe had his headquarters, to the Apthorpe House, another colonial homestead, at Ninety-first Street and Tenth Avenue, where Clinton and Cornwallis were stationed. Across this valley, just below us, known as The Hollow Way, on Bloomingdale Heights yonder, the Americans were intrenched.

"Washington was anxious to know what the British intended to do, and, in order to find out, selected Colonel Thomas Knowlton, of Connecticut, a gallant and active young leader, who had organized a small band of Rangers. At daybreak, on the 16th, Knowlton and his men made their way through the woods and approached the English pickets at One Hundred and Fourth Street and the Boulevard, then called the Bloomingdale Road. An alarm was given, and two or three British companies hurried forward and began firing. Knowlton made up his mind that there would be no running away on this occasion, and called on his men to stand their ground and show their mettle.

"For half an hour a brisk action took place. A thousand shots were fired, several soldiers fell, and then, the enemy having been strengthened, an orderly retreat was executed by Knowlton's men. The English followed and occupied this hill near Grant's Tomb, whereupon one of their buglers sounded the notes of the fox chase, a contemptuous signal of triumph that was distinctly heard in the American camp.

"Washington then planned a little surprise for the exultant bugle blowers. A body of volunteers was sent forward into The Hollow Way to tempt the British down the hill, while about two hundred men under Knowlton and a brave Virginian, Major Andrew Leitch, were ordered to make a circuit and catch the enemy in the rear. The English rushed down the hill, as they were expected to do, the Americans keeping them busy, and actually driving them back, so that the second detachment, appearing suddenly on some rocks at One Hundred and Twenty-third Street and the Boulevard, struck the enemy's flank instead of his rear. Knowlton and Leitch at the head of their men plunged forward and made a fierce attack. Almost at once Leitch sank, hit by three bullets. A minute or two later Knowlton was mortally wounded. He fell like a hero, saying, 'I do not value my life if we but get the day.' An hour afterward he died, and two weeks later Leitch breathed his last.

"In spite of the loss of their leaders, the patriots fought bravely on. The English were behind a country fence, but they were forced to retreat, and next took their stand in a buckwheat field at One Hundred and Twentieth Street, now forming a part of the ground west of Columbia University. Here the main fight occurred, and it was a fierce battle, I can tell you. No flinching—no running away this time. The 'rebels' fought with pluck and determination, and again—three times in all—forced the proud redcoats back, until they were not far from the spot where poor Knowlton had surprised them in the morning. In fact, so enthusiastic were the Americans that with great difficulty were they kept from pursuing the British still farther.

"Such was the battle of Harlem Heights—not a great conflict, but a brilliant little action that put refreshing hope into the hearts of the Americans and filled the British with a keen sense of mortification."

George and Tom scanned the historic ground

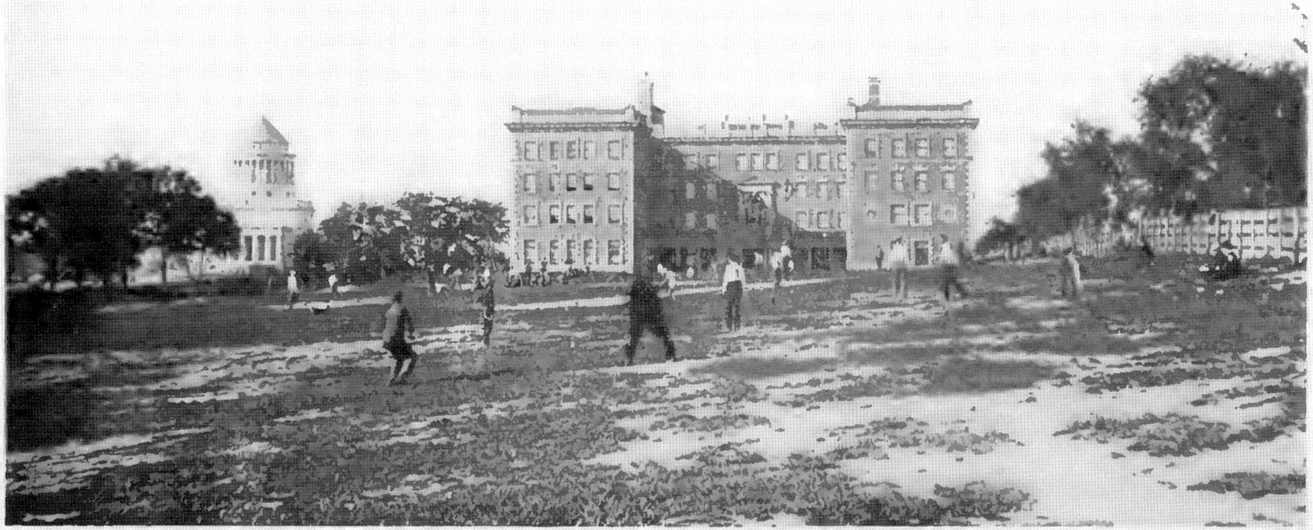

Harlem Heights battlefield looking north from One Hundred and Sixteenth Street, west of Broadway. Here the principal action took place. Barnard College in the center, Grant's tomb to the left. Photographed 1900.

around them, as if they were fighting the battle over again, while Emily sadly thought of the brave heroes that had given up their lives on this battlefield.

"Nothing of importance occurred during the next four days, but on the night of September 21st, the troops looking toward the south from their quarters on Harlem Heights, beheld a great spreading red glare in the skies over the city that made them wonder. The whole town seemed to be in flames. The fact was that fire had broken out in a frame house near Whitehall Street, and, fanned by the wind, had swept northeastward across the island, destroying Trinity, and consuming four hundred and ninety-three out of four thousand dwellings. The blame was thrown on the 'rebels,' and two hundred arrests were made, but no proof was found against a single individual. It is said, however, that while the fire raged many patriotic citizens were cruelly thrust into the flames by the angry soldiers. Two years later, in 1778, a second fire burned fifty houses more in the neighborhood of Coenties Slip.

"The great fire of September 21st was bad enough, but an event occurred the next day, Sunday, that left a deeper gloom behind it. In the neighborhood of what is now Third Avenue and Sixty-third Street, Nathan Hale, the martyr-spy, died an ignominious death for the sake of his country. Whenever I think of this brave youth I feel a sense of great grief. The news of Lexington awoke his patriotic spirit. He was then a tall, handsome young school-teacher of twenty. A short time before he had graduated at Yale, where he had been a bright student, a fine athlete, an amiable comrade. He was among the first to enlist, and in the course of time he received his commission of captain. The doubt, despair, and anxiety that followed the battle of Long Island depressed the whole army, and greatly worried Washington. He was anxious to know what Howe's next move would be, but to find out it was necessary to employ a spy. A volunteer was asked for, but none came forward. The officers were ready to fight, they said, but not to go among the enemy and be hanged like a dog. Hale took a different view of the matter: any service necessary for the general good he regarded as honorable. He went, was captured, brought before Howe, and condemned to be hanged. Short was the time given him to prepare for death, and to add to his misery a brute named Cunningham watched over him. Hale asked for a Bible, and was laughed at; he wrote letters to his dear ones, including a fair young girl to whom he was engaged, and they were torn up before his face. When he was led out to be executed his savage jailer jeered at him, saying that this was a fine death for a soldier. 'I only regret that I have but one life to lose for my country,' was his noble answer."

The boys were silent, and Emily's eyes were moist.

"The Sons of the Revolution," continued the professor, "have lately honored Nathan Hale by placing a beautiful statue in City Hall Park. I always stop before it and look reverently at that calm, young, heroic face. No shout of victory rang in the

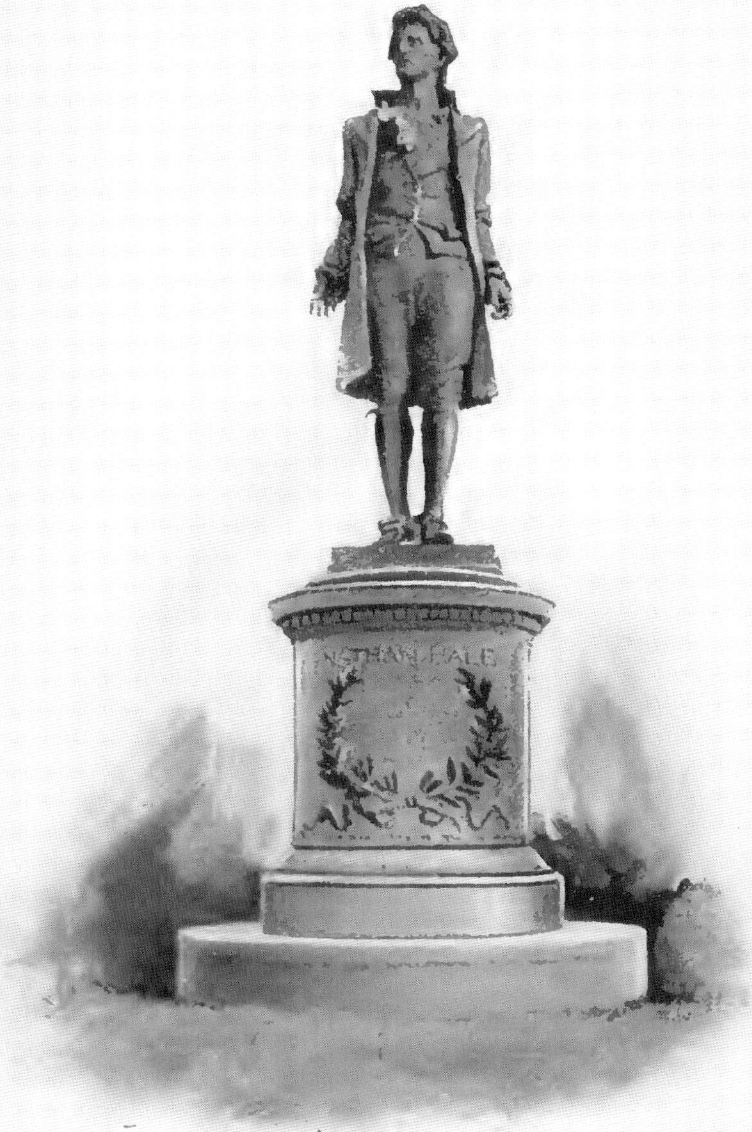

Statue of Nathan Hale in City Hall Park.

martyr's ears when he expired; he died the death of a spy, but to my mind he was a hero, and deserves a hero's place on the nation's roll of honor."

"Surely he does," said Emily.

"Here's a sentiment," said the professor, referring to his little memorandum book, "with which I think you will agree:

> "'Forgotten? Ne'er while Freedom's stars
> Shine forth in deathless light
> From out the flag he loved so well,
> For which he struggled, fought, and fell.
> His guerdon was the soldier's scars,
> And death, far from his native vale—
> Brave heart that beat for love and right,
> Brave soldier, Nathan Hale!'"

"Isn't there a tablet somewhere in honor of Knowlton and Leitch?" asked George.

"Yes, on yonder building," said the professor, pointing toward the Columbia University grounds.

We now mounted our wheels, rode past Grant's Tomb, which we had all visited previously, and going eastward through One Hundred and Twentieth Street to the Boulevard, stopped at the Engineering Building, in front of the beautiful bronze memorial near the entrance.

"There's poor Leitch," said the professor, pointing to the fallen major. "See, his face shows the pain of coming death. And there is brave Knowlton, sword in hand, leading on his patriotic followers, while that stolid creature opposite him is one of those paid Hessians who, for a few dollars, came over here to fight a people who had never injured them; whom, indeed, they did not even know."

"Ugh!" grunted Tom contemptuously.

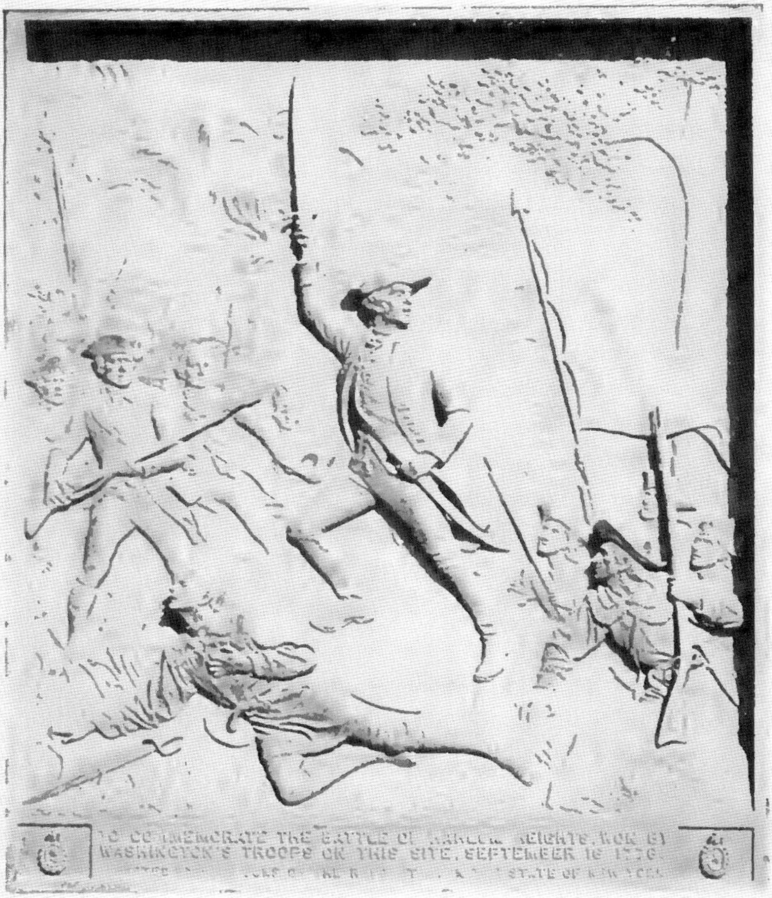

Tablet to commemorate the battle of Harlem Heights, Columbia University. Photographed 1900.

"All along here there was fighting," continued the professor, pointing to the Boulevard; "and over there where you see that open space to the south of

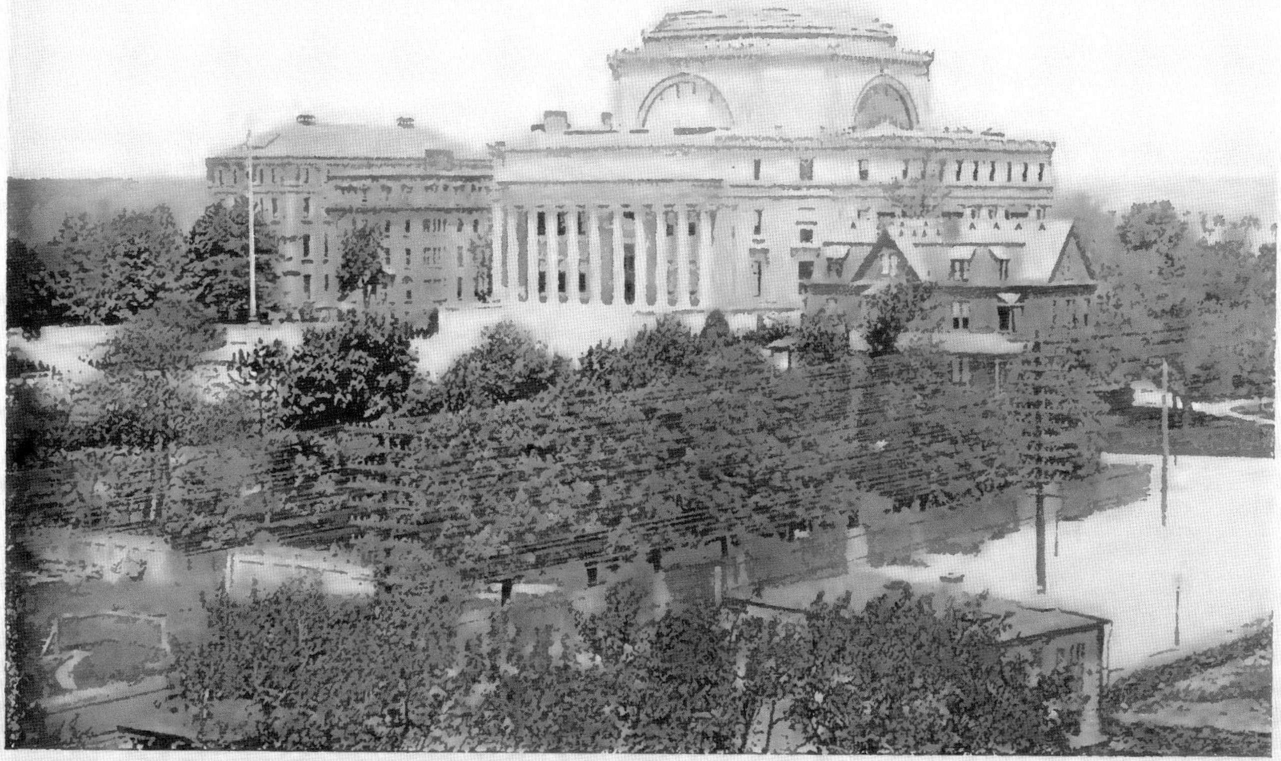

Library, Columbia University. From a recent photograph.

Barnard College was the famous buckwheat field where the main battle took place."

Entering the college grounds we seemed to feel the "learned atmosphere" of our surroundings, and, pausing on the terrace before the impressive Library Building, George read the great inscription over the columned entrance, which is as follows:

KING'S COLLEGE FOUNDED IN THE PROVINCE OF NEW YORK
BY ROYAL CHARTER IN THE REIGN OF GEORGE II.
PERPETUATED AS COLUMBIA COLLEGE
BY THE PEOPLE OF THE STATE OF NEW YORK
WHEN THEY BECAME FREE AND INDEPENDENT.
MAINTAINED AND CHERISHED FROM GENERATION TO GENERATION
FOR THE ADVANCEMENT OF PUBLIC GOOD AND
THE GLORY OF ALMIGHTY GOD.

CHAPTER VII

Leaving the grounds at One Hundred and Twentieth Street and Amsterdam Avenue, we rode over to the Point of Rocks at One Hundred and Twenty-seventh Street and Convent Avenue, from which elevation Washington and his generals watched the fight on September 16th. Following the smooth path that leads around the Convent of the Sacred Heart, we then wheeled north as far as One Hundred and Thirty-fifth Street, and going east one block to Hamilton Terrace, had a fine view of modern Harlem, which lay below us.

"We seem to be making as many discoveries up town as we did down town," remarked George, admiring the scene at our feet.

"Yes, indeed," assented Emily; "I had no idea there was so much of New York that I did not know."

"There is more ahead of us," remarked the professor, turning again in the direction of Convent Avenue. Just beyond One Hundred and Forty-first Street he stopped and pointed out Hamilton Grange, now used as a school.

"All this section from One Hundred and Thirty-eighth to One Hundred and Forty-fifth Street was

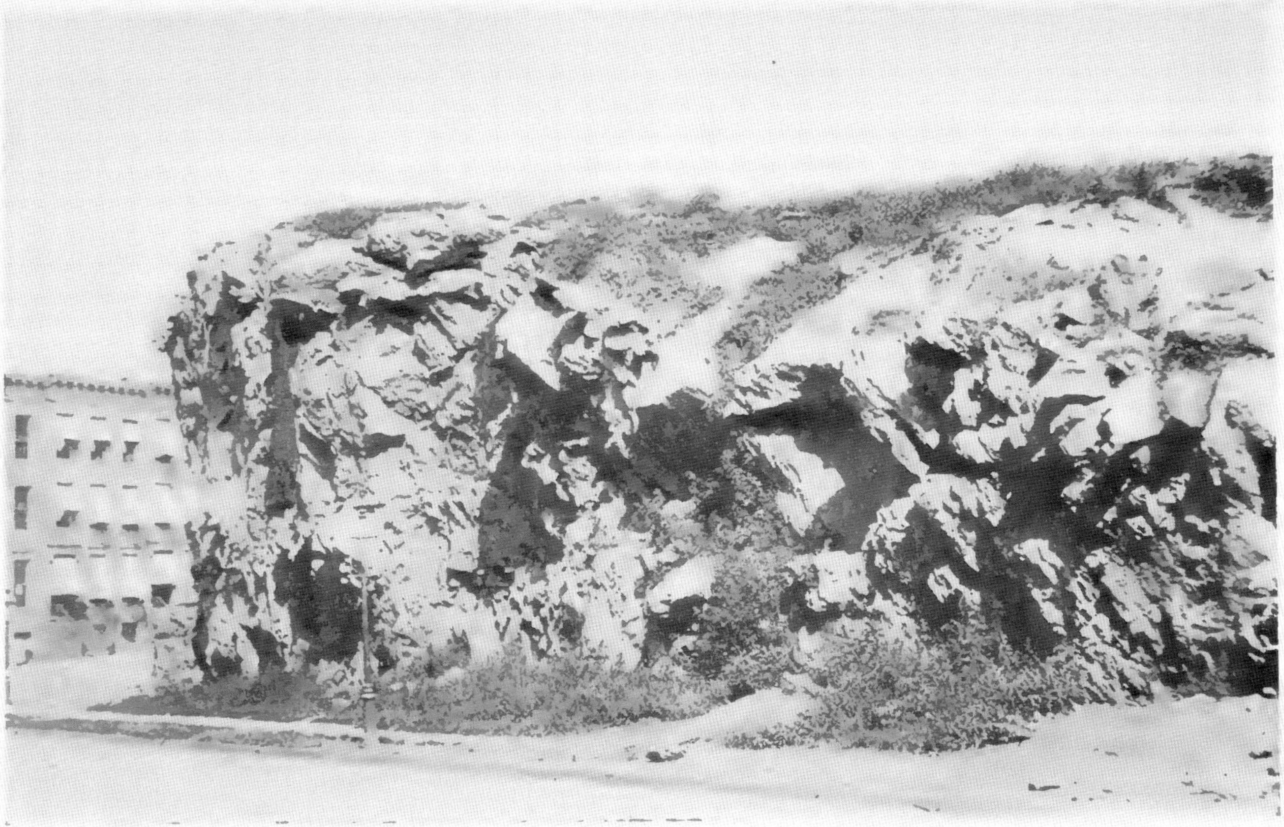

Point of rocks, One Hundred and Twenty-seventh Street and Convent Avenue. Photographed 1900.

owned by Alexander Hamilton. He built the house in 1802, and named it 'The Grange,' in honor of his uncle's seat in Scotland. It was a grand homestead in its day, almost square, sixty feet in width, with a broad piazza around it. The view in all directions must have been fine. Just across the avenue over

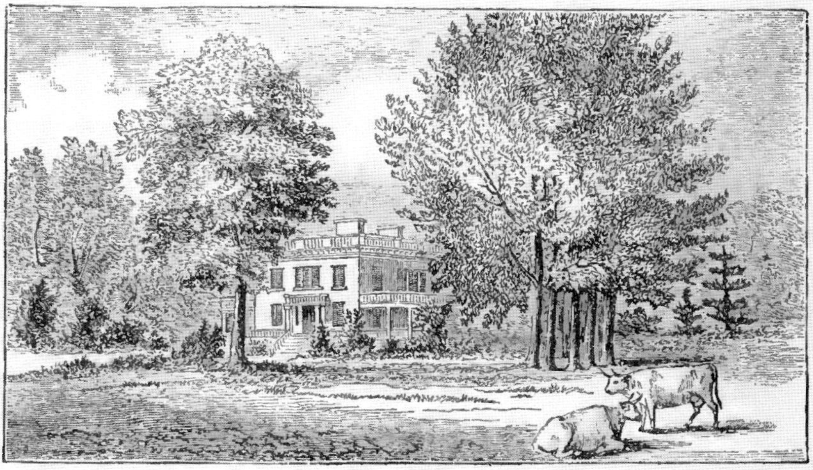

The Grange, as it appeared in Hamilton's time. From an old print.

yonder, near One Hundred and Forty-third Street, are the famous thirteen trees, representing the thirteen original States. For a time relic hunters threatened their destruction, but now, as you see, they are fenced in. Recently they became the property of a private citizen, who may some day place a bust of Hamilton within the inclosure, and thus add to the interest of this historic spot."

We lingered here for some time, the boys expressing a strong desire to settle down in the neighborhood, but at length the professor led us away, our next stopping place being the police station at

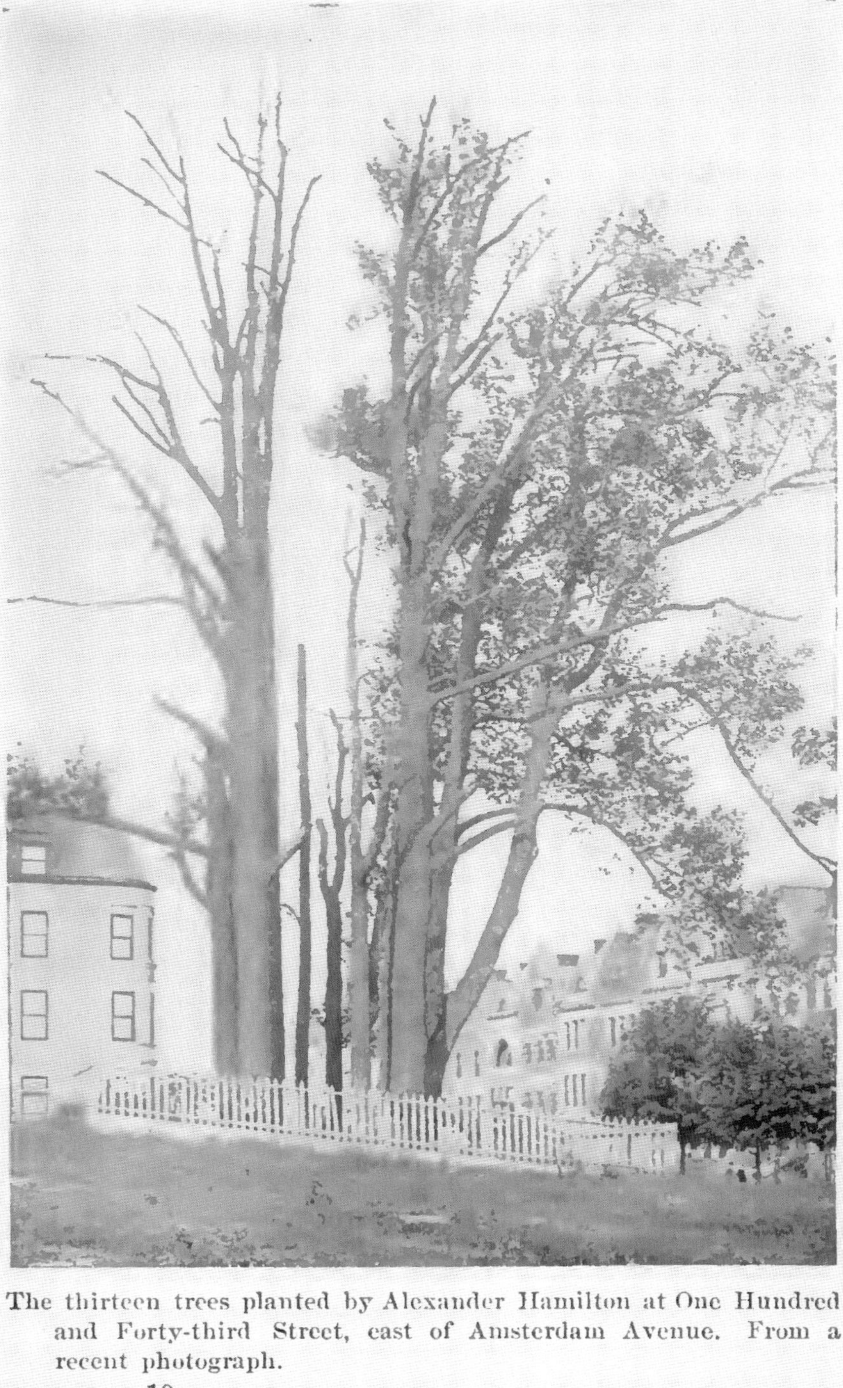

The thirteen trees planted by Alexander Hamilton at One Hundred and Forty-third Street, east of Amsterdam Avenue. From a recent photograph.

One Hundred and Fifty-second Street and Amsterdam Avenue, where, leaning up against the building in a neglectful sort of way, is an old stone bearing the date 1769, and the inscription "Nine miles to New York."

Going west, we presently reached Trinity Cemetery, which extends from One Hundred and Fifty-third to One Hundred and Fifty-fifth Street, and from Amsterdam Avenue to the North River. Before entering, we paused before a bronze tablet imbedded in the wall on One Hundred and Fifty-third Street, which contains this legend:

IN HONOR OF
COLONEL THOMAS KNOWLTON
AND MAJOR ANDREW LEYTCH*
OF THE
AMERICAN ARMY
KILLED SEPT. 16, 1776,
AT THE
BATTLE OF HARLEM.
ERECTED BY THE SONS OF THE REVOLUTION.

"Why was this tablet placed away up here?" asked George.

"Because, at one time it was thought the battle was fought in this neighborhood."

Within the beautifully kept cemetery we found much to interest us. Here was the tall monument, containing carved images of birds, erected in

* The name is generally spelled Leitch. A new tablet is soon to be substituted.

honor of the world-renowned ornithologist, Audubon. Here, too, were the tombs of Philip Livingston, signer of the Declaration of Independence; Stephen Jumel, John Jacob Astor, General Dix, and the cenotaph of President Monroe. The last named died in this city July 4, 1831, at the house of his daughter in Prince Street, east of Broadway. Twenty-seven years later the State of Virginia claimed the remains of her illustrious son, and under military escort they were transferred to Richmond.

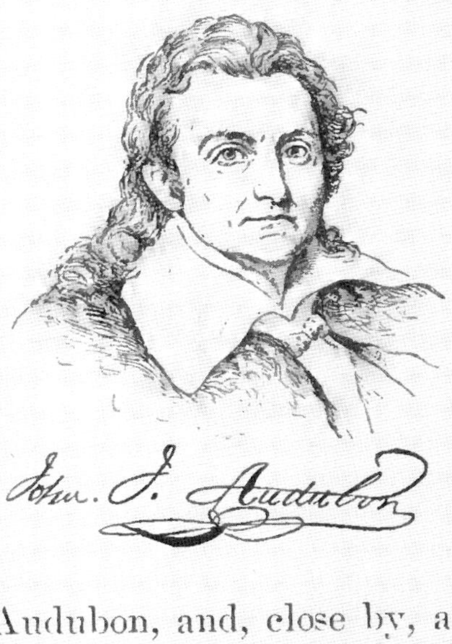

Before leaving this section we wended our way through the quiet paths of Audubon Park, extending from One Hundred and Fifty-fifth to One Hundred and Fifty-eighth Street along the Hudson. Here, in the southwest corner of the park, we saw the home of Audubon, and, close by, a Revolutionary redoubt, near which is a group of handsome houses and well-kept grounds, whose owners have never found it necessary to build fences or erect barriers of any kind against their neighbors.

Our next stopping place was at One Hundred and Sixty-first Street, just east of St. Nicholas Avenue, where, inclosed in a fine garden, we beheld a well-preserved and picturesque colonial mansion standing aloof from its modern surroundings.

"This," said the professor, "is one of the most interesting houses on Manhattan Island. It was erected in 1758 by Roger Morris, husband of Mary Philipse, a highly educated and very beautiful lady, who belonged to the well-known Philipse family. A few years before, Washington, while in New York, had met Miss Mary, and, so the story goes, fallen in love with her. It is even said that he proposed to her and was refused, but this fact has never been established. Duty soon called Washington away to Fort Duquesne, giving Captain Morris, who had been Washington's fellow aid-de-camp under Braddock, an opportunity to woo and win the fair lady. Morris became a royalist, and in 1776 his estate was forfeited. That same year Washington used the house as his headquarters, and later the Hessian general, Knyphausen, occupied it. After the Revolution, under its hospitable roof, Washington, John Adams, John Quincy Adams, Thomas Jefferson, General Knox, Alexander Hamilton, and other distinguished men and their wives were entertained. In 1810 it became the property of Stephen Jumel, a wealthy man, who had married a charming and brilliant young lady from Rhode Island. Then it numbered among its guests Louis Philippe, Lafayette, Talleyrand, Joseph Bonaparte, and Louis Napoleon. After a while the Jumels went to France and, returning some years later, brought with them eight chairs that had belonged to the great Napoleon, a table procured by Napoleon in Egypt, a clock from the Tuileries, and many other historically interesting and valuable furnishings.

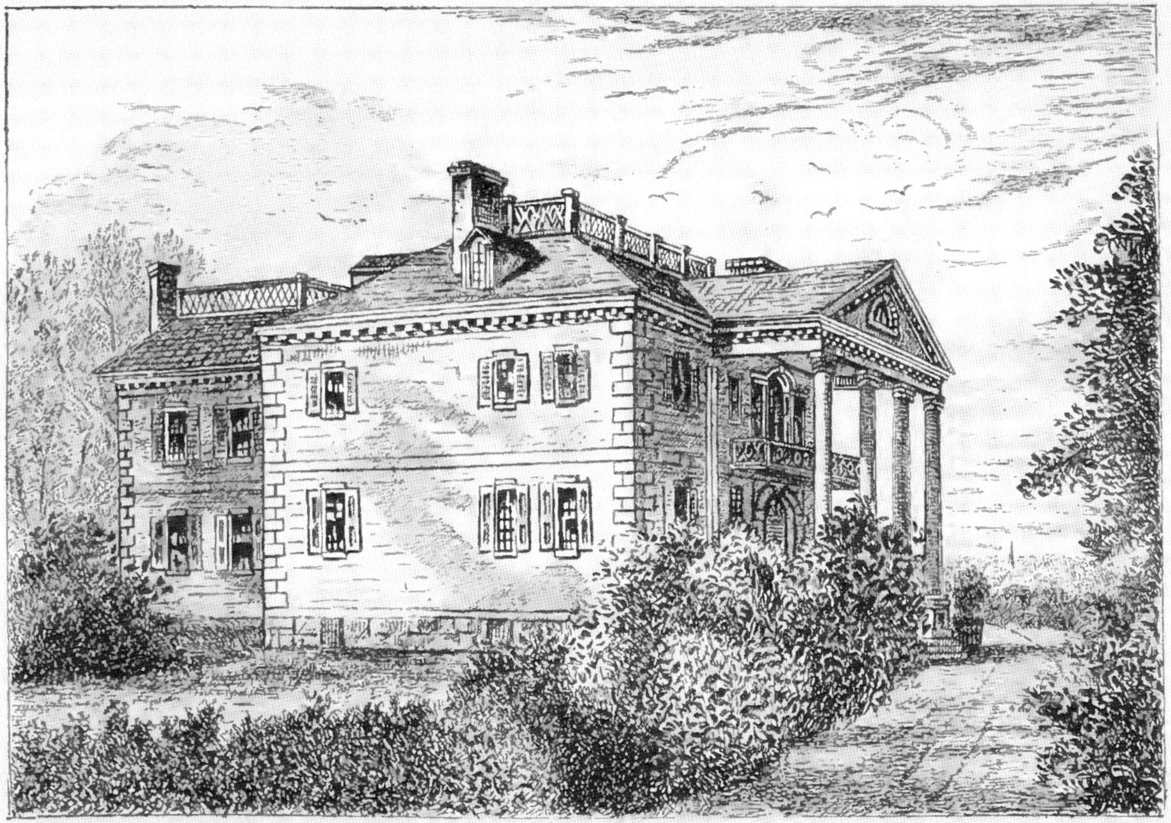

The Jumel Mansion. From an old print.

"Just below here," continued the professor, "at One Hundred and Fifty-ninth Street, you will notice a remarkable semicircle of fine, tall cypress trees. Ere the cutting through of streets was begun the circle was complete, and a little lake occupied the center. The trees, it is said, were brought from Egypt by Napoleon and presented to Jumel, who transferred them to his estate and planted them in the unique manner I have described to you.

"After Jumel's death his widow continued to live here. One day she surprised her friends by marrying Aaron Burr, the latter then being a very old man. For a time thereafter it was called the Burr Mansion—not for long, however, as the pair soon separated. Then John Jacob Astor became its owner, and here, tradition says, his secretary and friend, Fitz-Greene Halleck, wrote the immortal poem 'Marco Bozzaris.' At present the house belongs to General Earle, and is known as Earle Cliff."

During its long existence, and in spite of changes of ownership, the venerable residence has remained a landmark of colonial days. Some modern features have been added, but the original character of its early architecture prevails. There is a spell about the place that readily touches the imagination and brings to mind notable figures and interesting scenes of the past.

"Before we leave this historic spot," suggested the professor, "let us examine the fine tablet that adorns the old mansion."

To the right of the doorway, with its mullioned side-lights and elliptical transom of colonial fashion, we found a profile bust of Washington, wreathed with sprays of myrtle and laurel, and beneath it a plate with this inscription:

> WASHINGTON'S HEADQUARTERS.
> THIS TABLET IS DEDICATED BY THE
> WASHINGTON HEIGHTS CHAPTER
> DAUGHTERS OF THE AMERICAN REVOLUTION
> TO THE MEMORY OF
> GENERAL GEORGE WASHINGTON.
> WHO OCCUPIED THIS MANSION AS HIS HEADQUARTERS
> FROM SEPTEMBER 16TH TO OCTOBER 21ST, 1776.
> BATTLE OF HARLEM HEIGHTS, SEPTEMBER 16TH.
> COUNCILS OF WAR.
> PRESIDENT WASHINGTON VISITED THIS MANSION
> ACCOMPANIED BY HIS CABINET, JULY, 1790.
> MORRIS HOUSE, 1758. | JUMEL MANSION, 1810.
> EARLE CLIFF, 1900.

Again we mounted our wheels and pushed northward along St. Nicholas Avenue, Emily calling our attention to the fact that we were now "out in the country," as she called it. In truth, there was little to remind us of the fact that we were but a few miles away from the noise and rush of the city proper. Going down Depot Lane and north to Bennett Lane, we found, after some little investigation, the old, original Fort Washington, now a neglected embankment guarded by silent sentinels in the shape of trees. Two of the five corners of the bastioned earthwork can still be seen.

"This was the last stronghold," said the professor, "held by the Americans on Manhattan Island, the main army having been withdrawn to Westchester. Directly across the river from this spot were Fort Lee and Fort Constitution, and there General Greene was in charge. On the 13th of November, 1776, Washington visited these forts and had a conference with Greene. The former wanted to evacuate Fort Washington, believing that it was difficult to hold, and under the circumstances not important, but unfortunately he was persuaded to the contrary.

"Colonel Magaw was in command here, and had with him about two thousand men, many of whom were in outworks on the hills that surround us. On the 16th of November the British moved forward in four divisions, all of which were ordered to attack at the same time. The Americans made a gallant defense, but one by one the hills were taken by the superior numbers of the enemy, and at length the patriots were forced back to the fort. While this was going on, Washington was anxiously watching through a telescope the movements of one of the American divisions. He saw the men make a determined stand, but presently their line broke, and, being outnumbered, they slowly retreated. Then the Hessians rushed upon them, cut them down, and, like brutal beasts, bayoneted the wounded soldiers, though they begged for quarter. So completely was Washington overcome by the sight that, it is said, he wept with the tenderness of a child.

"The fort was now at the mercy of the enemy, and Magaw, realizing that it was useless to hold out, surrendered. Thus, Manhattan Island yielded up its last stronghold to the British, and the brave defenders were made prisoners of war and treated with fearful cruelty."

The professor's story cast a gloom over our little party, and we were glad to turn away and follow him along a path that after a while brought us to Fort George. Here the fine view of the river, valley, and hills changed our mood to one of keen pleasure. Below us the old King's Bridge Road followed its winding course, and beyond a stone castle tipped the crown of a hill. Our guide informed us that one of the outposts, afterward called by the British, Fort Tryon, occupied the opposite heights we were admiring, and showed us, a little to the south, the site of an old redoubt. We found here, also, in the restaurant, a case containing cannon balls and other Revolutionary relics that had been dug up in the neighborhood.

"With the capture of Fort Washington," said the professor, resuming his story, "the entire island passed into the hands of the British, and the city became a military post, Howe having his headquarters at the commodious Kennedy House. Royalist families soon began to drift in from all directions, the king's party was triumphant, and the patriots apparently had been swept out of existence. There was one powerful reminder in the town, however, of the great fight for liberty, in the shape of some five thousand prisoners of war, captured on Long Island and at Fort Washington. These unfortunates were intrusted to Cunningham, the brutal provost marshal, who had so cruelly tormented Nathan Hale during his last hours.

"Cunningham had his office in the New Jail, now the Hall of Records. Here many officers, including Ethan Allen, of Ticonderoga fame, were confined, and so closely were they packed that when their bones ached at night from lying on the hard planks and they wished to turn, it could only be done by word of command, 'Right' or 'Left,' whereupon they all changed their positions. Not content with allowing his helpless prisoners slowly to starve and freeze to death, this fiend Cunningham is said to have poisoned many and to have continued drawing their

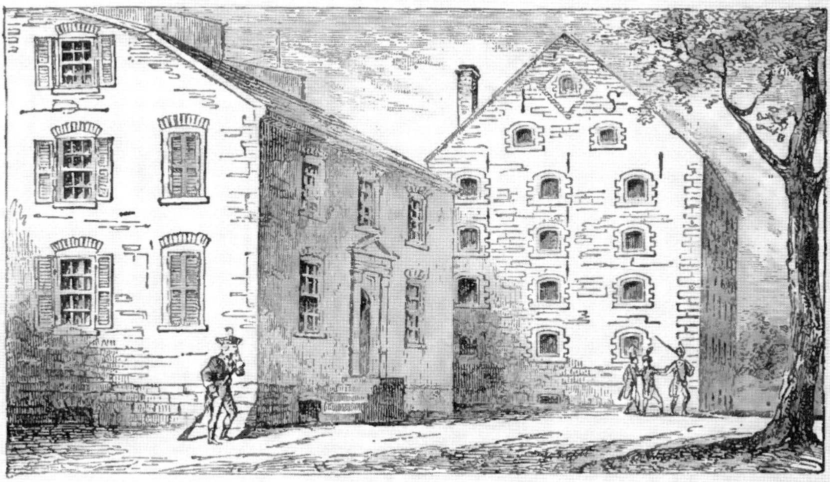

Rhinelander sugar house used as a prison during the Revolutionary War. From an old print.

rations, which he sold. He is reported to have boasted that he had thus killed more of the 'rebels' than had been slain by all the king's forces.

"Nearly every public building was turned into a prison, and all the big sugar houses were filled with suffering soldiers. Cold, hunger, foul air, putrid water, and disease quickly thinned their ranks. Every morning the dead-carts came to carry away the corpses and throw them into trenches, where no sign of identification marked their neglected graves.

"More awful still were the prison ships—foul, neglected hulks, where men were crowded worse than we would house the lowest beasts. The Jersey, anchored in the neighborhood of the Brooklyn Navy Yard, was the most famous or rather infamous of these floating dungeons. I can not describe to you the ghastly scene of filth, rags, and pestilence that characterized the Jersey, or tell you the sufferings of those poor, wan patriots who were once strong, hale, and happy men. Philip Freneau, the poet of the Revolution, has left behind a story of the prison ships in verse, of which I will read you a few lines:

> "'Here doom'd to starve, like famished dogs we tore
> The scant allowance that our tyrants bore.
>
> . . . .
>
> Three hundred wretches here deny'd all light,
> In crowded mansions pass th' infernal night.
> Some for a bed their tattered vestments join,
> And some on chests and some on floors recline;
> Shut from the blessings of the evening air,
> Pensive we lay with mingled corpses there:
> Meager and wan, and scorch'd with heat below,
> We looked like ghosts ere death had made us so.'

"Every morning the prisoners were awakened with the cry, '*Rebels, turn out your dead!*' These sufferers, relieved from misery, were hastily thrown into a pit near the shore, where the washing of the next tide often uncovered their bodies.

"Heaven alone knows the suffering, the hard-

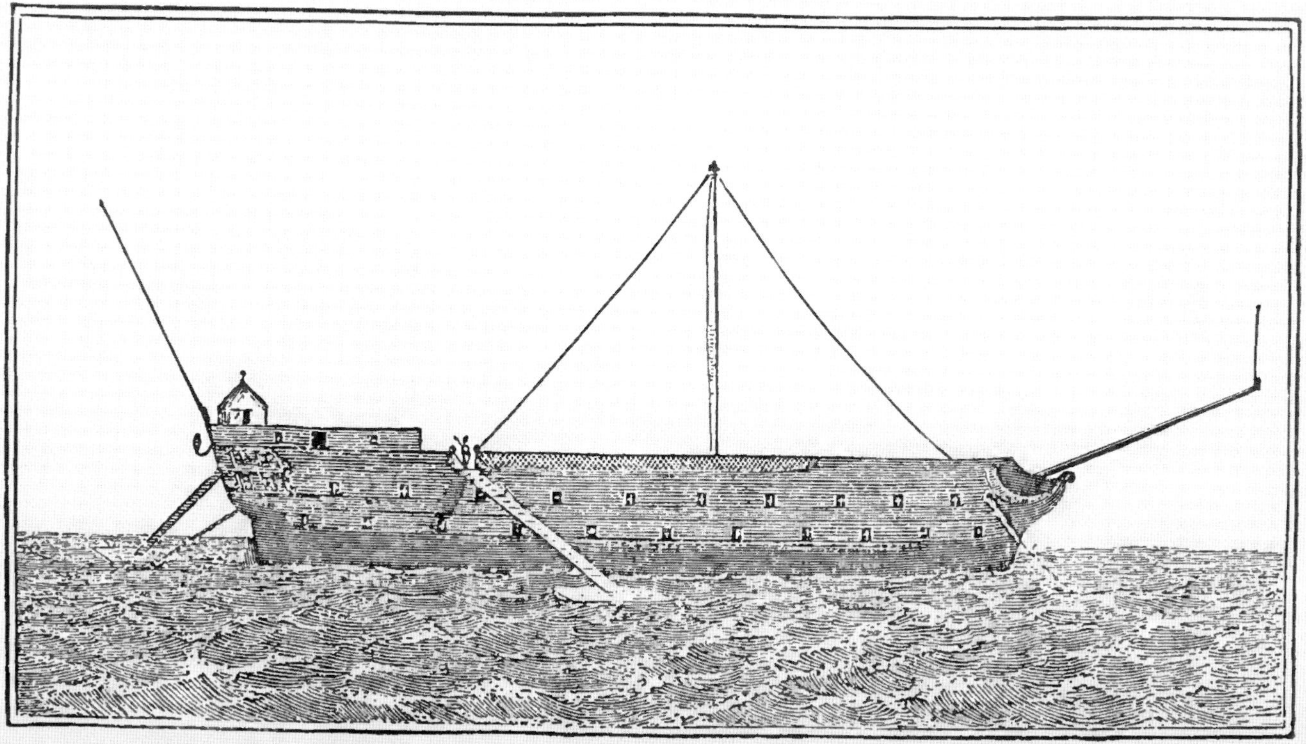

The old prison ship Jersey. From an old print.

ships, and sacrifices of the patriots that fought for the independence we enjoy. They are all worthy of our unceasing reverence, and none more so than the tortured wretches in New York's sugar houses and prison ships. It is said that their fearful treatment was a deliberate plan to make them desert the 'rebel' cause and join the forces of the king, tempting promises being held out to them. If so, the scheme failed, for almost to a man they resisted all attempts to win them from the cause of patriotism. But a day of reckoning came for Cunningham. Some years after the war he was convicted of forgery in London and executed.

"While the poor prisoners thus suffered, the king's officers found amusement in acting farces at a theater in Nassau Street, in attending bull fights, playing tennis, and in riotous living at the taverns. They also wantonly destroyed a library that had been established in the City Hall, by taking away valuable books, a knapsack load at a time, and selling them for liquor. This library had been founded in 1700, and comprised many interesting volumes. In 1788 it was reorganized under its old name of The New York Society Library, and it is in existence to-day, its building being in University Place near Twelfth Street. It owns extensive files of old newspapers and many important historical and biographical works.

"For seven long years the war dragged on, the patriot 'Continentals in their ragged regimentals' fighting the enemy, as well as the biting winds of winter and the gnawing pangs of hunger. At last, in the spring of 1783, the struggle came to an end, and the glad tidings of peace and triumph spread through the colonies. On the 19th of April, exactly eight years after the battle of Lexington, the news was officially published.

"The British lingered on for some months, and not until November were they ready to evacuate New York. On the 19th Washington arrived at Day's Tavern, corner of One Hundred and Twenty-fifth Street and Eighth Avenue. The troops, consisting of some eight hundred bronzed veterans in new blue coats, white vests and breeches, took up their station at McGowan's Pass, whence some of them perhaps had fled on that 15th of September when the British had rushed forward, driving the Americans before them. Four trophies, in the shape of six-pounders taken from the enemy, and engraved with the time and place of their capture, bore evidence of the changed state of affairs.

"Every day, it was thought, the English would depart, but not until the 25th of November did they take their much-desired leave, accompanied by hosts of royalist New-Yorkers, who were afraid to face their triumphant countrymen. At eight o'clock the drums at McGowan's Pass sounded, the soldiers fell into line, General Knox at the head, and with happy hearts marched down the old Post Road in the crisp autumn air into the Bowery, where they halted. To the west, where Grand Street crosses Mulberry, was a strong redoubt known as Bunker Hill, and to the south stretched a line of works just vacated by the British. At one o'clock the troops formed again, and the procession into the town began. Down the

Bowery, into Chatham and then into Queen (now Pearl) Street they marched, to the strains of merry music. I need not tell you that the people were out in force. Their clothes were perhaps a little shabby, but powdered wigs, white ruffles, cocked hats, silver buckles, and flowing silk dresses of varied hues are always attractive, even if somewhat worn. Onward, through the double row of cheering citizens, came the veterans. Proud was their step and erect their forms. Presently they swung into Wall Street, passed the mutilated statue of Pitt, and marched up to Broadway, halting at Rector Street.

"Two companies were now ordered to proceed to Fort George at the Battery, where an interesting ceremony was to be performed. The last British boats had just left the strand, the fort was empty, but something was wrong."

"I know!" exclaimed Tom; "the English flag was up on the flagstaff."

"Yes; and some mean individual had greased the pole and cut the halyards. But Yankee ingenuity soon overcame a trifle like that. The English in the boats were grinning, but their looks quickly changed when they saw a sailor lad, John Van Arsdale, hammer cleats to the slippery pole, and in short order reach the top. Then the insolent royal flag came down, and the Stars and Stripes soon waved in its stead, never to be replaced by any other ensign. For many years, each Evacuation Day, John Van Arsdale was intrusted with the pleasant duty of raising the flag at the Battery; then his son, and after him his grandson, enjoyed the privilege.

"I have some verses here," continued the professor, "that tell the story of Evacuation Day in spirited language. Let me read them to you:

"'Beat of drum and thrill of fife
  Down the Bowery lane;
Tramp of troops, in exile long,
  Marching home again.
Battle-seasoned soldiers these,
  In their buff and blue;
Victors in a wasteful war,
  Tried, triumphant, true.
Heroes here of Harlem Heights,
  Sons of Liberty!
Trusty troops that trapped Burgoyne,
  Sons of Victory!
Veterans of Valley Forge,
  Warriors marked by fame;
Guardians of the Neutral Ground,
  Worthy of the name.
Beat of drum and waving flags
  Down the Bowery lane;
All New York is out to shout,
  "Welcome home again!"

"'Tramp of troops in buff and blue,
  Marching down Broadway;
Down where but an hour before
  Redcoats ruled the day.
Halting at the Battery's edge,
  Watching from the strand
British hosts and Hessian hordes
  Slipping from the land.
All is well—but no, a sound;
  Hark! a mocking laugh:
Briton's flag is floating still
  From the Battery's staff.
Halyards cut, a greasy pole—
  This the parting grace—
Futile trick; swift Yankee limbs
  Reach the slippery place.

Down the lingering emblem drops,
  Vanishing from view,
While a shout rings out to greet
  The red and white and blue.'

"A few hours after the arrival of the soldiers a great civic procession followed. General Knox, leaving the troops, rode back to Bull's Head Tavern near Canal Street in the Bowery, later transformed into the Bowery Theater, and still a house of amusement, where he met Washington, George Clinton, recently elected Governor of New York, and other important personages and citizens. This procession followed the route of the troops and was greeted with a new burst of enthusiasm. Then came addresses, and later a dinner at Fraunces's Tavern, given by Clinton, at which thirteen patriot toasts were proposed and heartily answered. On December 2d a great display of fireworks was arranged at Bowling Green, and on the 11th public thanksgiving services were held.

"Thus Washington saw the glorious triumph of his long and sometimes ill-appreciated efforts. Glad, no doubt, was he at the success he had achieved, yet sad, too, he must have felt as he walked through the streets of New York, once so gay, bright, and prosperous in appearance, but now showing evidences everywhere of seven years of foreign occupation. The track of the great fire was still visible; canvas roofs covered the ruined buildings and gave to the charred district the name of Canvas Town. The shattered walls of Trinity marred Broadway; most of the churches, robbed of their pews and foul with filth, were unfit for use; fine mansions were going to decay, wharves were deserted, warehouses were vacant, and the streets were silent. It was a city sorely wounded, but not bereft of life.

"Washington remained in New York but a few days. On December 4th he met the principal officers of the army in the 'Long Room' at Fraunces's Tavern and said farewell to them. It was a touching scene. He parted from them as tenderly as if they were his brothers. Silently they followed their beloved chief as he left the room and passed through a double line of light infantry to Whitehall Ferry. Here he entered a barge, and, while he was being rowed away, stood up, took off his hat and waved a silent adieu to the sorrowing group that watched him go."

CHAPTER VIII

> "With wars and horrors overspread,
> Seven years, and more, we fought and bled,
> Seized British hosts and Hessian bands
> And all—to leave thee in their hands."

"IN these words," said the professor, "the poet of the Revolution, writing in 1783, grieved over the fate of New York. It took the town fully four years to get over the mischief done by the soldiers, but then, having regained most of its lost resources, it went forward with a stride that astonished the rest of the country, including Philadelphia, at that time the largest city in the colonies. No one was more struck with the change than Washington when he returned in 1789 to be inaugurated President.

"But I see," said the professor, "that I am running a little ahead of my story. The peace of 1783 did not bring with it either tranquillity or contentment. The yoke of King George had been thrown off, it was true, but there was something wrong. There was a Colonial Congress, but it had no power and was not respected, while the colonies were neither friendly nor neighborly. New York, for instance, made Jersey farmers pay a tax on the vegetables they brought into the State.

"It was now felt that a stronger central Government was necessary, and a convention met in Philadelphia in 1787 to consider the matter. The best men of the country were there, and they had a gigantic task before them—a battle of brains instead of a conflict of arms. One of the most conspicuous figures in that body of wise men was Alexander Hamilton of New York, then not yet thirty years old. He led the Federalists—that is, those who wanted a strong confederation. Opposed to them was the party that upheld the rights of the individual States, and wanted to yield as little as possible to the national Government. In other words, a big State like New York did not like the idea of being placed on the same level with a little State like Rhode Island.

"As you can readily imagine, many other suggestions and plans met with opposition and caused long discussions—too long to be repeated here. The story of the framing of the Constitution is very interesting and instructive, and some day I trust you will read all about it in Bancroft's great history. This fact, however, I want to impress upon you at present, that New York city played a great and honorable part in helping to establish the union of the States, and in this connection you ought particularly to remember the names of Alexander Hamilton and John Jay.

"Assisted by Madison, who afterward was elected President, they wrote and published a series of brilliant letters, explaining all about the new Constitution, which produced a profound effect. These letters, under the title of The Federalist, are now to be had in book form. I am sure you'll find it in your father's library."

"Oh, yes, I have seen it," said George, "but I haven't read it."

"Now, while Hamilton, Jay, and others were working to get the State Legislature, which was sitting at Poughkeepsie, to adopt the Constitution, the merchants and mechanics of New York city organized a grand procession to help Hamilton, whom they regarded as their special champion. Almost every industry was represented—the butchers, the bakers, and the candlestick makers. Each had a float, or an emblem, or a motto. The sailmakers, to give you an example, had a stage drawn by four horses, bearing a flag, on which was painted a ship under full sail, called New Constitution; also a picture of Hamilton, and this motto:

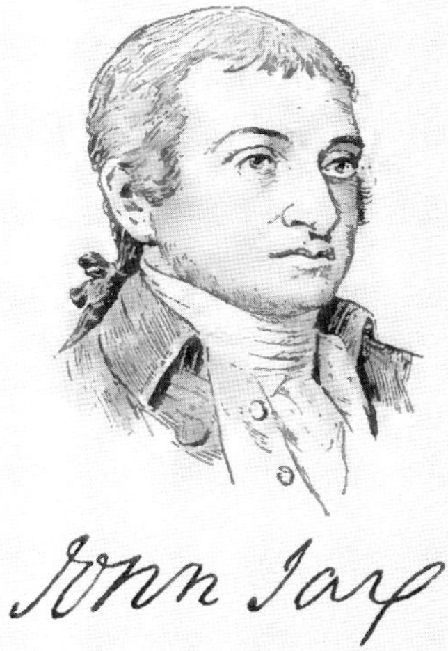

"'Let steadiness our steps pursue,
May justice be our guide;
The Federal plan we keep in view,
We fall if we divide.'

"But the most interesting and original feature of the procession was the Federal ship Hamilton, a frigate, twenty-seven feet long, fully rigged, carrying thirty-two guns, manned by thirty mariners, and mounted on a truck drawn by ten horses. As the procession moved through the principal streets, salutes were fired and the sails changed as if the vessel were afloat. Later in the day a great banquet was held, during which thirteen toasts were proposed, the first being 'The United States'; the fourth, 'General Washington'; and the last, 'The Day; may the Union of the States be Perpetual!'

"This took place on the 23d of July, 1788. Three days later the glad news was received that the Legislature had adopted the Constitution, New York being the tenth State to join the Union."

"It ought to have been the first," remarked Tom.

"No doubt," said the professor; "but the fact of being slow did not mean lack of enthusiasm afterward. This was proved when, in April, 1789, Washington having been chosen President, New York, as capital of the new federation, prepared to welcome the great patriot who was 'first in peace as well as first in war.'"

"And first in the hearts of his countrymen," added Tom.

"Washington's journey from Mount Vernon was one continuous ovation. At Elizabethtown Point, in New Jersey, a committee of both Houses of Congress and many public officials met him. Here he embarked in a splendid barge built for the occasion, manned by thirteen pilots in white uniforms. Other barges, beautifully decorated, followed, and, accompanied by music, this remarkable flotilla moved up the broad and beautiful bay of New York. The barge landed at Murray's Wharf, and here, amid the ringing of bells, the roaring of cannon, and the shouting of the people, Washington stepped ashore, where he was welcomed by his old friends, Governor Clinton, General Knox, and other comrades of the Revolutionary War.

"Carpets had been spread to a carriage, but Washington preferred to walk. I need hardly tell

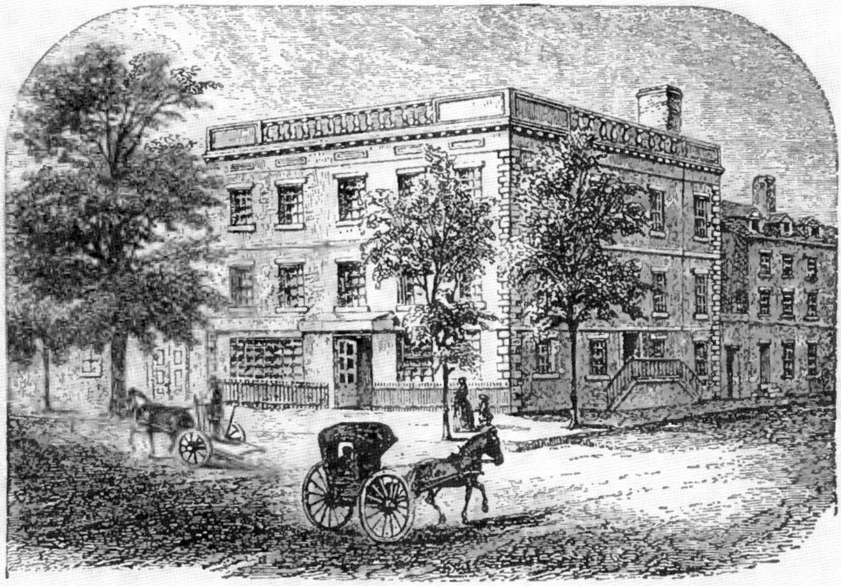

Washington's house in Cherry Street. From an old print.

you that the streets were decorated. All sorts of flags, silken banners, and garlands of flowers bearing his name were everywhere to be seen. Washington bowed every few steps, and of course took off his hat to the ladies, many of whom shed tears of enthusiasm as they waved their handkerchiefs and threw flowers. At No. 1 Cherry Street, corner of Pearl, where now one of the piers of the Brooklyn Bridge rests, he paused and entered the house that had been prepared for him."

"Was it a fine house?" asked Emily.

"Oh, yes, and a fine neighborhood, but rather far up town, as the inhabitants then thought.

"People came from all directions to see the inauguration ceremonies, and the little city was soon overcrowded, every public-house, boarding-house, and private dwelling being more than filled with guests. Some, it is said, slept in tents. The taverns were jammed to their utmost capacity, and each had a special song of welcome of its own. Here is a verse from one of the rhymed greetings:

"'Thrice welcome to this shore,
Our leader now no more,
But ruler thou.
O truly good and great,
Long live to glad our State,
Where countless honors wait
To deck thy brow!'

"A short delay occurred, but on the 30th of April all was ready, and the inauguration took place. At nine o'clock there were religious services in all the churches; at twelve the city troops paraded before Washington's door, and, soon after, the committee of Congress and the heads of departments came in carriages. A half hour later Washington entered the coach of state, and then the procession, the foreign ministers, and a long train of citizens bringing up the rear, moved on toward the City Hall in Wall Street. Federal Hall, as it was then called, had been considerably enlarged and improved, so as to

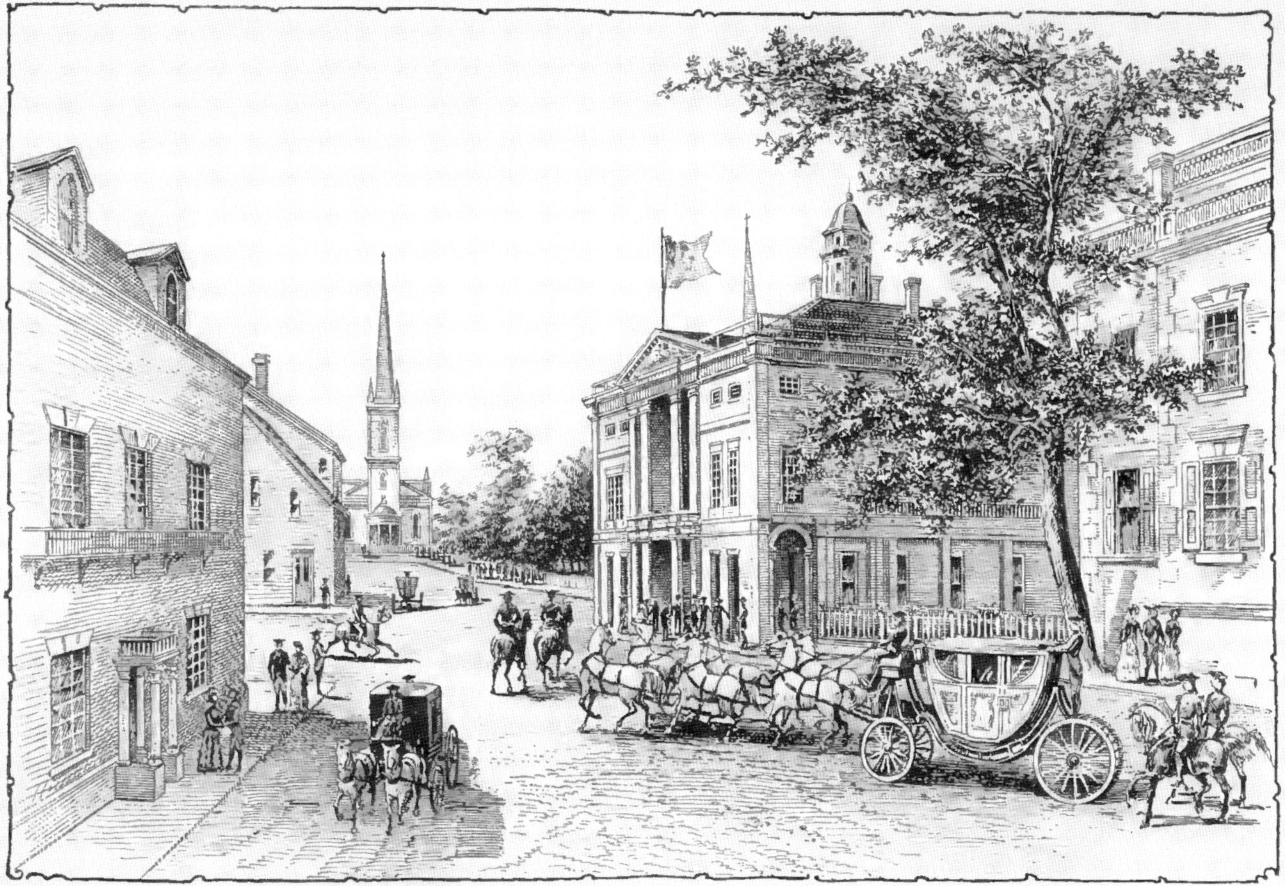

Wall Street in 1789, showing Federal Hall. From an old print.

serve the needs of the Senate and the House of Representatives.

"A large crowd of citizens had gathered, occupying the street, windows, and even the roofs of nearby houses, and all eyes were directed to the balcony in front of the Senate chambers. One of the most interested spectators was Alexander Hamilton, who looked on from his residence opposite, at the corner of Wall and Broad Streets.

"Just before the oath was to be administered it was discovered that there was no Bible in Federal Hall. Fortunately, the chancellor, Robert R. Livingston——"

"Was he the same that had helped prepare the Declaration of Independence?" interrupted George.

"Yes. Fortunately, as I have said, he was a Freemason, and knew that there was a Bible at St. John's Lodge near by. It was brought and, as you can imagine, it is treasured by that lodge to this day.

"The oath was solemnly pronounced by the chancellor, Washington bowing reverently and kissing the Bible. Then Livingston stepped forward, waved his hand and cried out, 'Long live George Washington, President of the United States!' At the same moment a flag was displayed on the cupola of the building, which was followed by a discharge of artillery at the Battery. The bells now began to ring out peals of joy and the people shouted and cheered.

"Washington then delivered his inaugural address to both Houses of Congress, after which the whole assemblage proceeded on foot to St. Paul's, where special services were held."

"Why not to Trinity?" asked George.

"It had not yet been completely rebuilt. After the services a general jubilee took place, and in the evening there were brilliant illuminations and fireworks. Thus New York honored him who had defended her in time of war, and now in time of peace, having been elevated to the highest post in the land, dwelt within her gates."

"Did Washington like living in New York?" asked Emily.

"I imagine he liked it quite well, but his preference was, undoubtedly, his beloved Mount Vernon. Still, he enjoyed going to the John Street Theater, and, in spite of those who have tried to make him a man without humor, it is known that he laughed heartily at the good points of the play. He was fond, too, of walking to the Battery, or going on horseback to the upper part of the island, where Harlem Heights and Fort Washington must have called up vivid memories of war and hardship, now happily but shadows of former anxieties. Then, too, there were visits to Vice-President Adams at Richmond Hill, the beautiful residence in Greenwich village that once served as Washington's headquarters. There was one custom also that pleased him very much, and that was the New-Yorkers' way of celebrating New Year's day, by calling, wishing each other a Happy New Year, and extending a hospitable welcome to every visitor. The President said he hoped New York would never give up this genial custom, but a few years ago it began for some reason to go out of style, and it has now been completely dropped.

"About a month after Washington's arrival, Mrs. Washington and her two grandchildren, Eleanor and George Washington Parke Custis, reached the city, using the same barge that had brought the President. Receptions and dinners were now the order of the day; the foreign ambassadors and many of the most distinguished men of the country resided here, and there was plenty of society life in town. There is a celebrated painting of Lady Washington's first grand reception, by Huntington, that contains sixty-four portrait figures of well-known persons. A study of this picture will make you acquainted with nearly all the prominent people that graced New York during that time.

"After a few months the Cherry Street house was found inconvenient, and the Washingtons moved to the McComb Mansion, No. 39 Broadway, which, being six stories high, was regarded as a wonderful building."

"Wasn't that the place where the first houses were built, and where there is a tablet now?" asked Emily.

"Yes, close by," said the professor. "Washington celebrated his birthday in the year 1790 by moving into his new residence. At the same time another form of celebration was going on elsewhere. A new society, known as Tammany, or the Columbian Order, organized about two weeks after Washington had taken the oath of office, held a meeting on the Twenty-second of February, at which it was decided to commemorate the day regularly every year. Thirteen toasts were then drunk in home-made porter.

"Tammany was organized as an intensely patriotic American society, and, instead of adopting any such foreign dignitary as St. George or St. Andrew, as had been the custom, it turned a well-known and highly respected Indian chief, Tammany, into a saint

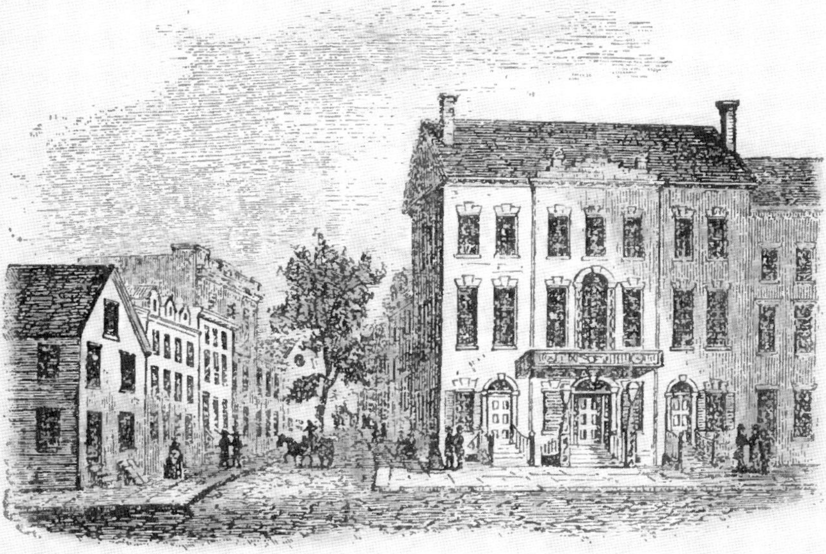

Tammany Hall in 1830; present site of the New York Sun Building. From an old print.

and accepted him as its patron. Furthermore, in order not to ape any European ways, the members dressed in Indian costume, the home of the society was called a wigwam, and the presiding officer the Grand Sachem. The first permanent wigwam was where the Tribune Building stands to-day, the second where the Sun is now established, and the third its present home in Fourteenth Street. The early history of Tammany is very interesting. It founded a museum, engaged in charitable work, and in the year 1808 gave proper burial to the remains of the unfortunate victims of the prison ships. For years their ashes had been literally blown about, no one considering it his duty to inter them. Under the auspices of Tammany a vault was built in Hudson Avenue, Brooklyn, a notable funeral procession organized, and the coffins reverently deposited in this Tomb of Patriots.*

"But to go back to the year 1790. New York was then the city of official gatherings and state affairs; still, there wasn't a bath room, a furnace, a gas jet, or a match in town. Latchkeys were unknown, steel pens were not in use, and coal had not been introduced. To reach Harlem one was compelled to go on horseback or in a carriage; to visit Albany, the quickest conveyance was a sailboat which generally took a week; to send a letter to Savannah, thirty-three cents in postage was required."

"I don't think I should have liked New York very much in those days," remarked Tom.

"Still, other cities were jealous of New York, and before the end of the year 1790 Congress decided to honor Philadelphia by making it the capital. So Washington once more bade farewell to Manhattan Island, the Senators and the Representatives

---

* During the summer of 1900, while excavations were going on in the Brooklyn Navy Yard, a large number of additional skeletons were unearthed. Under the auspices of the Prison-Ship Martyrs' Association and officials from the navy, on June 16th, the remains were placed with becoming ceremonies next to those previously interred. A movement is on foot to erect a monument to these martyrs.

followed suit, likewise the foreign ambassadors, and all the officials of the national Government, leaving New York to make the best of her natural resources, and to depend on the energy and enterprise of her own citizens."

CHAPTER IX

"HERE'S a curiosity," remarked the professor, the next time we met, handing George a thin pamphlet.

"The New York Directory," said George, reading the title-page.

"Can you decipher the date?"

"1786."

"This is a reprint of the first directory ever issued in New York city. It has about eighty pages, some nine hundred names and addresses, includes an almanac, a table of coins, arrivals and departures of the mails, a list of the professors of Columbia College, the officers and directors of the Bank of New York (the only one in the city), and other interesting matter. It contains, also, a curious coincidence. Turn to page 63, George, and read, under the head of 'Lawyers,' the first name."

"Aaron Burr, Esq., 10 Little Queen Street."

"Little Queen is now Cedar Street," explained the professor. "And what name is next?"

"Alexander Hamilton, Esq., 57 Wall Street."

"You will notice that these two names are not in their alphabetical order, which makes the coincidence all the more remarkable. Perhaps the pub-

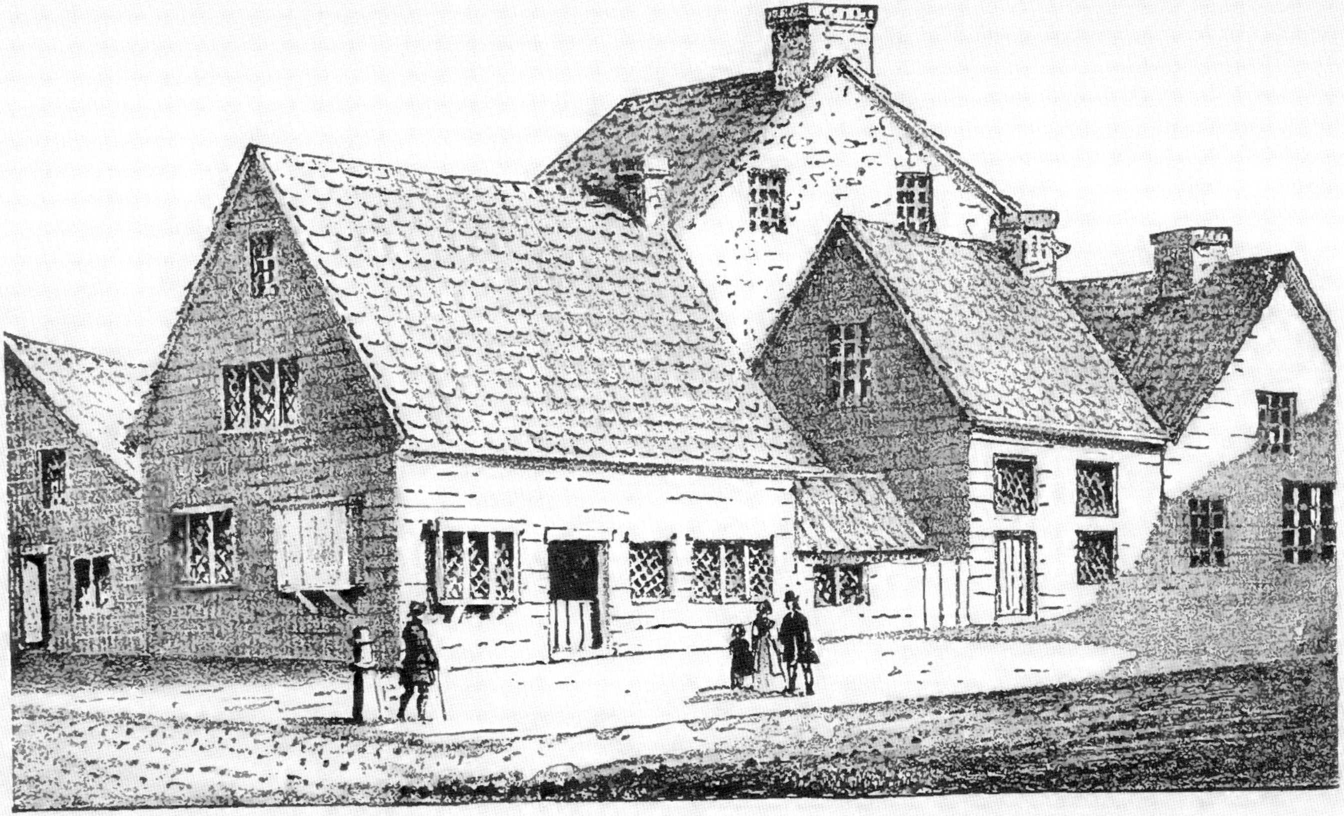

View of old buildings in William Street, between Liberty Street and Maiden Lane, in the year 1800.
From an old print.

lisher of the directory placed them together because they were the two most brilliant lawyers of their day. At any rate, there they are, and now we are ready to talk about their deplorable duel. I have already pointed out to you the difference between the Federalists, who believed in a strong *national* Government, and the Anti-federalists, who thought more of the *States* than of the *United* States. Hamilton was an ardent Federalist, Burr was on the other side. They were thus political enemies. Burr had been chosen Vice-President of the United States, but he believed that if it had not been for Hamilton he might have had the presidency. By and by he sought the governorship of New York, and again Hamilton crossed his path and defeated him. Burr then heard that Hamilton had referred to him as a dangerous man, and demanded an explanation. No doubt Hamilton, broad-minded statesman that he was, *did* think Burr, who stooped to the lowest tricks of a ward politician, a dangerous man, and he was too honest and too courageous to deny it. Then followed a challenge and the duel at Weehawken.

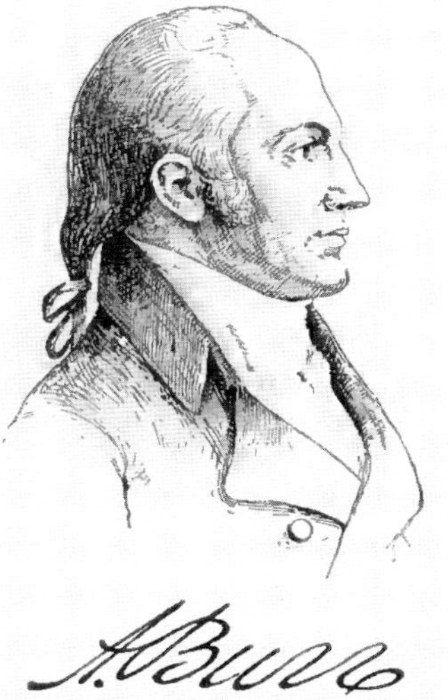

"Early on the morning of July 11th, when the birds were singing and all Nature was smiling, a boat left the neighborhood of Hamilton Grange, another that of Richmond Hill, now Burr's country house, and crossed the Hudson. An hour later they returned, one bearing the fatally wounded Hamilton. There is proof that he made no effort to hit his antagonist; Burr shot to kill.

"When New York heard of the duel, the excitement became intense; when the people learned of Hamilton's death they were horror-stricken and too deeply grieved to express their sorrow, but their tongues were loosened when they thought of Burr, and their indignation was uttered in no uncertain terms. It seems that Burr had supposed himself so popular that nothing could harm him. Suddenly, to his astonishment, he discovered that he was hated and despised; fear took hold of him, he became afraid of his own shadow; and, finally, like one who dreads the hand of justice, he ran away, and was loathed ever afterward.

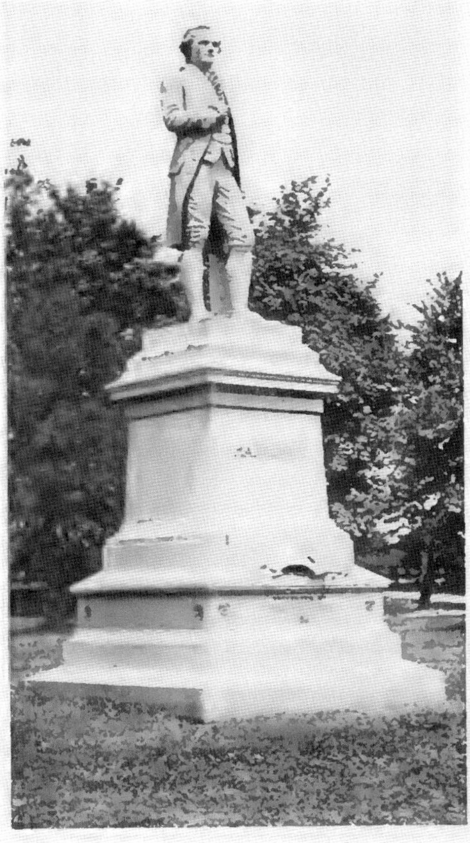

Statue of Alexander Hamilton in Central Park. Erected 1880. Photographed 1900.

"Meanwhile the name of Hamilton has been

cherished, his fame has spread and the wonderful achievements of his brilliant mind are still of service to his country, constituting a monument that needs no inscription."

"It seems too bad, though," said Emily, "that he should have died in such a way."

"I quite agree with you," remarked the professor. "This benefit came of it, however: it put an end for all time to dueling in this city. It seems really that to improve matters on this earth some sort of sacrifice is necessary.

"Hamilton's funeral took place on July 14th. Amid the doleful booming of cannon an imposing and sorrowful procession moved slowly down Broadway to Trinity. Every organization in the city was represented, and the whole community was in mourning. On a platform in the church sat the four sons of the great statesman, the youngest only four years of age. Gouverneur Morris, one of Hamilton's best friends, delivered the funeral oration. The body was interred with military honors in the churchyard, and a monument was afterward erected over his grave by the Society of the Cincinnati. A memorial was also erected over the spot where he fell.

"Writing of this tragic place, one of our poets has said:

> "'When the great strife for freedom rose,
> Here scouted oft her friends and foes
> Alternate, through the changing war.
> And beacon fires flashed high and far;
> And here, when Freedom's strife was won,
> Fell, in sad feud, her favor'd son.

"'There last he stood. Before his sight
Flowed the fair river, free and bright;
The rising mart, and isles and bay,
Before him in their glory lay—
Scenes of his love and of his fame—
The instant ere the death-shot came.'"

"What is the Society of the Cincinnati?" asked Emily.

"An organization," answered the professor, "formed in 1783 by the officers of the Continental army. It was named in memory of an illustrious Roman, *Lucius Quintius Cincinnatus*, who retired from war to the peaceful pursuits of the citizen. Its objects were to preserve the rights and liberties for which the patriots had so nobly fought, to promote and cherish national honor and union among the States, to maintain brotherly kindness, and to extend relief to members or their families in need of it. Men distinguished for patriotism or special talents were admissible as honorary members. The first president, I need scarcely add, was George Washington.

"As I remarked before," continued the professor, "a sacrifice is generally necessary to gain some benefit. It almost appears as if mankind objects to being helped. As an instance, take the case of Robert Fulton. He was insulted and ridiculed because he audaciously planned to run a boat by steam."

"Was he really laughed at?" asked Tom, incredulously.

"Oh, yes," answered the professor; "right here in New York. It was a time when some of the master minds of the world were trying to solve the

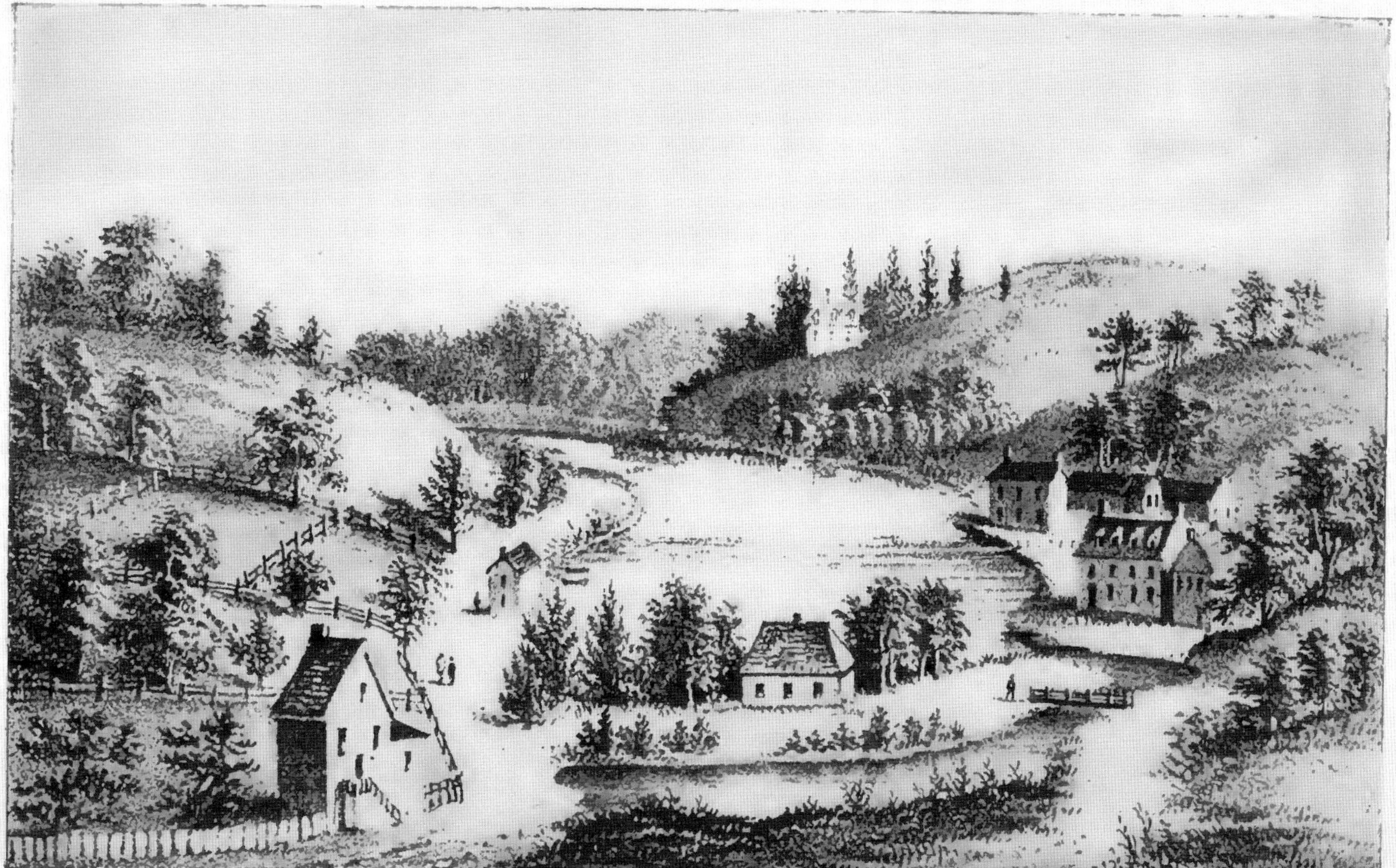

Collect Pond, 1800. From an old print.

problem of overcoming space; but the people, not understanding the matter, laughed at the experiments. Robert Fulton began life in Pennsylvania on a farm. At an early age he showed a decided talent for painting, later for invention. He was not the first, however, to build a steamboat. One had been operated in Europe as early as 1543. In 1796 New York had seen a boat go by steam. John Fitch had built it and propelled it around the Collect Pond, carrying with him as a passenger Chancellor Robert R. Livingston, who, besides attending to affairs of state, was greatly interested in steam. Livingston and Fulton met in Europe and there planned to build a steamboat that would carry passengers and freight up and down the Hudson. The result was the construction of the Clermont in 1807, a boat one hundred and thirty-three feet long, with two clumsy-looking paddle wheels and a very tall smokestack. The doubting Thomases called it 'Fulton's Folly.' A great crowd gathered at the wharf on the day of her first trip, and some made sarcastic remarks which Fulton overheard. At his command, however, the boat moved, reached midstream, and plowed her way through the water *against the wind*, going about five miles an hour. The people were surprised to see her keep on and finally disappear; they were fairly astonished to see her back again four days later with proof that she had been to Albany and back. Here was a modern miracle; no one had dreamed such a thing possible. Her appearance as she glided up the Hudson literally astounded the natives, especially at night. The sparks shooting up from the tall smoke-

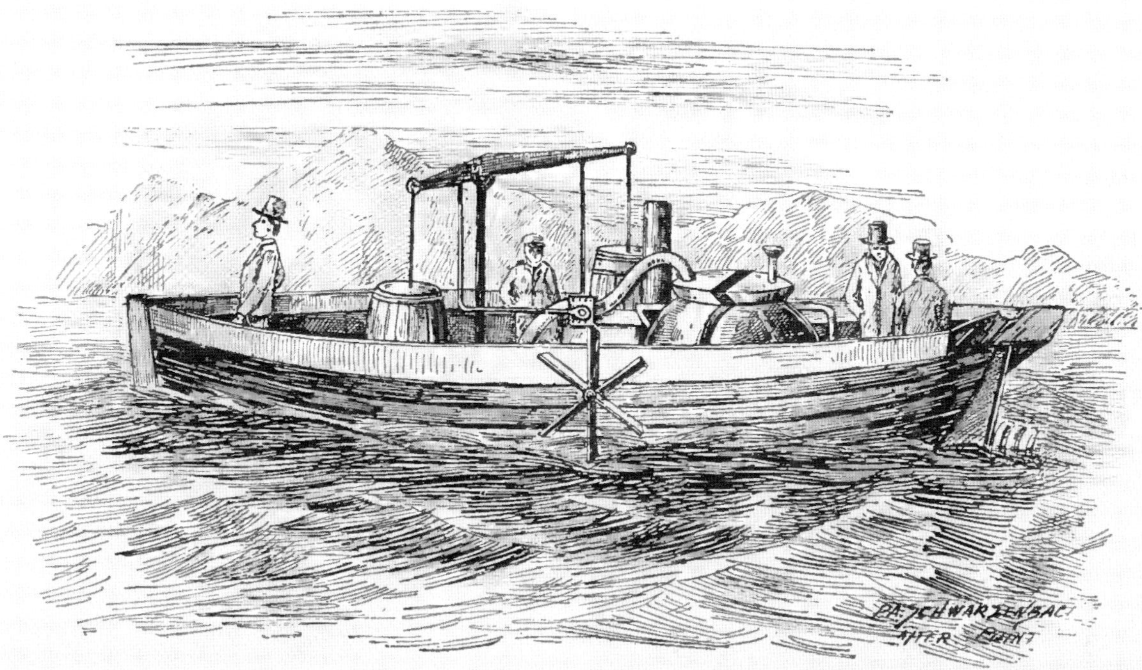

First boat propelled by steam. From an old print.

stack, and the noise of the machinery, so startled the terror-stricken observers that some of them fell on their knees, thinking that a fearful monster was upon them.

"Thus Fulton, in his forty-second year, achieved a success that aroused the attention and admiration of the whole world. It was the first *practical* step in the direction of reducing space on the water, and New York enjoyed the honor of seeing the effort crowned with success; and yet, strange to say, New York has never seen fit to raise a memorial of any sort to this illustrious citizen."

"How did the sailboat men like the new steamboat?" asked George.

"Not at all; in fact, they did all in their power to damage it, and often the Clermont arrived at Albany or New York with one paddle wheel smashed or missing. There was a certain sailboat man, however, who acted in a different spirit—namely, young Captain Cornelius Vanderbilt.

"Vanderbilt was a boy of thirteen when Fulton's boat made its first trip to Albany. Vanderbilt senior was a Staten Island ferryman, and the boy's highest ambition in life was to own a boat like that of his father. At the age of sixteen he begged his mother to lend him the considerable sum of one hundred dollars wherewith to buy a boat. She agreed to do so, if he would plow, harrow, and plant with corn a certain field within a certain time. It was a rough, tough, and stony field, but young Vanderbilt was not dismayed. He induced some of his boy friends to help him, and the work was done on the day agreed upon. Furthermore, it was well and thoroughly done. Vanderbilt now bought his boat and began his career. There were forty other boatmen in the

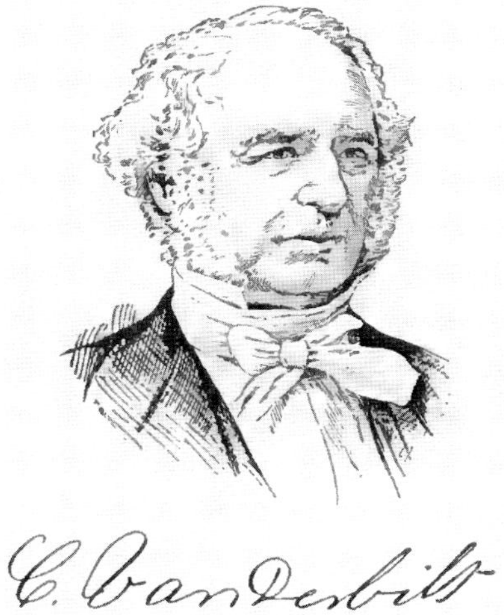

business ahead of him, but soon his close attention to his duties and the care he took of the money he earned told in his favor. For several years he gave most of his receipts to his parents. In the meantime his way of doing whatever he undertook thoroughly and satisfactorily brought him more and more business.

"Eight years passed. Vanderbilt was now twenty-four, and the owner of several of the best sailboats on the river and of nine thousand dollars in cash. Suddenly he gave up his profitable business and accepted a position as captain of a steamboat, at one thousand dollars a year, or one third of the amount he had been earning before. He had made up his mind that the steamboat had come to stay, and that the path of success was in the new direction. In the course of time he owned steamboats instead of sailboats. Again, later, when the railroad began to offer better facilities than the steamboat, he forsook the latter and became an owner of railroads. In this way, through doing what he undertook thoroughly and well, and being alert as to the best means of serving the public, he built up his colossal fortune."

"And how about Astor?" queried Tom.

"He began somewhat earlier," said the professor. "He was born in the little German village of Waldorf, in 1763, and arrived here when he was twenty-one years old—the year after the Revolutionary War came to an end. He had a brother in New York in the butcher business, who found a place for the lad in a fur establishment, where he received two dollars a week and board for beating furs. Other boys had filled this position before Astor, but the world has not heard of them. Young John Jacob made up his mind the very first day he went to work that he would learn all there was to know of the fur business. And he did. His employer found out, ere long, also, that this was no laggard of a lad, and advanced him rapidly. Three years after his arrival Astor swung out his own sign, and within sixteen years he had acquired a quarter of a million dollars, a great fortune in those days.

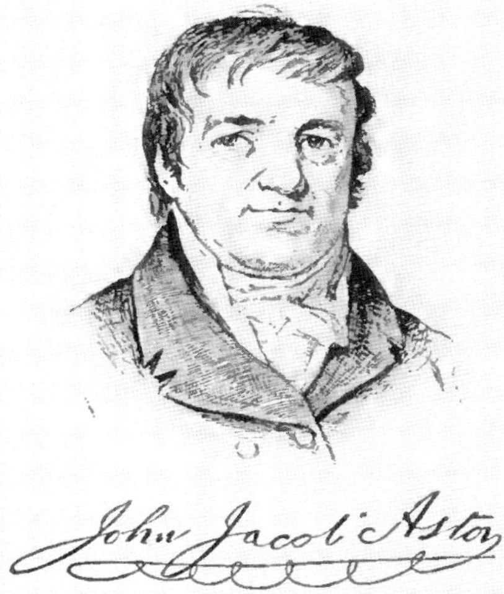

"Here was another case of doing things thoroughly and of studying conditions. For instance, Astor carefully watched the growth of the city. One day he sold a piece of property in Wall Street for eight thousand dollars. The purchaser remarked, after the papers were signed, that he thought he had made a good bargain, prophesying that in a few years the lot would be worth twelve thousand dollars. 'True,' replied Astor, 'but with your eight thousand dollars I shall buy eighty lots above Canal Street, which, by the time your lot is worth twelve thousand, will be worth eighty thousand.' And so it proved to be.

"It was not, however," continued the professor, "the making of fortunes that led me to speak of Vanderbilt and Astor, though the success that crowns industry is always interesting; nor was it to point out in this way the commercial development that was taking place in New York, but to show you to what splendid use money may be put. When the War of the Rebellion broke out Vanderbilt was able to show his patriotic spirit by presenting the Government with a fine steamer, while his descendants enjoyed the privilege of contributing nearly two millions of dollars to the College of Physicians and Surgeons in this city, thus rendering it one of the finest medical institutions in the country. The Astor Library embodies the generous donations of the Astor family, amounting to about a million and a half dollars. The Cooper Union Library and Free Schools, and the Lenox Library with its rich treasures, are similar examples of the immeasurable good that wealth may provide. Furthermore, I would have you remember that it was love for the city and a desire to enlarge its resources of learning and art, to benefit its citizens, to elevate their tastes, to increase their knowledge, and to add to their happiness, that prompted these grand and munificent bestowals."

"If ever I have a fortune," remarked Tom seriously, "I shall do something for the city."

"Don't wait until you get your fortune," said the professor. "Begin by doing small things and

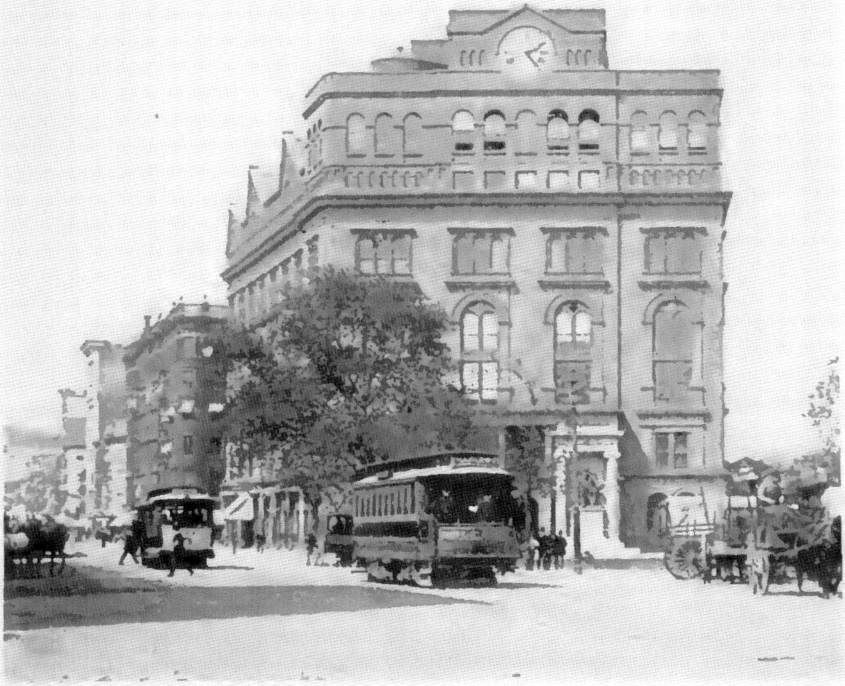

Cooper Union and Peter Cooper's statue. From a recent photograph.

the greater ones will follow. Only a few days ago I read in one of our newspapers of a modest little club of boys that had been formed downtown somewhere by some kind-hearted people. A sculptor became interested and showed the lads how to work in clay. One little fellow, possessing the precious gift of genius, was in that club. From the club he went to

Cooper Union, then to the Academy of Design, and to-day he is on the high road to fame."

"Was Peter Cooper a poor boy?" asked Emily.

"A very poor boy," answered the professor; "so poor that in all his youth he had but six months of school life. While he was an apprentice, receiving the pitiful sum of fifty dollars a year, he bought a tallow dip, and by the light of this dip he educated himself. It was during these days, while acquiring knowledge in this hard way, that he made up his mind, if ever fortune bestowed sufficient means upon him, to found a night school for mechanics who like himself were ambitious to learn. Many other men have been stirred to make similar resolutions while undergoing privations and hardships in early life, but later, in the enjoyment of prosperity, have forgotten all about their fine intentions. Peter Cooper did not forget—he never swerved from his early purpose.

"But we have been wandering. Let us go back to old New York and become better acquainted with another of her brilliant sons, whose name has already been mentioned—De Witt Clinton. In 1790, at the age of twenty-one, he became private secretary to his uncle, Governor George Clinton; at twenty-eight he entered the State Assembly, at twenty-nine the Senate, at thirty-two he was sent to the United States Senate; at thirty-three he was appointed Mayor of New York; and at the age of fifty-five he was elected Governor of the State by the greatest majority ever given to a candidate up to that time.

"Busy as Clinton was with the affairs of state, he still had time for other matters. He was one of the most active organizers of the Historical Society, likewise of the Academy of Fine Arts. He enjoyed the honor, too, of being the first President of the Public School Society, formed in 1805.

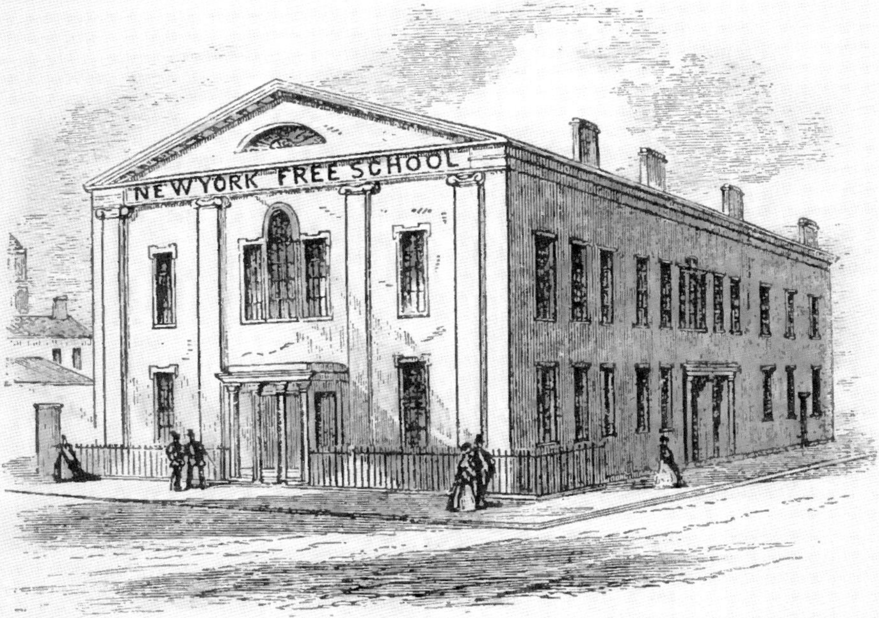

New York Free School No. 2, Chatham Street, 1808. From an old print in Valentine's Manual for 1866.

"Before this time the churches had established schools, but the children of the churchless poor were allowed to grow up in ignorance. Some Quaker ladies started the first movement to provide an education for the city's waifs, and Clinton, together with others, joined in the good work. Thus was begun what is now one of New York's proudest institutions, a system that provides primary, grammar, and high schools, where two hundred and eighty thousand children receive free education; night schools, where those who work during the day may learn; vacation schools for the summer months, and free lectures for winter evenings; also two colleges, where the higher branches of knowledge are taught, and where young

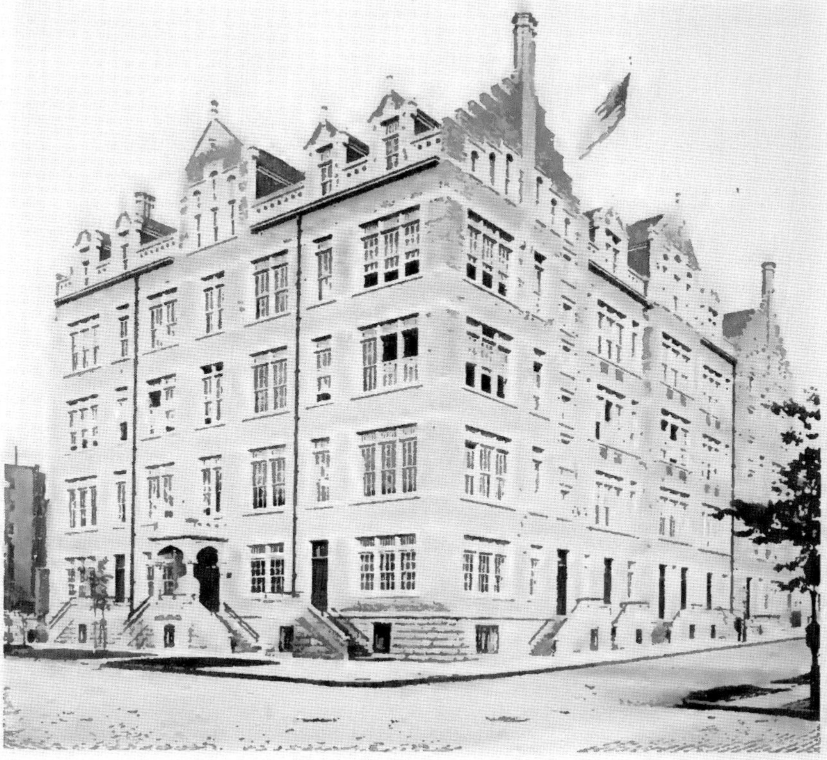

Modern schoolhouse. At West End Avenue and Eighty-second Street. From a recent photograph.

men and young women are fitted for professional careers. Over five thousand teachers are employed in this vast work which is carried on in one hundred and eighty-one buildings.

"While Clinton was mayor—in 1812—our present City Hall was completed, and it remains to-day

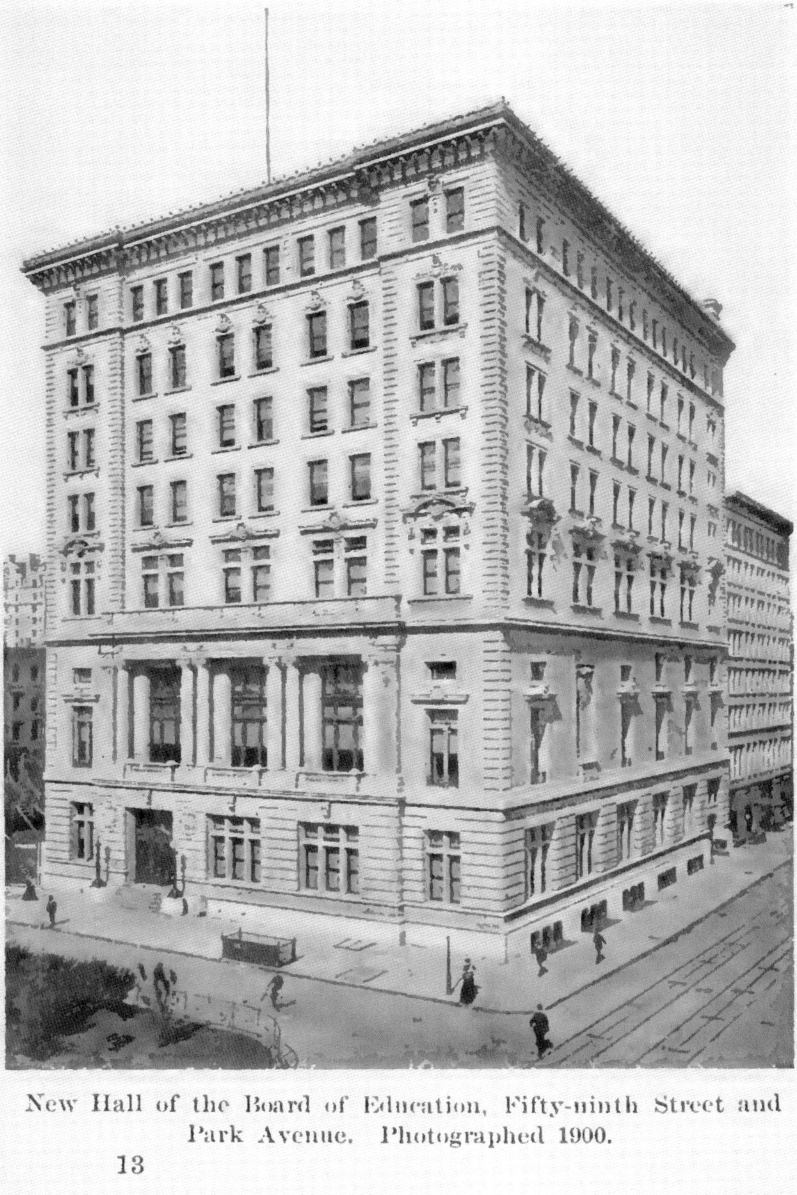

New Hall of the Board of Education, Fifty-ninth Street and Park Avenue. Photographed 1900.

among the most beautiful architectural features of the metropolis. The front and sides are of marble, but the rear is of sandstone. The latter was used for economical reasons, the belief being that the uptown side was of little consequence, as the city would be a long time growing north of the new building. In 1890 the brownstone was painted white."

"They'd stare if they were to see New York today, I guess," said Tom proudly.

"The brownstone idea seems all the more curious when we are told that in 1807 a commission laid out our present gridiron plan of numbered streets and avenues up to One Hundred and Fifty-fifth Street. The committeemen apologized, it is true, for having done so much 'laying out,' and acknowledged that probably not for centuries would most of these streets be occupied. Less than one century has passed and nearly every inch of ground is now covered with its pile of brick and mortar.

"In 1814, while the war with England was in progress, New York was thrown into a fever of excitement by a rumor that the Island of Manhattan was to be invaded by the British. As usual, the defenses were poor and few. Clinton issued a stirring address to the people, asking their help to complete the unfinished fortifications. Four days later three thousand persons were at work; and even the newspapers suspended publication, so that their men might help. Among the enthusiastic volunteers were—

> "'Plumbers, founders, dyers, tinners, tanners, shavers,
> Sweeps, clerks and criers, jewelers, engravers,
> Clothiers, drapers, players, cartmen, hatters, nailers,
> Gaugers, scalers, weighers, carpenters, and sailors.'

"In short, every one who could handle a pick or a spade, or carry earth on a shingle, did so. Such was New York's display of patriotic spirit, and every

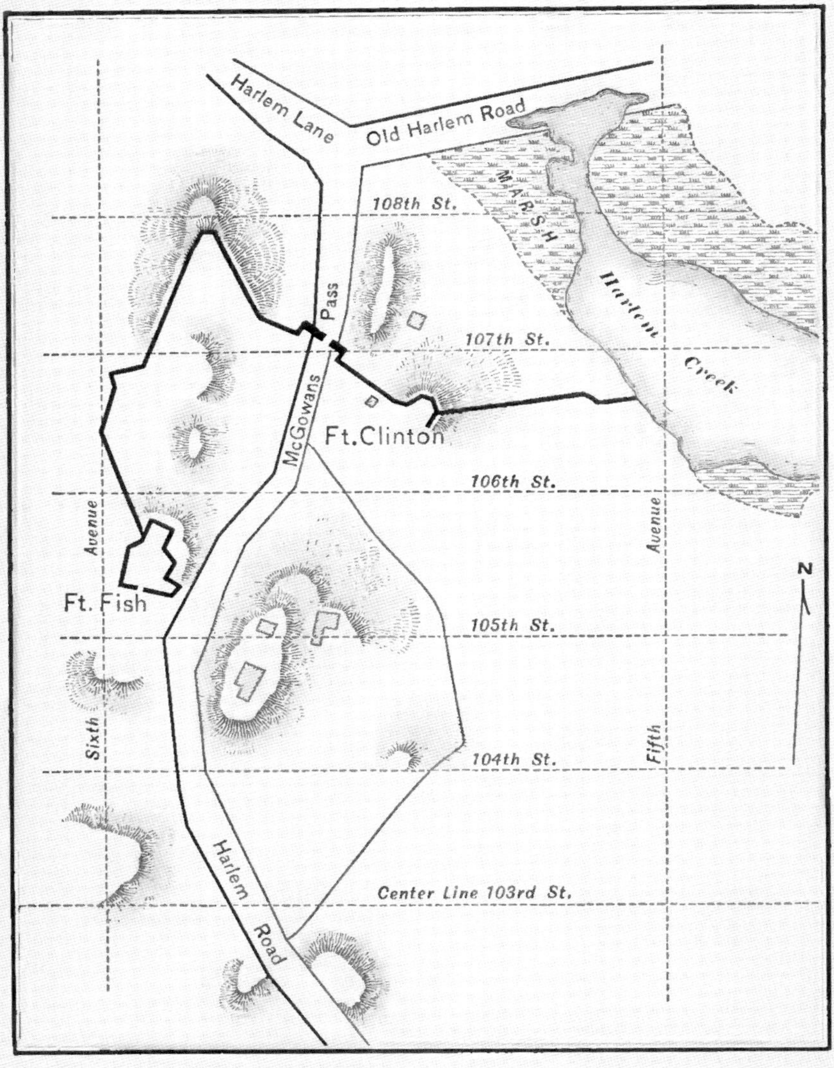

Map of McGowan's Pass and Forts Fish and Clinton. Copied from a chart of 1814.

lad who was able to shoulder a musket offered his services. The Narrows and Hell Gate were protected, and all the hills on the island bristled with earthworks and cannon.

"There are some interesting landmarks of this period in Central Park and just beyond it, which I now purpose showing you," said the professor.

We were always ready for an excursion, and eagerly accompanied our guide to the site of McGowan's Pass, which we remembered as an important feature of Revolutionary days.

"This vicinity was particularly well fortified," began the professor. "As the map shows you, there was a fort on either side of the pass, the two being connected by a line of breastworks. "Would you like to see the site of one of these works—Fort Clinton?"

There was an immediate assent.

The professor, acting on his suggestion, led the way to the little pond just above the Fifth Avenue entrance at One Hundred and Fifth Street and pointed to a hill opposite, from the top of which rose a flagstaff.

"It doesn't look very warlike," remarked Emily, impressed by the calm beauty of the scene.

"Let us climb to the top," suggested the professor by way of reply.

We did so, and were surprised to find near the flagstaff several old cannons, the appearance of which was sufficiently indicative of war to satisfy all of us.

We now made our way to the old Blockhouse, situated near One Hundred and Tenth Street, and

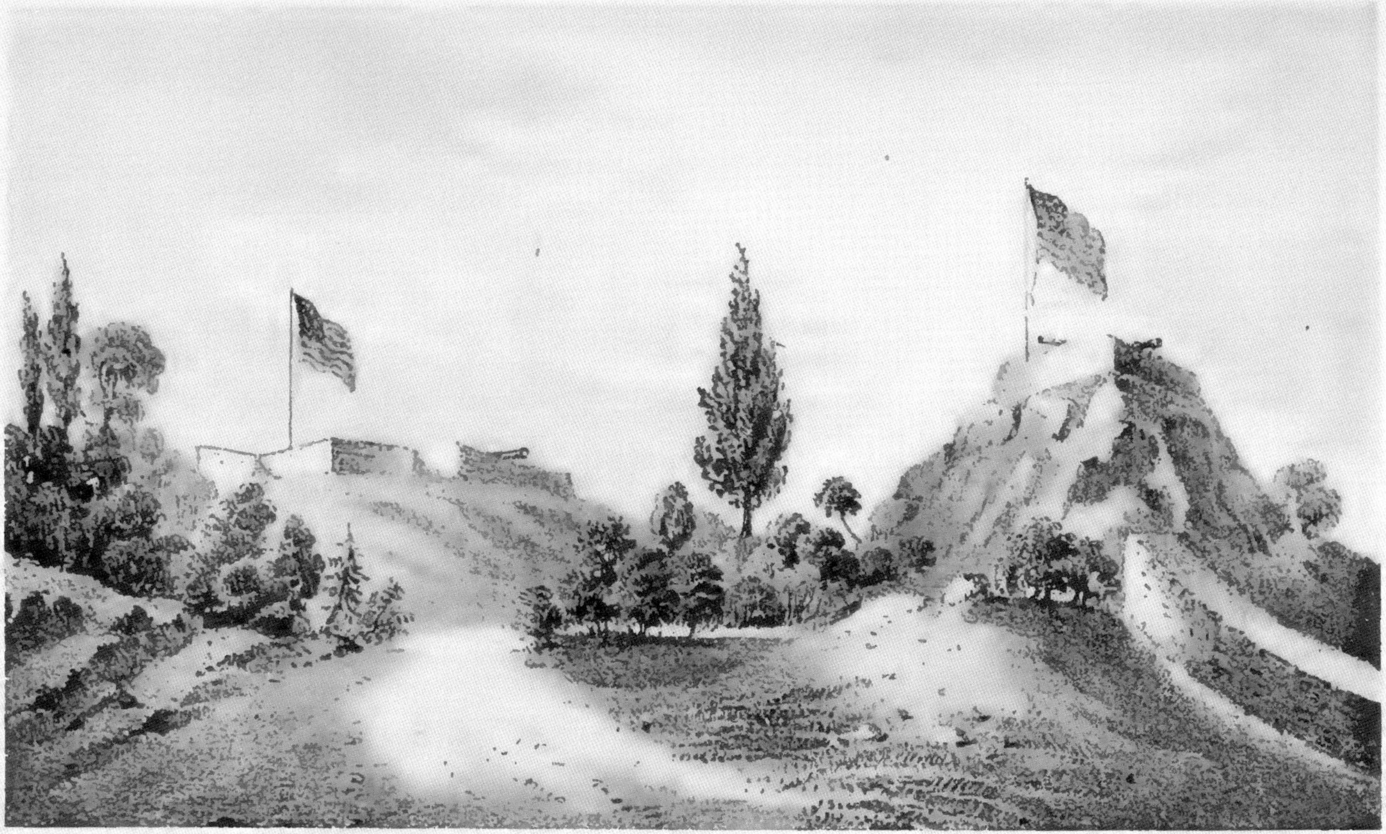

Fort Fish. Fort Clinton.

Fortifications at McGowan's Pass, 1814. From an old painting.

were forcibly reminded of its excellent position by the steep ascent to its lofty perch. This was one of several, the professor explained, that guarded the roads during the War of 1812 from Hell Gate on the east to the heights near the spot where Grant's Tomb is located on the west.

"On the Fourth of July last," continued the professor, "I came up here before daybreak to see the ceremony of raising the flag. I arrived at four o'clock, and ten minutes later heard the inspiring music of fifes and drums. Then through the entrance at One Hundred and Tenth Street came the Washington Continental Guard and some detachments of the naval militia. At 4.33 the moment of sunrise, the flag was run up, and the drum corps played 'Yankee Doodle.' It was a simple but a touching act; the freshness of morning was about us, the Stars and Stripes floated beautifully in the air of freedom; I stood upon historic ground and felt the true feeling of patriotism.

"The Guard soon marched off to another Blockhouse, which we shall visit next," said the professor, leading the way down. At One Hundred and Twenty-third Street, near Amsterdam Avenue, we paused, and saw firmly fixed on a prominent base of rocks the second Blockhouse. It had a decidedly warlike look, and but little stretch of the imagination was required to fancy the presence of cannons and soldiers.

"In addition to the forts and blockhouses there were strong gates that were used as barriers. One blocked McGowan's Pass, and the other helped to protect Manhattanville.

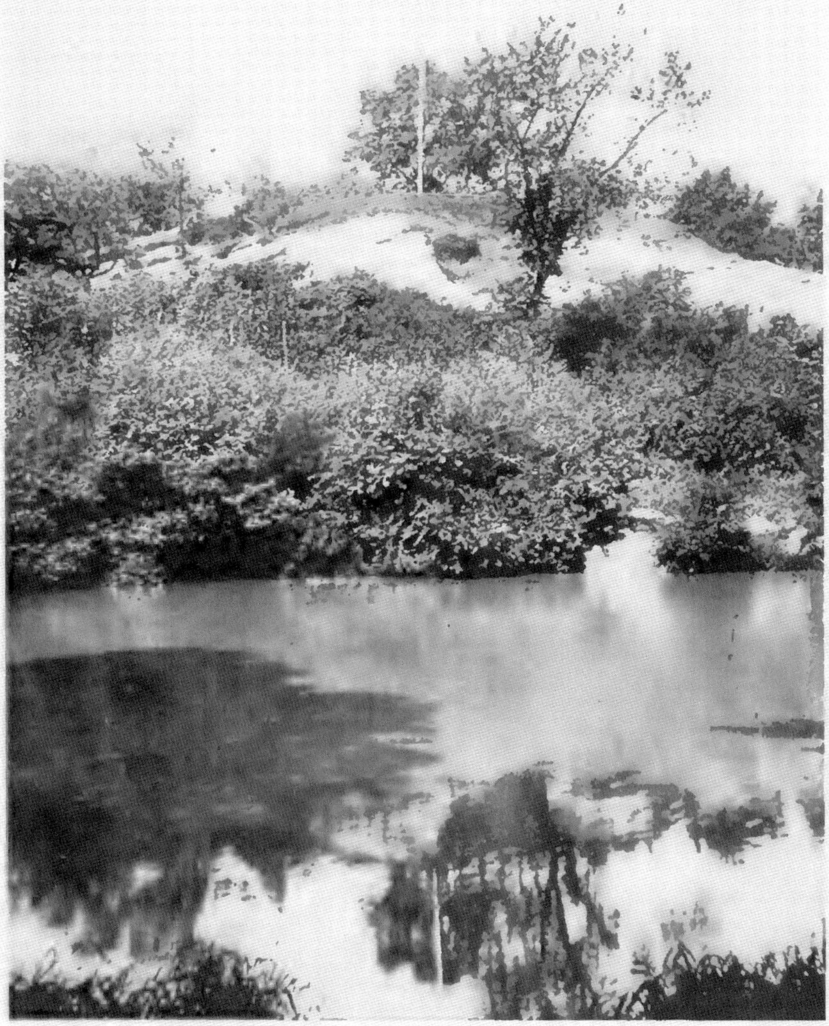

Site of Fort Clinton in Central Park, between One Hundred and Sixth and One Hundred and Seventh Streets, near Fifth Avenue. Photographed 1900.

"A little to the northwest, situated on a mass of rocks was Fort Laight, named in honor of Lieutenant-Colonel E. W. Laight, of the city militia. A few years ago the remains of this fort were still visible, near the south side of One Hundred and Twenty-fifth Street, one hundred and twenty yards east of Eleventh Avenue.

"Enough of war, however," remarked the professor, "and of warlike memorials. Let us turn our attention once more to the achievements of peace. Clinton's wise administration, as I have indicated, had contributed much to the prosperity of the city, but he was destined to render it a greater service than any already to his credit. To cut a canal through New York State and thus to unite the Great Lakes and the Hudson was his dream and his ambition. In 1800 Buffalo was a village and Rochester a mere clearing with a single log cabin. The great fertile regions in that section, now rich with wheat, were almost bare, because it cost too much to transport the grain to Albany. At last, in 1810, after a great deal of work, the Legislature was induced to appoint a committee of investigation. Gouverneur Morris, one of New York's worthy sons, and De Witt Clinton, untiring and never satisfied that he had done enough, were on this committee. Later on, Robert Fulton was also appointed.

"The plan contemplated a canal four hundred and forty miles in length, and an expenditure of six million dollars. Clinton saw clearly what an enormous benefit the city would derive, but his political enemies, who referred to his project as 'The Big

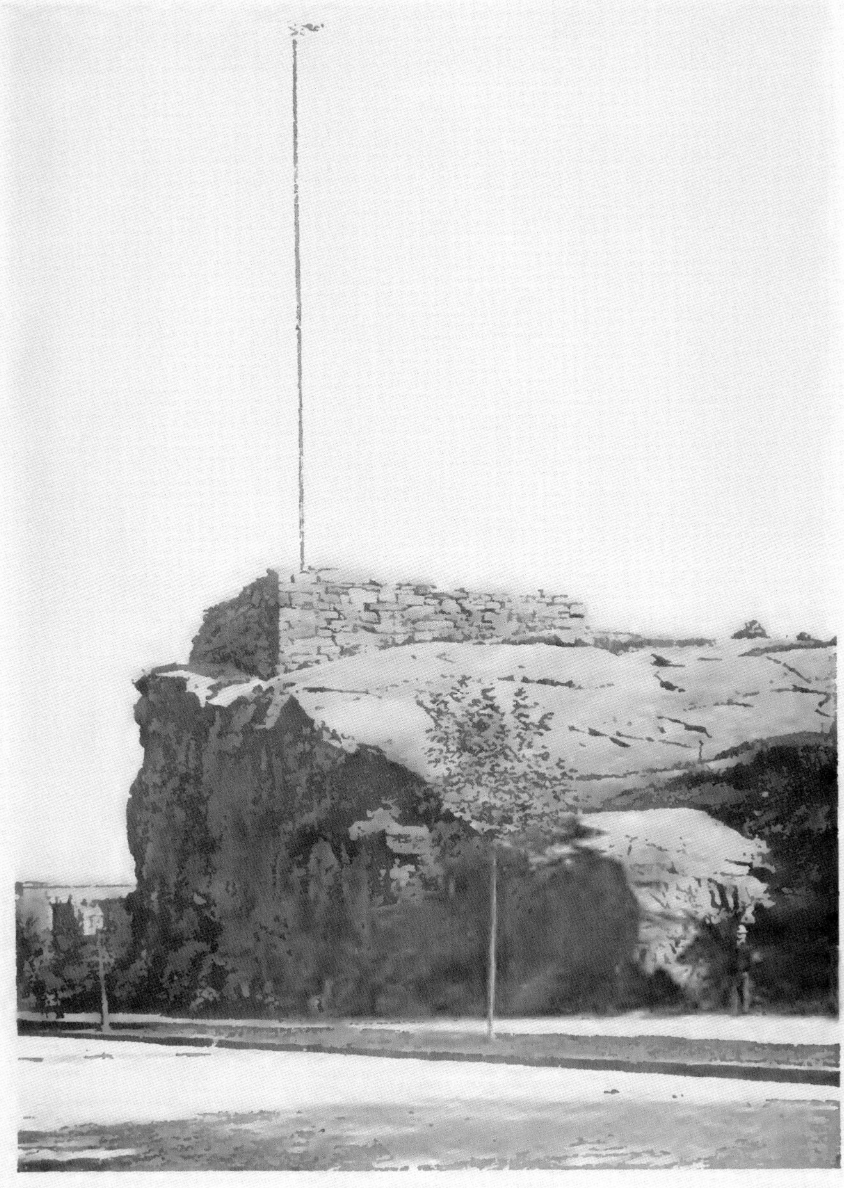

Blockhouse, One Hundred and Twenty-third Street, east of Amsterdam Avenue. Photographed 1900.

Ditch,' hampered him at every step, and in 1824, after he had worked for fourteen years, succeeded in having him removed from the committee."

"What a shame!" exclaimed Emily.

"Ay, but they hurt themselves more than they hurt him. When the people heard what had been done, indignation meetings were held, and when election time came they gave him that big majority for governor that I have already mentioned.

"But to return to the canal. On October 26, 1825, everything was ready to let the waters of Lake Erie into the channel that had been dug. A great celebration had been planned. There being no telegraph in those days, cannons had been placed all along the route to give notice of the great event. At ten o'clock the first gun was fired; at eleven o'clock the Albany signal rang out; all the way down the Hudson the flashes told the story, and at 11.21 New York heard the glad tidings. In the meantime four canal boats, carrying a distinguished company, started from Buffalo. Everywhere along the route crowds were gathered to welcome the proud little fleet; it seemed, in fact, as if the people of the whole State had turned out to rejoice. At Albany there was a congratulatory address, a public dinner, and a grand illumination in the evening. On November 5th the canal boats reached New York. Then a great procession of all sorts of vessels, covered with flags and banners, formed, moved down the bay and out beyond Sandy Hook, salutes greeting it from the forts.

"Here Governor Clinton, whose tall, well-pro-

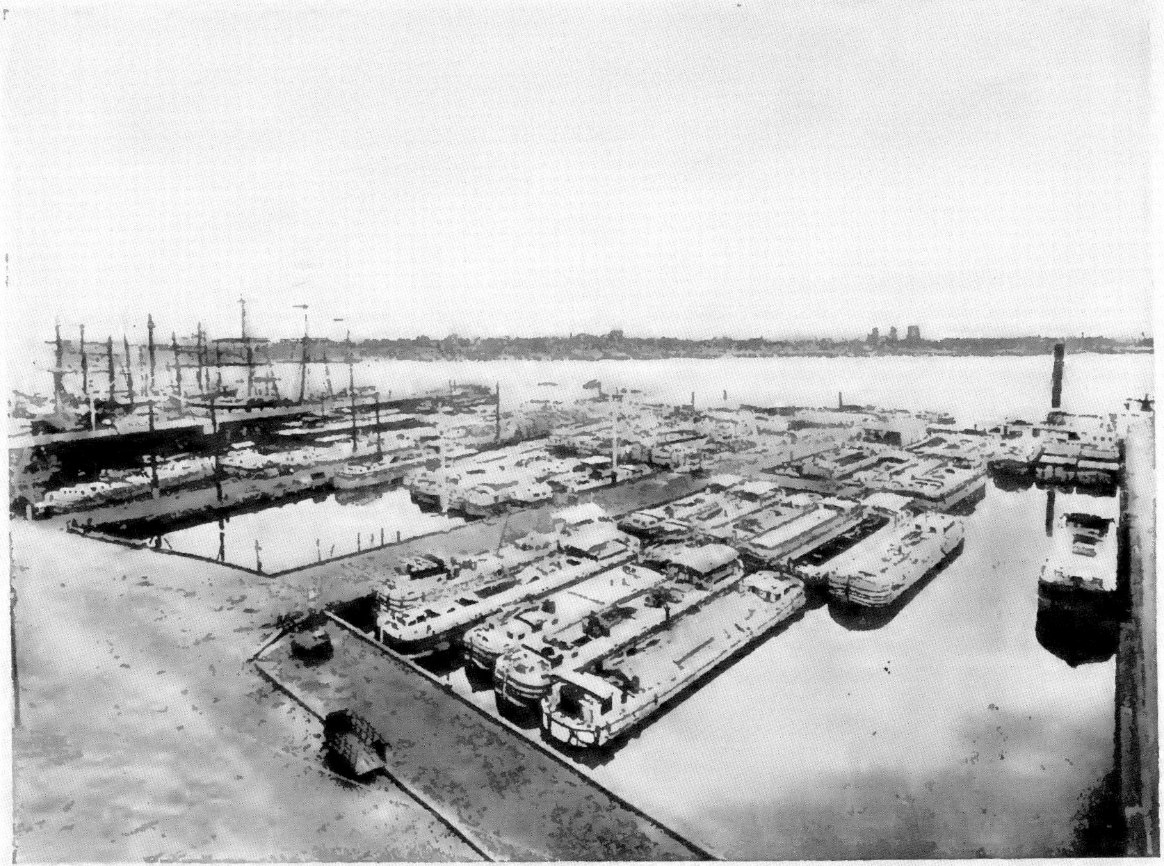

Canal boat village, Coenties Slip. From a recent photograph.

portioned figure always commanded attention, stepped forward, lifted on high a keg of water brought from Lake Erie, and poured the contents into the ocean, thus mingling the two waters. In the meantime a celebration no less impressive was taking place on land. A procession four and a half miles long paraded with banners and music through the principal streets. In the evening fireworks and illuminations followed, and the whole city wore an air of festivity.

"It is well-nigh impossible to measure the benefits of the Erie Canal; it turned a wilderness into a vast fertile area, and brought into New York the produce of these new fields. Without doubt it contributed more than any previous achievement to increase the commercial interests of the city.

"From an ode written for the Canal Celebration I have copied the following verse that thrills with the spirit of the time:

> "''Tis done! 'Tis done! The mighty chain
> Which joins bright ERIE to the MAIN,
> For ages shall perpetuate
> The glory of our native State!'

"While New York was thus progressing in one direction, it was still backward in many ways. Its sanitary conditions were very bad, and it suffered from fearful epidemics. Smallpox, cholera, and yellow fever in turn played awful havoc among its inhabitants. The year 1822 marked a climax and became known as 'the year of the yellow fever.' Everybody who could, rushed out of town. A procession of carts and carriages moved up Broadway to Greenwich village, which was known to be a healthful spot. At Liberty Street a high board fence was stretched across the island as a quarantine measure. Meanwhile, Greenwich suddenly developed into a town. Houses were put up as if by magic; banks, newspapers, and wholesale firms sprouted overnight. Bank Street, so named because the banks selected that row, is a reminder of the yellow-fever year. Thus Greenwich began to grow; it grew, furthermore, in its own peculiar way, and when in later years it came in contact with the upward-moving city, its streets, having followed a direction of their own, could not be made to harmonize with those of the town, which explains why West Fourth and West Tenth Streets, instead of running parallel, deliberately cross each other, to the utter confusion of people who are not well acquainted with old Greenwich ways.

"Gradually greater attention was paid to sanitary measures; foreign vessels were inspected on their arrival; but twenty years passed ere a system of running water was introduced, and not until 1866 was the Board of Health established.

"In 1825 a new wonder surprised the town. The house at No. 7 Cherry Street was lighted by gas. In it lived the President of the New York Gas Company, a recently organized corporation. About this time pipes were laid in Broadway from Canal Street to the Battery, and New York for the first time in its history beheld a well-lighted street. Gradually other streets were thus favored, though for years the

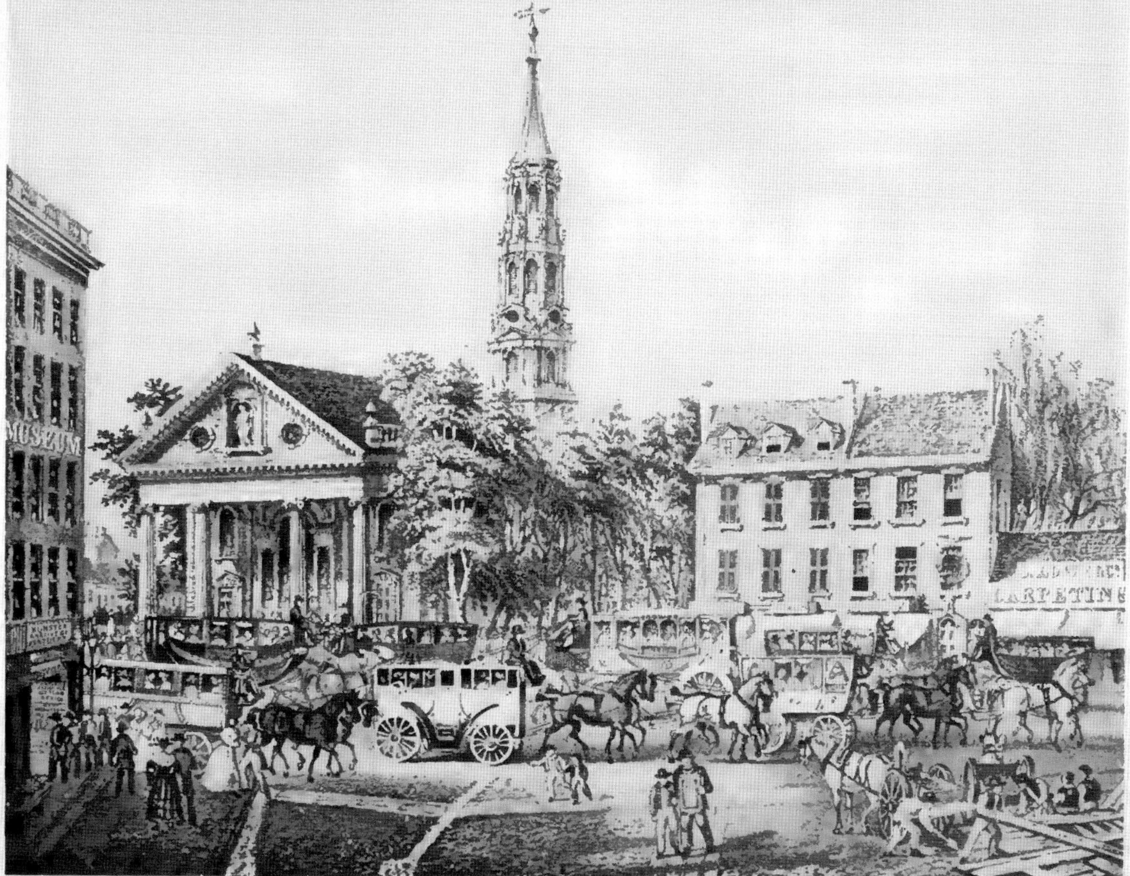

View of St. Paul's church and the Broadway stages, 1831. From a lithograph print in Valentine's Manual for 1861.

town presented a checkered appearance, one block being dimly lighted with ancient oil lamps and another brilliantly illuminated from the works of the new gas company.

"On December 16, 1835, a terrible fire suddenly broke out in the neighborhood of Pearl and Wall Streets and wrought awful havoc. It was intensely cold; the little water that could be obtained quickly froze, and the flames spread without check. For three days the conflagration continued, and was only stopped by blowing up a number of buildings with gunpowder. Six hundred and fifty houses were destroyed and twenty million dollars' worth of property consumed. The Dutch Church in Garden Street and a Marble Exchange in Wall Street, containing a statue of Hamilton, were among the ruined structures.

"A poet of that time thus gave expression to his sad thoughts on viewing the ravages of the flames:

"'Alas! that pillar'd pile! how, as I gazed
Upon the blacken'd shafts, did I recall
The sculptured marble there, whose brow was raised
So like a god's, within that shadowy hall!
Immortal HAMILTON!—though crumpled deep
In the red chaos of that billowy night,
It needs no chisel's memory to keep
Thy spirit's nobler outline vast and bright!
No time—no element can mar the fame,
Gathered, like fadeless sunlight, round thy spotless name!'

"In Pearl Street, almost opposite the William Bradford tablet, there is a gray limestone memorial, consisting of a female figure, beneath which appears the following inscription:

DESTROYED 1835
IN THE CONFLAGRATION 16, 17 DEC'BER.
650 BUILDINGS CONTAINING MERCHANDISE
WERE CONSUMED IN ONE NIGHT.
LOSS 20,000,000 OF DOLLARS.
REBUILT 1836.
AGAIN DESTROYED BY FIRE 1853.

"The lack of water on this occasion was one of the chief causes that led to the construction of the Croton Aqueduct. Its starting point was forty miles from the City Hall, and it involved the tunneling of solid rocks, the crossing of valleys by embankments, and of brooks by culverts. At the Harlem River it necessitated the building of High Bridge, fourteen hundred and fifty feet long and one hundred and fourteen feet above high water. It also required the erection of two reservoirs: one south of Eighty-sixth Street, called the Receiving Reservoir; the other (now being torn down to make room for our great Public Library) at Forty-second Street and Fifth Avenue, used as a distributing basin. Since then the big reservoir, extending from Eighty-sixth Street to Ninety-sixth Street, designated as the Retaining Reservoir, has been added to the system. It covers one hundred and nine acres, and has a capacity of one thousand million gallons.

"The year 1842 saw the completion of the great undertaking, and in October the city, always ready to celebrate, organized a monster demonstration. A procession, including representatives of all the various trades, with floats and banners, marched through the streets and was reviewed by the governor, members of Congress, and mayors of neighboring cities. City Hall Park was the center of interest, for here an ingeniously constructed fountain had been built, the main jet throwing a column of water sixty feet into the air, while, by shifting a plate, the spouting waters could be made to assume seven different shapes.

"The people of to-day can hardly picture the city without its Croton, nor do we realize that our light touch taps a stream whose pure and wholesome source is forty miles away. The rejoicing when this blessing was bestowed upon New York is well described by the poet George P. Morris, whose words I'll read you:

"'Water leaps as if delighted,
While the conquered foes retire;
Pale Contagion flees affrighted
With the baffled demon Fire.
Water shouts a glad hosanna,
Bubbles up the earth to bless;
Cheers it like the precious manna
In the barren wilderness.

"'Round the aqueducts of story,
As the mists of Lethe throng;
Croton's waves, in all their glory,
Troop in melody along.
Ever sparkling, bright and single,
Will this rock-ribbed spring appear,
When posterity shall mingle
Like the gathered waters here.'

"A memento of the old style of water supply is still in existence in the shape of a solitary hand pump at the corner of Trinity Place and Cedar Street."

CHAPTER X

"THE newspapers of the first half of the century were very different from those of to-day. They were serious sheets intended for business offices, were expensive, and were delivered by special messengers. As a rule, none but merchants subscribed for them. The man who first thought of a bright, newsy, *cheap* paper is almost unknown. He was Horatio D. Sheppard, and, strange to say, was not a journalist. He was a student of medicine, who used to pass through Chatham Street, where all sorts of things were sold for a few cents. He noticed that the cheapest article sold most readily; nobody seemed to mind spending a cent. Suddenly the thought of a one-cent newspaper came to his mind—to be sold by boys just as peanuts and candy were sold.

"Sheppard had but little money, and consequently sought to interest the printers of the town in his plan. They laughed at it, as people had laughed at Fulton when he spoke of a steamboat. To sell newspapers like cakes and candy seemed a ridiculous proposition.

"There was one young printer, however, who listened to Sheppard. This was Horace Greeley. He was born in New Hampshire in 1811, came to New

York when he was twenty, excited ridicule by his homespun clothes and his peculiar appearance, but soon convinced people that he knew what he was about. Greeley had a friend named Story; the two formed a partnership in 1832, and agreed to publish Sheppard's paper, but they insisted that the price must be two cents. On January 1, 1833, The Morning Post was issued amid a terrible snowstorm. There were few people in the streets, while the newsboys were soon chilled and were glad to run home. The Post lived just two weeks and three days, and then appeared no more.

"Still, the effort was not in vain. Nine months later The New York Sun was established as a one-cent paper, while Horace Greeley owed his start in business to Sheppard and his idea. In 1834 Greeley formed a new partnership and planned a weekly paper called The New-Yorker. About this time James Gordon Bennett, then a newspaper writer, came to Greeley, showed him a fifty-dollar bill and some smaller notes, and invited him to join in the project of establishing a paper to be called The New York Herald. Greeley declined, being too much taken up with his own idea.

"The first number of The Herald, price one cent, appeared in May, 1835. The office was in a cellar in Wall Street. The office furniture consisted of a chair and a plank placed across two barrels. Here Bennett wrote editorials and attended to customers. He worked sixteen or seventeen hours a day. From five to eight in the morning he wrote short, crisp editorials that attracted and amused his readers; during the regular morning business hours he wrote advertisements, sold papers, and prepared material for the printers; about one o'clock he sallied forth and picked up Wall Street paragraphs; from four to six he was back at his office; while in the evening he visited a theater, a ball, a concert, or a public meeting, and gathered news and gossip. Thus The Herald began its career.

"In 1841 Greeley, assisted by Henry J. Raymond, launched The Tribune. The first edition consisted of five thousand copies, and with difficulty were the papers distributed. A rival journal sought to kill the new enterprise by sending men to fight the little fellows who were trying to sell the new journal. Greeley published the whole story, and the circulation began to grow at an astonishing pace. At the end of seven weeks its edition was eleven thousand, which was the utmost a press of that day could print. The country boy, who a few years before was so poor and so wretched-looking that no one wanted to hire him, was now the most prominent editor in New York.

"It has been said of Greeley that he was able to produce more good editorials per year than any other editor of his time. Raymond, just fresh from college, was a born journalist, and was able to do an astonishing amount of excellent work. In 1851 he founded The New York Times. Some time later Charles A. Dana joined Greeley's staff. His brilliant services subsequently as editor of The New York Sun have everywhere been acknowledged. Bayard Taylor and Margaret Fuller also contributed to the columns of The Tribune, and helped to make it a great power and a fine newspaper. Thus, this little band of gifted and intensely hard-working journalists laid the foundation of the cheap press—cheap in price, but wonderful in every other way.

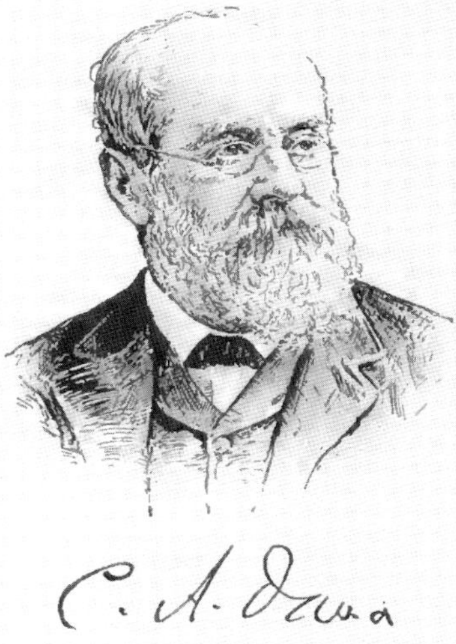

"Of course, at first, news, such as we understand the term, was impossible to get, but in the year 1844 the introduction of the telegraph system by Samuel F. B. Morse changed the whole situation. Morse, like Fulton, devoted his early years to art, and then became interested in science. In 1832, during a trip across the ocean from Europe, he met a gentleman who explained to him certain experiments that had been conducted in Paris with the electro-magnet. The marvelous speed of the electric fluid along a wire suggested to Morse's inventive brain the idea of thus overcoming space, and on his return to New York he at once began experimenting in his studio.

"It took him five years to invent and perfect an alphabet of dots and dashes, and an instrument that would properly record them. At last, however, the little key obeyed the touch perfectly, and clicked its messages as clearly as the human voice. Then Morse showed his device to the public, but, as usual, the ignorant laughed and would not believe. In 1843 a bill was introduced into Congress appropriating a sum of money to establish an experimental line between Washington and Baltimore. The last day of the session arrived, one hundred and twenty bills were still ahead of it, and Morse, after waiting until a late hour, went away discouraged. But the next morning came a surprise. News was brought to him by Miss Ellsworth, daughter of the Commissioner of Patents, that the bill had been passed. In May, 1844, the line was completed, a message prepared by Miss Ellsworth was successfully forwarded, and the world was in possession of a new marvel.

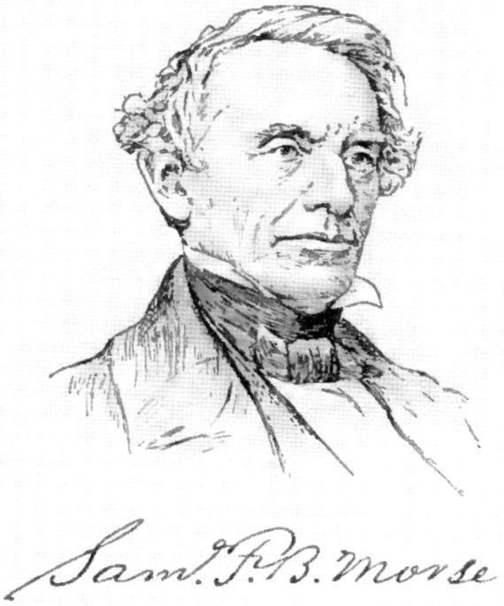

"Morse's residence was in New York. At No. 5 West Twenty-second Street you will find a tablet that tells this story:

> IN THIS HOUSE
> S. F. B. MORSE
> LIVED FOR MANY YEARS
> AND DIED.

"In 1853 a World's Fair was opened in New York in a magnificent structure of glass and iron, called the Crystal Palace, located out in the country near Forty-second Street and Fifth Avenue. It was completely destroyed by fire in 1858.

"In 1856 our beautiful Central Park was laid out. The committee that took charge of this important undertaking consisted of the Mayor, the Commissioner of Streets, Washington Irving, the author; George Bancroft, the historian; and William Cullen Bryant, the poet and author. The design was the handiwork of Calvert Vaux and Frederick Law Olmstead, who originated the science of landscape architecture, which became recognized throughout the country. The success of their plan lay in the fact that they preserved all that was beautiful in Nature instead of trying to create artificial results.

"In 1856 the first statue of modern New York was erected—namely, that of Washington in Union Square; and about the same time a monument was placed near Madison Square to honor the memory of General Worth, of this State, who had distinguished himself in the Mexican War.

"In 1857 two of New York's best-known citizens, Cyrus W. Field and Peter Cooper, conceived the idea of connecting Europe and America by cable. In August, 1858, the connection was actually made, and great rejoicing followed. The City Hall was illuminated; a big parade, including bands, banners, and floats, marched through the streets, and a splendid banquet marked the occasion. The Queen sent a message of congratulation to President Buchanan, to which he replied in the same vein; and then, strange to tell, the cable stopped working. Eight years of additional and costly experimenting followed ere the wire under water would carry messages satisfactorily. At last, however, success was attained and two thousand miles of ocean were overcome. Three years later, in 1869, New York and San Francisco were joined by the tracks of a great railroad, and the two ends of the continent, three thousand miles apart, were linked together.

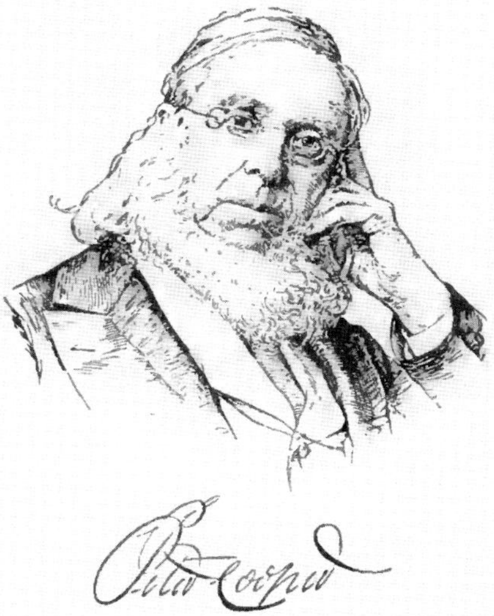

"But I see we have been traveling a little too fast. Let me take you back to the year 1861, when the news reached New York that Fort Sumter had been fired upon. Many a heartache was caused by these tidings. Was the Union, for which Washington and his noble comrades had fought so hard, going to pieces? It seemed so. New Yorkers had met and sent earnest appeals to their brethren in the South, asking them to pause and consider, but all to no purpose. Now it meant fight, and New York was ready to do her share. In April the troops began to leave for the front. People who saw the favorite Seventh depart, say it was an experience never to be forgotten. To quote the words of a member of the regiment: 'It was worth a life, that march. Only one who passed, as we did, through that tempest of cheers, two miles long, can know the terrible enthusiasm of

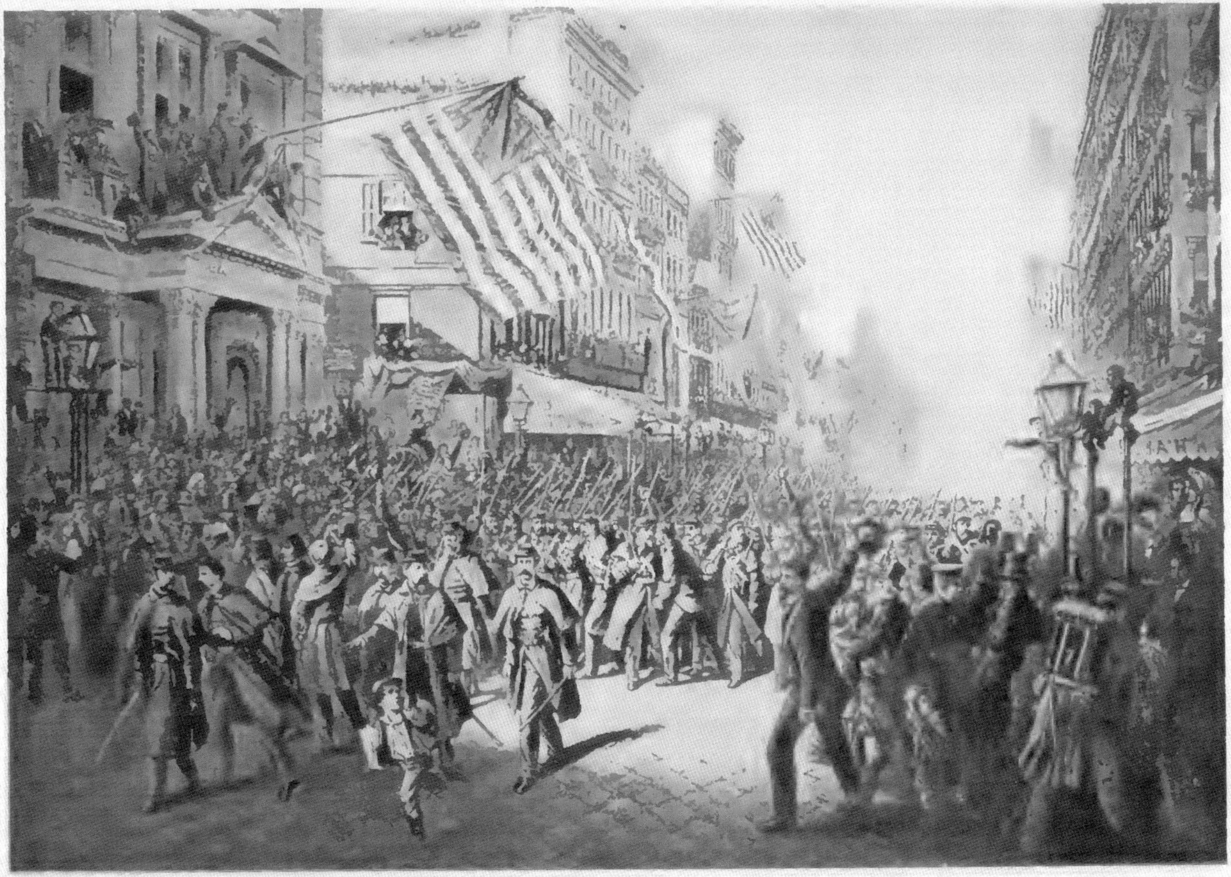

Departure of the Seventh Regiment. Reproduced from an engraving in the History of the Seventh Regiment.

the occasion. I could hardly hear the rattle of our gun carriages, and only once or twice the music of our band came to me muffled and quelled by the uproar. We knew it now, if we had not before divined it, that our great city was with us as one man, utterly united in the great cause we were marching to sustain. This grand fact I learned by two senses. If hundreds of persons roared it into my ears, thousands slapped it into my back. . . . So we said good-bye to Broadway, moved down Cortlandt Street under a bower of flags, and at half past six shoved off in a ferryboat.'

"The place where the Seventh Regiment began its existence has been marked by a tablet, which you can see at the southwest corner of Fulton and Nassau Streets. It reads as follows:

ON THIS SITE IN THE
OLD SHAKESPEARE TAVERN
WAS ORGANIZED
THE SEVENTH REGIMENT
NATIONAL GUARD, S. N. Y.
AUGUST 25, 1824.

"To help on the cause of the Union, not men only but money in abundance was forthcoming. During the first year New York loaned the Government the astonishing sum of two hundred and ten million dollars—over four times as much as all the other sections of the country put together.

"The women of New York also did their share of good work. Early in April, 1861, they formed a

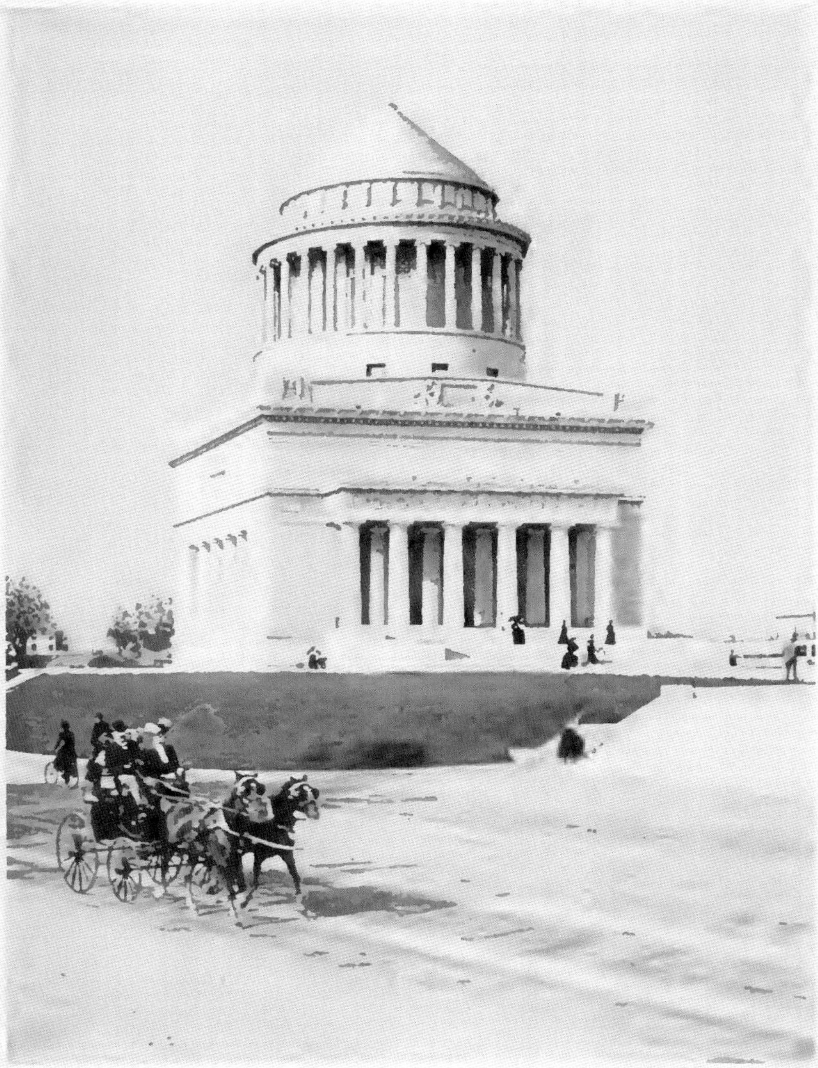

Grant's tomb, Riverside Drive. From a recent photograph.

Central Relief Association, and soon thousands of women, and even children, were busy scraping lint, knitting socks, making garments, and preparing delicacies, while scores of tenderly reared maidens volunteered as nurses.

"Every war, unfortunately, furnishes its sad memorials. In the hall of the College of the City of New York, at Twenty-third Street and Lexington Avenue, there is a marble tablet that bears a list of names and tells the following legend:

IN MEMORY
OF
THE GRADUATES
OF THE
COLLEGE OF THE CITY OF NEW YORK
WHO LOST THEIR LIVES
IN THE
SERVICE OF THEIR COUNTRY
DURING THE
WAR FOR THE UNION.

"I wish the story of the war could end here, but truth compels me to tell you of an occurrence that will always cause true New-Yorkers to blush for the fair record of the city. In 1863 it was found necessary, in order to raise troops, to introduce the draft system, whereby men drew lots that decided whether they were to serve or not. Two enrolling offices were established: one in Broadway near Twenty-eighth Street, the second at the corner of Forty-sixth Street and Third Avenue. A certain element, largely foreign, assisted by roughs, who were ready for any mischief or worse, planned to resist the draft. From July 13th for four days a series of bloody, destructive, and brutal riots took place, in which over one thousand persons were killed, a great number wounded, and two million dollars' worth of property was destroyed. This crowd of brutes attacked the police, insulted women, pursued negroes, and hanged such as they caught to the nearest lamp post. I know of nothing more barbarous that could have happened in a land of savages."

"Was this the only riot that took place in the city?" asked George.

"Unfortunately not," replied the professor. "The first disturbance of this sort was known as the 'Doctors' Riot,' which occurred in 1788. The New York Hospital, then located in Broadway near Duane Street, had been completed shortly after the Revolutionary War, and a small medical school had been opened. Rumors that bodies were being stolen from the Potter's Field and dissected, horrified the masses, and a mob attacked the doctors. The militia had to be called out, and, before order was restored, five rioters were killed and eight wounded. The year 1834, noteworthy because it marks the granting of the right of the citizens to *vote* for mayor, is also known as 'The Year of Riots.' First came an 'Election Riot,' followed by an attack on those who opposed slavery; and then a 'Stonecutters' Riot,' occasioned by the refusal of workmen to use marble as building material. In 1835 jealousy among the militia regiments led to a fracas; and in 1837 a

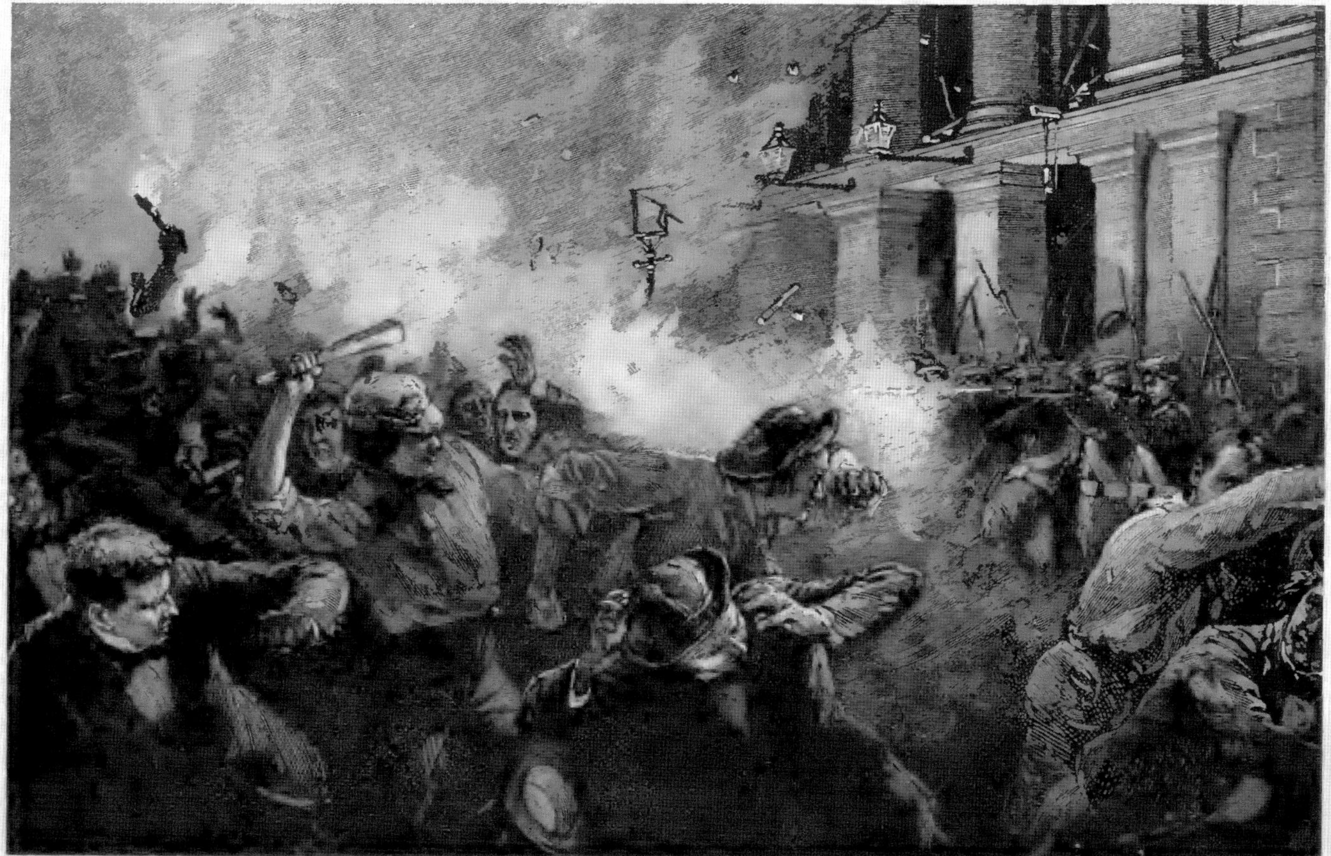

Astor Place Riot, 1849. From an old engraving.

'Bread Riot,' brought about by the high price of flour, created trouble and destruction of property. In 1849 the great Astor Place Riot shocked the community. This occurred at a theater that occupied the site on which the Mercantile Library is located, and was caused by the rivalry of two actors. Macready was an Englishman who had been well received in America. Forrest was an American who had been insulted in England owing to Macready's hostility. In view of this fact, the latter showed poor taste in revisiting America, and a number of indignant citizens decided to show their resentment. The demonstration began with groans and hootings as soon as Macready appeared, and ended in a riot, in which twenty-two lives were sacrificed.

"But let us turn from mobs and lawlessness and consider something worthier of our attention—namely, our splendid Fire Department. It began its existence in 1656, when three 'worshipful' fire wardens were appointed to inspect the wooden chimneys of New Amsterdam. Two years later an order was divided among the shoemakers of the town to make one hundred and twenty-two leathern buckets, which were hung up in various places. In 1731 two fire engines were ordered in London, and a room in the City Hall was set aside for them. The engines consisted of boxes on wooden wheels, and handles that could be pushed up and down. Gradually improved devices were introduced and volunteer fire companies organized. These companies were made up of some of the best young men of the town, and great rivalry existed among the different organizations, each trying to be first at a fire. Often, collisions occurred, followed by blows, so that instead of fighting the flames the firemen fought each other. All this was changed in the year 1865, when a paid department was established and steam engines were introduced. Since then we have men trained especially for their work, and it is safe to say no braver, quicker, or finer force exists anywhere else in the world.

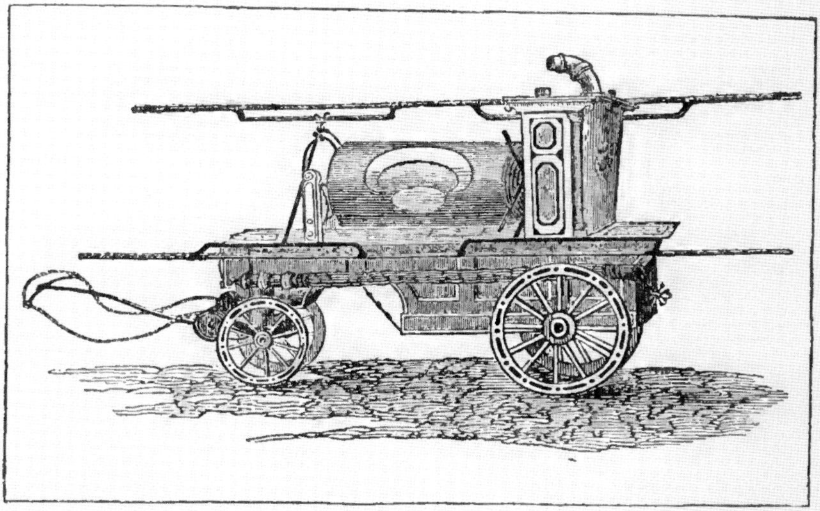

Style of engine used in 1812. From an old print.

"Most men, you will find, attend to their own little affairs, their own particular business, but there are a few who think of larger interests. These far-sighted individuals are the ones that send the world forward. One of these dreamers was William C. Kingsley. As far back as 1866 he began to plan a great bridge to connect New York and Brooklyn. Both places were growing rapidly, the ferry service

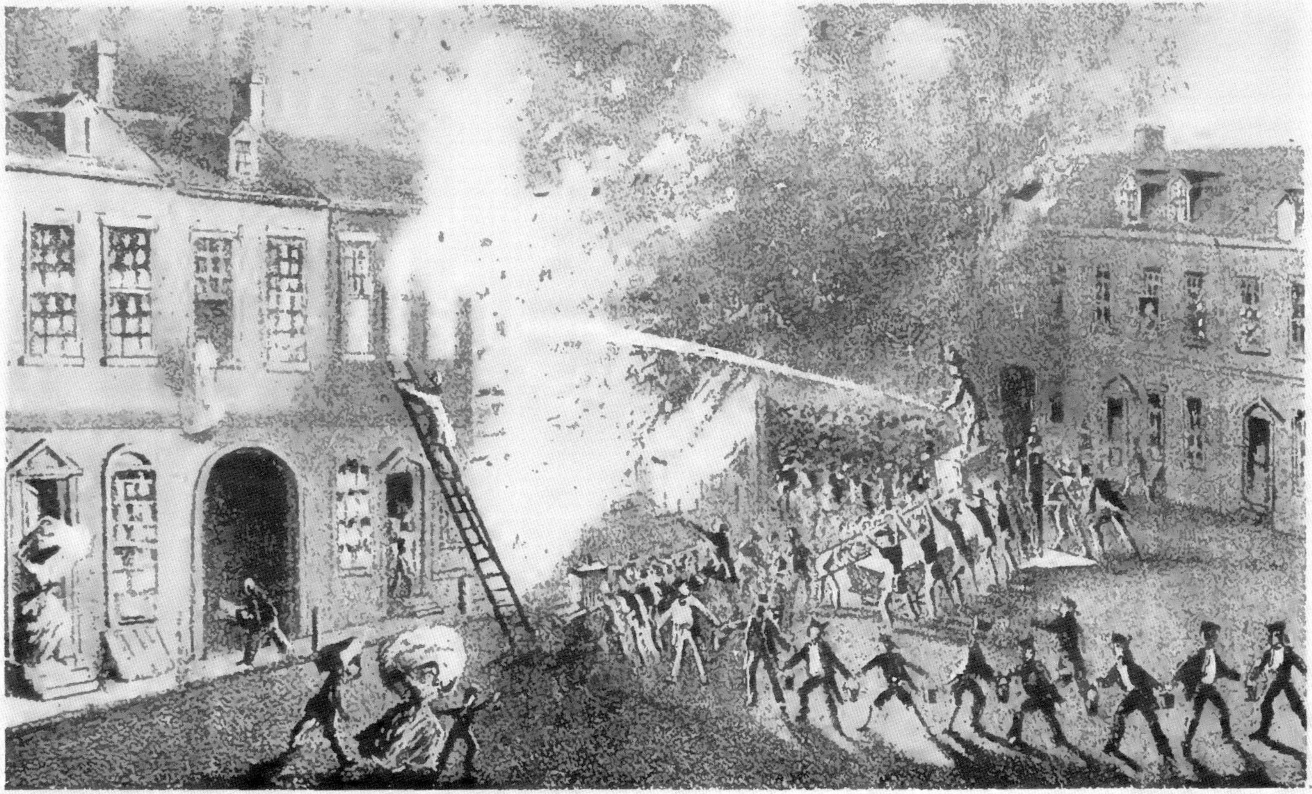

Scene at a fire, 1800. From a fireman's certificate of that date.

was not adequate, a better means of crossing was required. Kingsley interested John A. Roebling and his son, the engineers, and other influential men. In 1870 the work was begun; the first wire was run over in 1876; seven years later the bridge was opened to the public, and the same year the first train of cars crossed the span. From end to end the bridge measures a little more than six thousand five hundred feet, and up to date it has cost about twenty million dollars.

"Like one of Nature's perfect productions its beauty grows the more we look at it. As one of our poets has said, addressing it:

"'You thrill through all your cords of steel,
Responsive to the living sun;
And quickening in your nerves you feel
Life with its conscious currents run.

"'Your anchorage upbears the march
Of time and the eternal powers;
The sky admits your perfect arch,
The rock respects your stable towers.'

"The year 1866, apparently, was a favorable season for dreamers. About the same time that William C. Kingsley began to think of the possibility of a bridge, Andrew H. Green, now known as 'The Father of Greater New York,' saw in his mind's eye the union of New York, Brooklyn, Staten Island, and the Bronx, and during a period of thirty-two years he advocated it whenever he had a chance to do so. On January 1, 1898, his dream became a reality, and a few months later, on the occasion of his seventy-sixth birthday, a gold medal was presented to him at the City Hall as a token of appreciation of his services. Associated with him in planning Greater New York was James S. T. Stranahan, fondly called 'Brooklyn's First Citizen,' an active member, too, of the committee that designed and built the bridge.

"The idea of forming the greater city was not merely to be able to say that New York has a population of over three million inhabitants, but to unite under one head people who really belonged to one locality, whose business interests were on Manhattan Island, although their homes happened to be beyond one of the rivers that surround it. The union, too, was meant to stir up the pride and the love of the citizens for the greater city, and make it in every sense a grand and worthy metropolis.

"Let me give you an idea of what this *new* New York means. It embraces three hundred and twenty square miles, and has a population of three million four hundred thousand, making it the second city of the world. Its streets measure twelve hundred miles, it has over five hundred miles of street and elevated railroads, contains one hundred and sixty-seven thousand buildings, and the assessed value of its real estate is over three thousand million dollars. Its expenses per year are between eighty and eighty-five million dollars. Such has been its development from a curious little Dutch town during a period of two hundred and seventy-five years. What its size will be when it celebrates its five hundredth birthday is almost too much for the imagination.

"Large figures are always impressive, but good works mean infinitely more than great numbers. It is satisfying to know that to-day every citizen of New York has more opportunities of improving his mind than the city ever offered before. Art, science, music—in fact, every department of knowledge—offers him free entrance. His home, his health, his safety, his rights—all are more carefully and wisely protected than ever in the past. Let him then do his full share to help establish a truly Greater New York, and he will have the city that all good and loyal citizens devoutly desire."

CHAPTER XI

WE resumed our walks a few days after hearing the "Review of the Nineteenth Century," as the professor called his last talk.

"Here is Chelsea Square," said he, leading us down Ninth Avenue and turning westward into Twentieth Street.

A few steps farther and we saw one of the most picturesque scenes to be found in New York—a large, beautiful lawn, spreading trees, and a curtain of ivy, covering red-brick chapel walls. The church bell was ringing, and students in caps and gowns were crossing the campus.

"What is it?" asked Emily, deeply interested.

"This is the General Theological Seminary of the Protestant Episcopal Church, and each one of those young men hopes some day to be a bishop."

"It doesn't seem like New York at all," said Emily.

"In that you agree with Janvier, who has written charmingly of old New York," remarked the professor. "He says this section carries him in fancy across the Atlantic to one of the English university towns."

"Why is it called Chelsea?" asked George.

"About the year 1750 Captain Thomas Clarke, an American soldier, built a house in this neighborhood, and, desiring to give it a name that would suggest rest and quiet, chose Chelsea, having in mind, no doubt, the expression used by English military men, 'Dead as Chelsea.' About the year 1800 the property passed into the hands of Bishop Moore, and a dozen years later descended to his son, Clement C. Moore. The latter was a genial college professor, who published learned books, but his fame rests on a little rhyme written at Chelsea for his grandchildren, beginning with the well-known line—

"'Twas the night before Christmas.'

"Prompted in all likelihood by his father the good bishop, Clement C. Moore presented to the seminary, free of rent, the whole block it now occupies. The corner stone of the first building was laid in 1825. At that time the greater part of the lot was open ground, and it became known as Chelsea Square."

"It surely is a beautiful, restful place," said Emily.

We walked around the square, admiring its dignified halls, the chapel, and the campus, suggesting a mixture of church and student life, and entered Twenty-third Street, where the professor pointed out London Terrace, a row of peculiar but friendly-looking houses with deep gardens and tall trees. In Twenty-fourth Street we saw the Chelsea cottages, cozy two-story boxes, with comfortable bay windows and picturesque porches—quite unlike anything else one sees in modern New York.

"Most New-Yorkers of to-day are one-sided," remarked the professor, as he led us down Eighth Avenue—"that is, they are either east-siders or west-siders, and know little of the other side of the town.

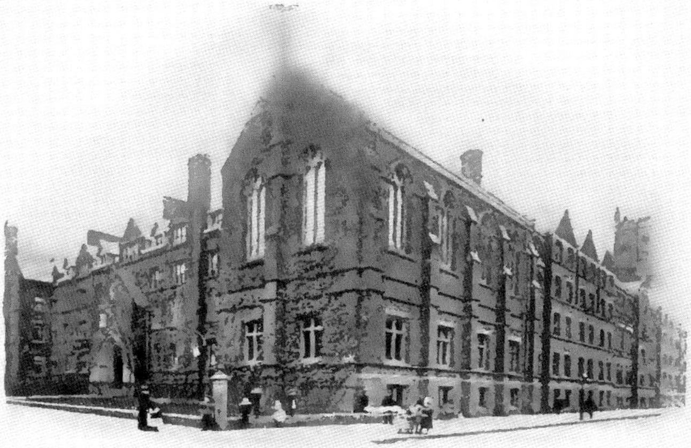

Theological Seminary, Twentieth Street and Ninth Avenue.

It is only by poking your nose into out-of-the-way corners that you can discover the landmarks of old New York. Here, for instance, is a very interesting example," he added, stopping at Twelfth Street.

"Abingdon Square," said George, glancing at a lamp post.

"This little triangular piece of green is all that is left of Greenwich village. Round about here at one time there were beautiful lawns and fine country houses; the air was filled with the scent of flowers, and near by Manetta * brook tempted the fishermen. About the year 1750 Sir Peter Warren, vice-admiral, having captured many prizes on the high seas,

* Sometimes spelled Minetta.

settled down in Greenwich village, built a fine mansion, and married Miss Susannah De Lancey, a member of the great De Lancey family. Here three daughters were born, the oldest of whom became the wife of the Earl of Abingdon. After a while Warren House and the estate were sold, and this square is the only memento we now have of them.

"About 1760 Richmond Hill was built. This, as you no doubt remember, was used by Washington as his headquarters. Later Vice-President Adams lived in it; still later Aaron Burr and his gifted daughter Theodosia occupied it; and finally John Jacob Astor bought it. Subsequently it became a theater, then a tavern, and then it was pulled down.

"The various epidemics of smallpox, cholera, and yellow fever that attacked the city at the lower end of the island spared the healthy neighborhood of Greenwich and helped, as you know, to build it up.

"Toward the close of the century a State prison was erected at the foot of Tenth Street, and a part of the old wall, it is said, still stands, being now a portion of a brewery.

"In 1816 a stage line was established connecting the city of New York with the village of Greenwich, and the blowing of the horn announcing the arrival of the 'bus never failed to cause general excitement.

"Here's a description in verse," added the professor, referring to his little book, "that furnishes a good picture of the rural charms of this favored spot:

"'In those days fair Greenwich village
  Slept by Hudson's rural shore,
Two miles out from New York city,
  With its bustle, rush, and roar!
Then great Gotham's "eighty thousand"
  Filled the New World with amaze,
And the City Hall was building
  "Out of town" in those "fast" days!
Then Canal Street was a tide creek,
  Famed for piscatory charms,
And Broadway a county turnpike
  Winding northward through the farms.
Then the stage from Greenwich prison
  Drove to Wall Street twice a day—
Now the somber "Black Maria"
  Oftener drives the other way!'

"Gradually the city began to grow up to the village, and then occurred that extraordinary tangle of streets of which I have already spoken. Old Greenwich, however, resisted the advances of the town for a long while, keeping up a sort of exclusiveness of its own. It claimed to be cleaner, nicer, and more patriotic than any other part of the island. It is said, in fact, that nowhere else were the Fourth of July and the Twenty-second of February more enthusiastically celebrated. But now its glory is gone. Many of the comfortable-looking three-story brick houses, with wrought-iron railings and oval windows over low doorways, are still here, but they are no longer clean or inviting. There is one relic, however, that I want to show you."

Walking down Tenth Street toward the river we soon arrived at Weehawken Street, and there beheld a row of low wooden houses, one or two with outside staircases, unlike any other buildings, it is safe to say, now to be seen on Manhattan Island. They are remnants of what was known as Upper Greenwich Village, and are nearly three quarters of a century old.

"They certainly look it," said Tom.

Passing into Christopher Street and then eastward, we turned into Hudson Street, and walked along this broad thoroughfare, noticing the names of unfamiliar streets and catching glimpses here and there of the smaller and more modest houses that suited our grandfathers.

At Leroy Street we came unexpectedly upon a park that looked as if a French garden had been

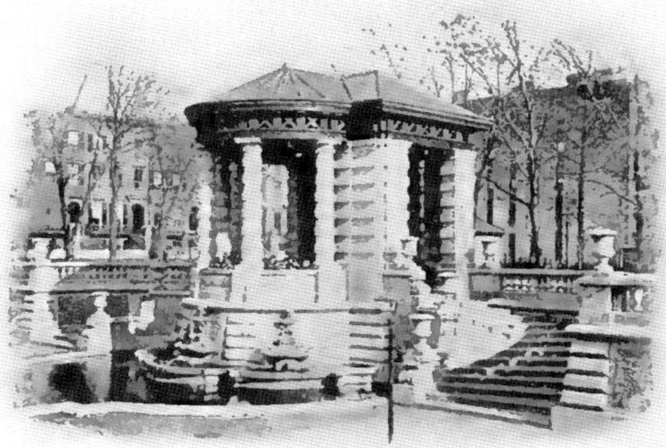

A glimpse of Hudson Park, Leroy and Hudson Streets.

dropped bodily into this New York opening. Here was a massive kiosk, gateways, steps, grassy slopes, pools, and water jets. Children were romping about, and old people were resting on the benches.

"Isn't it beautiful!" exclaimed Emily.

"What is it?" asked Tom.

By way of answer the professor led us along one of the pebbly walks to the eastern end of the square and showed us a stone memorial suggestive of a coffin, on which rest a fireman's hat and implements. It is a tribute to some brave fire laddies who lost their lives trying to save those of others.

"Was this a cemetery?" asked George.

"Read the inscription on the bronze plate," said the professor.

It is as follows:

IN MEMORIAM.

THE CITY OF NEW YORK
DEVOTED TO THE SERVICE AND COMFORT OF THE LIVING
THIS GROUND,
FORMERLY USED BY TRINITY PARISH
AS A BURIAL PLACE FOR THE DEAD,
WHOSE NAMES, ALTHOUGH NOT INSCRIBED,
ARE HEREBY REVERENTLY COMMEMORATED.
A. D. 1898.

"Dear me!" remarked Emily, a little shocked; "then this used to be a graveyard."

"So were Washington Square, Union Square, and Madison Square, and some of the other parks before they were turned into resting and breathing places for the living."

"Was Gramercy Park, too?" asked George. That neighborhood was of special interest to the young people, as they had once lived there.

"No," replied the professor. "Gramercy Park is part of an old farm called by the Dutch *Krom-*

messie, meaning a crooked knife, the form of which the farm resembled. In 1831 the present inclosure was given to owners of lots fronting it by Samuel B. Ruggles. Near the park gate there is a stone which tells this story:

GRAMERCY PARK
FOUNDED BY
SAMUEL B. RUGGLES
1831
COMMEMORATED BY THIS TABLET
IMBEDDED IN
THE GRAMERCY FARM BY
JOHN RUGGLES STRONG
1875

"This ground," continued the professor, recalling our attention to the park in which we were standing, "was formerly a cheerless old cemetery; as Hudson Park it does reverence to the dead and brings pleasure to the living."

"I remember a curious little graveyard over near Sixth Avenue," remarked Emily.

"In Twenty-first Street," added the professor. "That is a Jewish burial ground, or 'Place of Rest'; it has been there over half a century, and it is cared for as zealously to-day as when country fields surrounded it. There are two other 'Places of Rest' of this kind in the city; the oldest just south of Chatham Square—one can see it from the Elevated Railway—and the second at the southeast corner of Eleventh Street and Sixth Avenue.

"The subject of parks," continued the professor, "is very interesting and important. For many years, where they were most needed—that is, in the poorest districts—there were few or none; but now, through the efforts of earnest workers, this state of affairs is much improved. Lately a breathing place was opened in Mulberry Bend, in the heart of a densely packed tenement district, and another near the foot of Grand Street. Like Hudson Park, these new pleasure squares have been made beautiful as well as useful. Within the last few years, also, the river front has been used, and fine recreation piers have been built that have, no doubt, saved the lives of many sick and suffering children."

We remained here for some time, admiring the beauties of the place, and then continued our pilgrimage southward. As we crossed Canal Street, George asked:

"Was this a canal formerly?"

"Yes," answered the professor. "It was the outlet of Collect Pond, and originally was quite a deep stream. The Indians used it, and their great war canoes often passed up and down under the shelter of its banks. When the city grew up to it, pavements were laid on both sides, trees and flowers were planted, and it presented a far more beautiful appearance than it does to-day."

A few steps brought us to the corner of Varick and Laight Streets, where we found the dignified front of St. John's church, once a conspicuous and beautiful triumph of architecture, but now fairly choked by the "commonplace of trade."

"In 1803," said the professor, "Trinity erected this chapel. At that time it was so far uptown that people wondered where the congregation was to

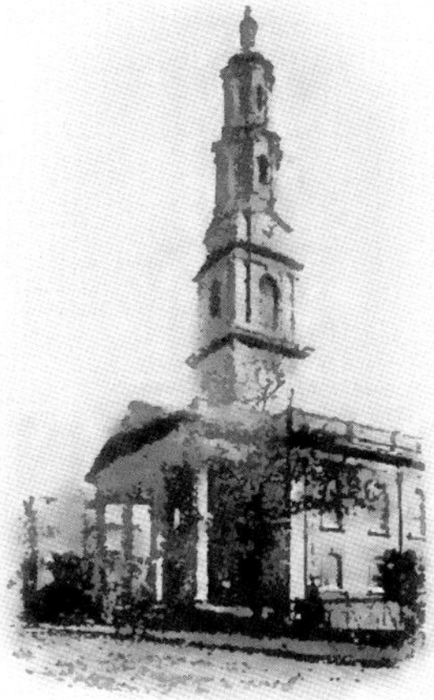

St. John's chapel, Varick Street.

come from, and in order to attract settlers to its vicinity a fine park was laid out where that ugly freight depot now stands. The park was a thing of beauty in its day, and soon many of the best people of the town moved into the neighborhood. Among those who came were the families of Alexander Hamilton and General Schuyler. Each family owned its house and possessed a key that opened the massive gates of the park, from which all outsiders were rigorously excluded. After a time, however, the uptown movement began, the character of the place changed, and the old square was deserted; but the church, faithful to its trust and unmindful of fashion and favorite localities, remained to fulfill its duty."

"So did St. Paul's and Trinity, did they not?" asked George.

"Yes, and that makes them particularly interesting from a historical point of view."

A short ride brought us to Broadway and Vesey Street, where we entered the gateway of St. Paul's.

"Why don't they have a door in front?" asked Tom.

"This isn't the front—it's the rear. When the church was built, in 1766, Broadway was not of much account, while the direction of the Hudson—there was a clear view then to the river—was regarded as the proper place for the portal. You can imagine the effect, after service, of walking out and seeing the noble stream flowing by at the foot of a gently sloping landscape."

We went into the simple house of worship, looked at the many memorials, but were particularly interested in two bronze tablets.

The first, erected in 1889, contains this legend:

IN COMMEMORATION
OF
THE CENTENNIAL OF THE INAUGURATION
OF
GEORGE WASHINGTON
THE
FIRST PRESIDENT OF THE UNITED STATES
APRIL THIRTIETH MDCCCLXXXIX
ERECTED BY
THE AISLE COMMITTEE AT SERVICES
HELD IN ST. PAUL'S CHAPEL, N. Y.

The second bears this inscription:

THIS TABLET
IS ERECTED IN COMMEMORATION OF
THE CENTENNIAL ANNIVERSARY SERVICES
OF THE
DEATH OF HIS EXCELLENCY
GENERAL GEORGE WASHINGTON
COMMANDER-IN-CHIEF OF THE ARMIES OF THE UNITED STATES
DURING THE WAR OF THE REVOLUTION
OBSERVED AT ST. PAUL'S CHAPEL,
ON THE BROADWAY, NEW YORK
DECEMBER 14, 1899.

GENERAL SOCIETY OF THE CINCINNATI	SONS OF THE REVOLUTION IN THE STATE OF NEW YORK

"These two bronze plates," remarked the professor, "are like two milestones on the path of time. The one calls attention to the date of Washington's inauguration; the other, erected ten years later, commemorates his death. The hundredth anniversary of this sad event, which caused the whole nation to mourn, has suggested some lines which you may like to know. Here they are:

"'Time dims the lengthening scroll of fame,
Year after year the honored tracings fade,
And many an erstwhile well-remembered name
Sinks slowly into faint and glimmering shade,
And is entirely forgot. Not so with thee:
Thy fame is like the everlasting hill;
A hundred years sweep on destroyingly,
And wreck the work of man, but thou art still,
In spite of time and death, a living power,
Whose force is felt throughout the broadening land,

Inspiring multitudes who bless the hour
  That placed the patriots' weal in thy safe hand.
A century its varying course has run,
But names thee still the nation's noblest son.' "

After listening to this worthy tribute, we passed slowly through the churchyard, pausing here and there to look at an old tombstone, and, reaching the Broadway section, stopped in front of the Montgomery monument.

"You know, of course," said the professor, "that Montgomery was one of those brave young officers who lost their lives in the Revolutionary War. He was born in Ireland in 1736, and assisted in the capture of Quebec in 1759. Just before the war he bought a beautiful estate on the Hudson, married a daughter of Robert R. Livingston, and looked forward to a life of peaceful happiness. But when the patriot cause called, he answered at once. He led an army into Canada, captured Montreal, and on the last day of the year 1775, in the midst of a blinding snowstorm, attempted to take Quebec. Placing himself at the head of his troops, and shouting, 'Men of New York, you will not fear to follow where your general leads—march on!' he fell, mortally wounded. His remains were interred with honor in Quebec, and rested there until 1818, when the State of New York had them transferred to St. Paul's. A special boat covered with emblems of mourning conveyed the body down the Hudson. Slowly it passed his beloved country seat, the strains of a sad dirge rising softly to the porch where sat his widow, quite alone, gazing down upon the coffin of her hero.

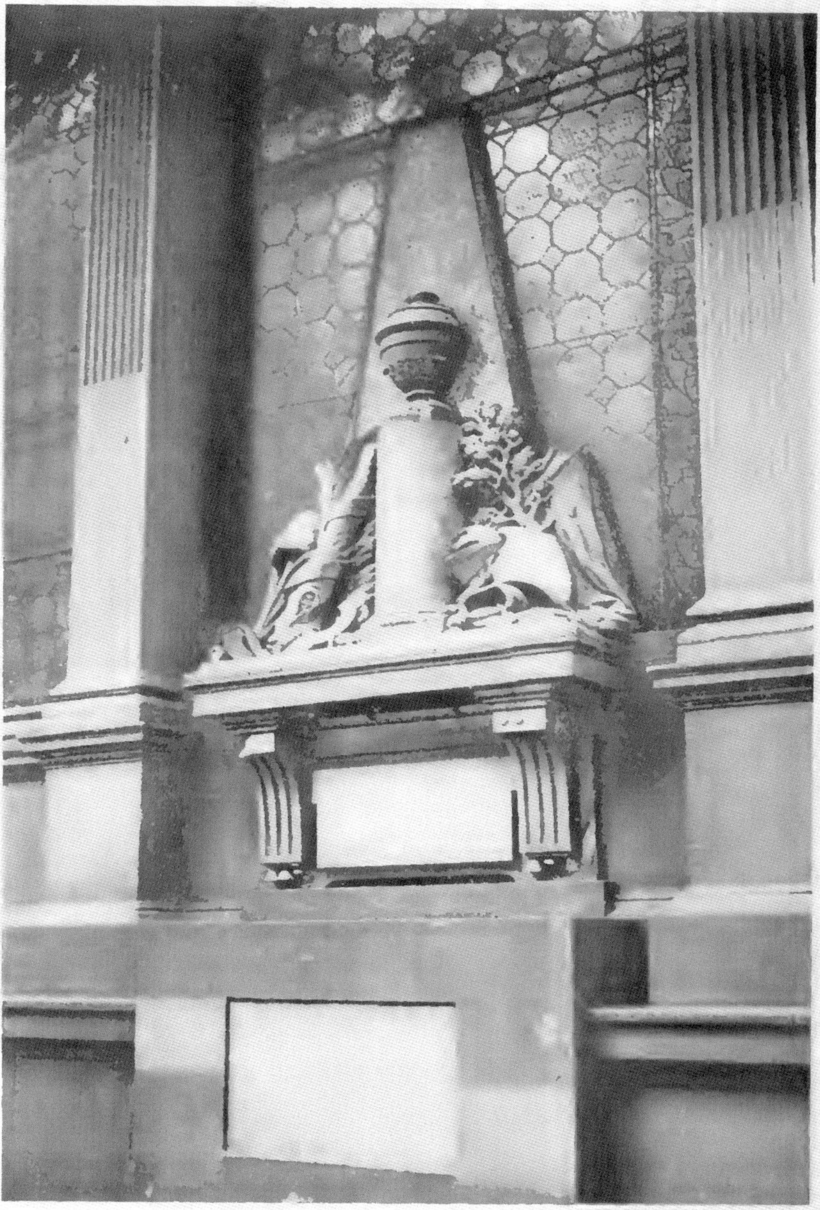

Montgomery's tomb, St. Paul's church. Photographed 1900.

Who will describe her feelings as that strange funeral boat drifted along before her tear-dimmed eyes? When her friends came to get her they found her lying prostrate in a swoon.

"Two other noble Irishmen are honored here," continued the professor. "That shaft to the left bears the name of Thomas Addis Emmet, and the one to the right that of William James MacNeven. These two distinguished men were leaders in the movement begun in 1795 to free Ireland. They came here about 1804 and won distinction, the first as a lawyer and the second as a physician. The inscription on MacNeven's monument must touch the patriotic spirit of every true American. 'In the cause of his native land,'" read the professor, "'he sacrificed the bright prospects of his youth, till in America he found a country which he loved as truly as he did the land of his birth.'"

"How interesting everything becomes when you know something about it!" remarked Emily, as we walked down Broadway toward Trinity.

"Yes, and it makes you like things you never cared about before," added Tom.

"How old is Trinity?" asked George.

"The first Trinity was dedicated in 1697, enlarged in 1737, and destroyed by the great fire of 1776. The second church was dedicated in 1790, in the presence of Washington, and for nearly fifty years served the congregation. In 1839 it was deemed unsafe and was pulled down, the present fine structure being completed in 1846.

"Trinity may properly be called a mother of

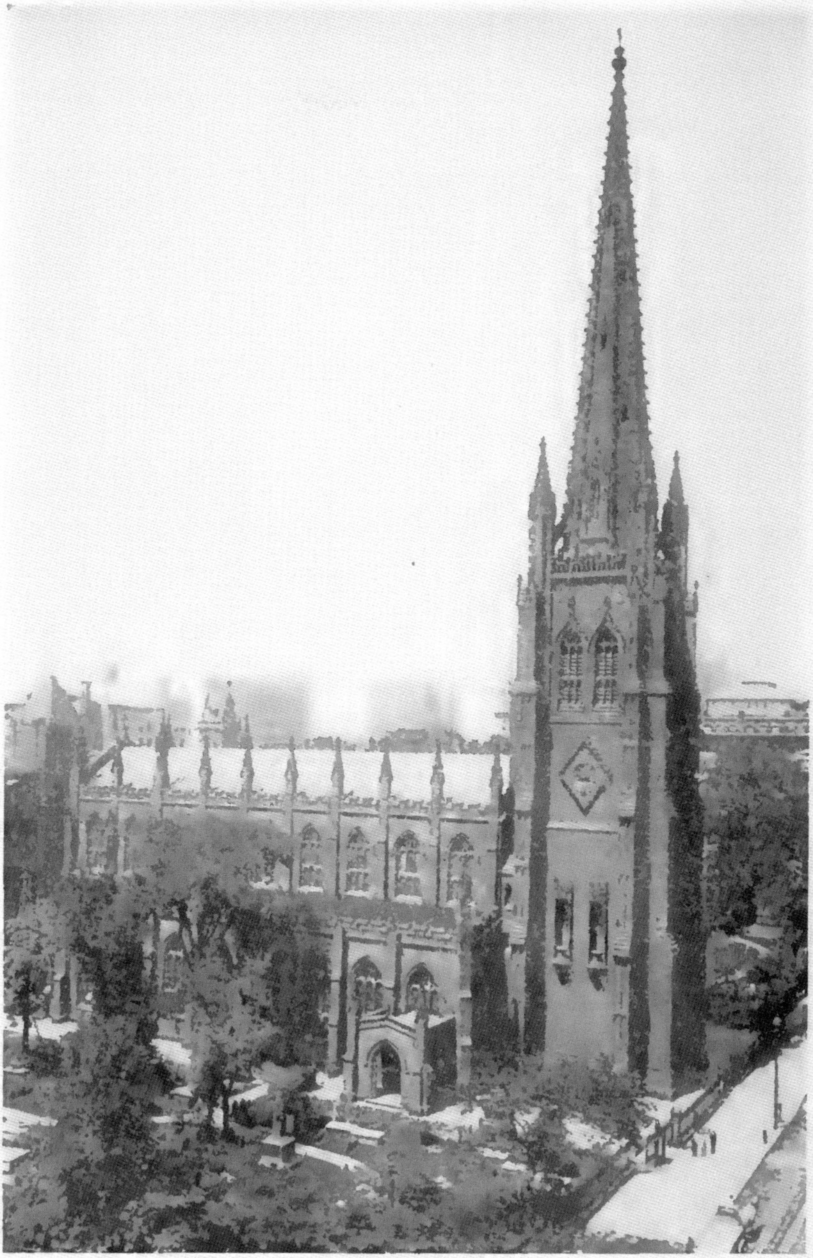

Trinity church. From a recent photograph.

churches, for to its aid and influence no less than fifty places of worship owe their existence, not to mention three colleges and several other public institutions."

"Look at these beautiful bronze doors," said Emily; "they are quite new."

"Yes, they were given a few years ago in memory of John Jacob Astor," explained the professor. "There is one at the south side entrance that I think will specially interest you."

Here we saw the fine tablets representing "Henry Hudson off Manhattan Island," "Washington at St. Paul's in 1789," and "The Consecration of Trinity in 1846." Entering the church, we remained some little time under its noble arches, im-

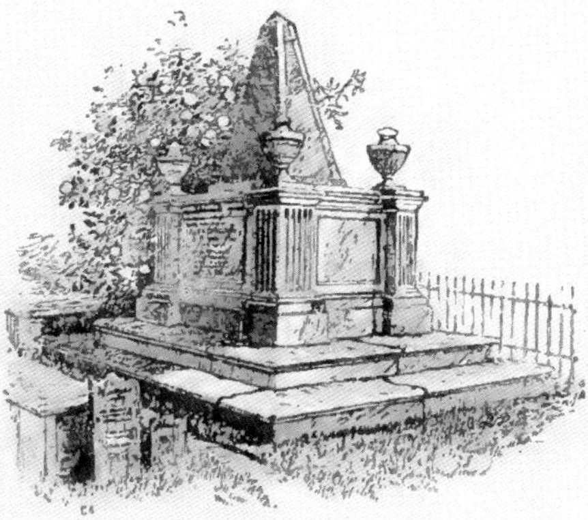

Hamilton's tomb.

pressed by the sacred quietness that reigned within, while out of doors all was hurry and bustle.

"Where is Hamilton's tomb?" at length asked George.

A few steps brought us to the simple monument

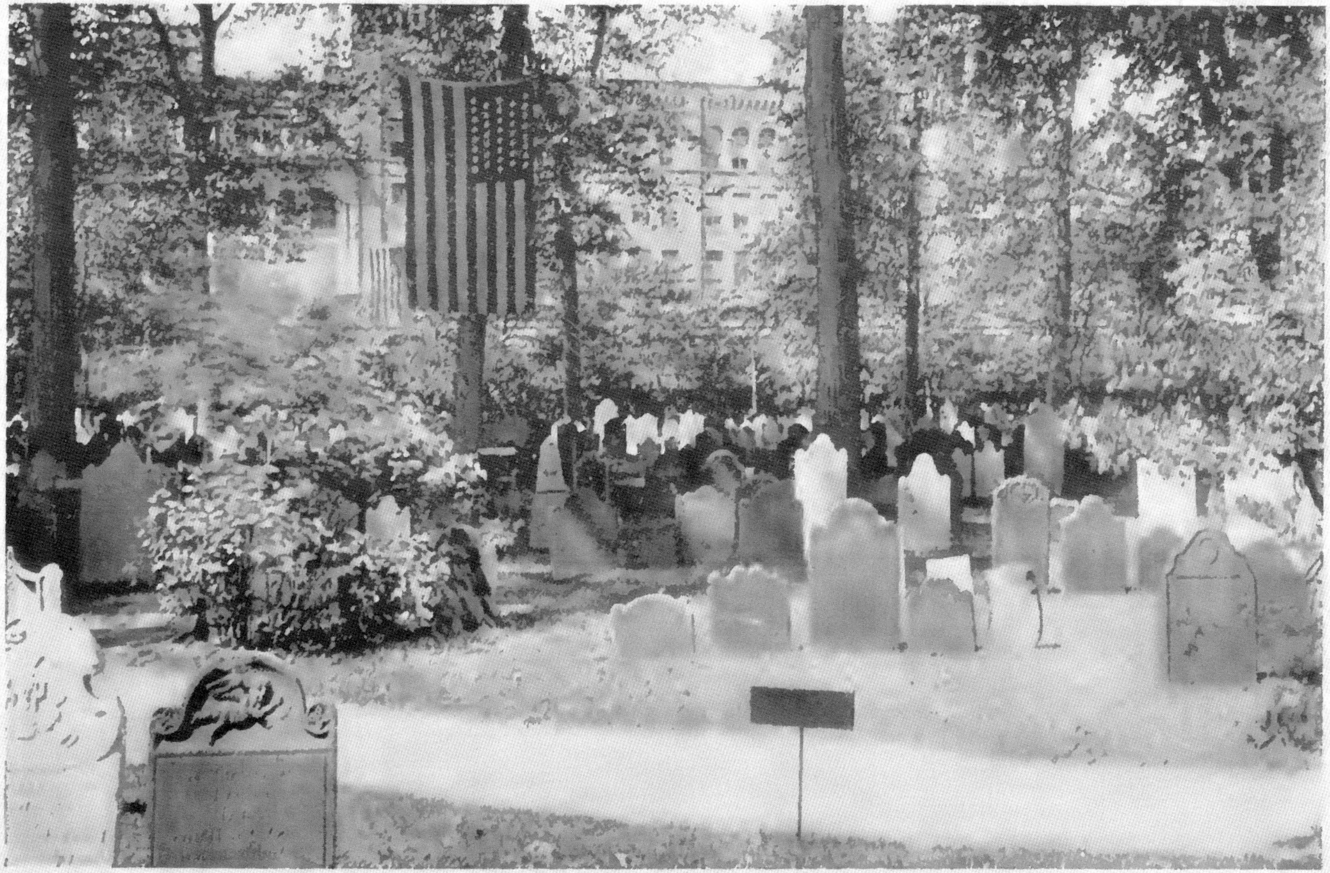

Trinity churchyard. From a recent photograph.

in the churchyard, and here we read this inscription:

> THE PATRIOT OF INCORRUPTIBLE INTEGRITY,
> THE SOLDIER OF APPROVED VALOR,
> THE STATESMAN OF CONSUMMATE WISDOM,
> WHOSE TALENTS AND VIRTUES WILL BE ADMIRED
> BY
> GRATEFUL POSTERITY
> LONG AFTER THIS MARBLE SHALL HAVE MOULDERED INTO DUST.

Wandering about we found many names that we recognized, such as De Lancey, Duane, and Beekman, which Tom remarked made him think of street signs.

All at once Emily beckoned to us and pointed to these tender words:

> "Here a pretty baby lyes,
> Sung to sleep with lullabys;
> Pray be silent, and not stirre
> The easie earth that covers her."

Then George called our attention to a new-looking stone over the grave of William Bradford, the first printer, which contains this verse:

> "Reader, reflect how soon you'll quit this stage;
> You'll find but few attain to such an Age.
> Life's full of Pain. Lo here's a Place of Rest.
> Prepare to meet your GOD, then you are blest."

A footnote calls attention to the fact that the original stone is in the rooms of the New York Historical Society.

"Charlotte Temple," said Emily, reading the name on a plain slab lying flat on the ground.

"The Shrine of Unhappy Love," added the professor. "Many people come here and drop a tear or a flower for poor Charlotte. The story is that she left her home in England and came here with an army officer, and that he then deserted her, leaving her to die in misery and poverty. A romance has been written telling the whole unhappy story, but whether it is true or not, and whether there ever was a Charlotte Temple, is a mystery that has not been solved."

Emily lingered for a time, but we wandered on, noting where Albert Gallatin, the great financier, lies at rest; where Robert Fulton is buried in the Livingston vault, and where the gallant General Kearny, who fell in Virginia in 1862, is interred. In this neighborhood stands the bronze statue of Dr. John Watts, first Judge of Westchester County, and founder of the Leake and Watts Orphan House; and near the Broadway entrance is the tomb of Captain James Lawrence, the heroic commander of the Chesapeake, who, dying, spoke those undying words, "Don't give up the ship!"

"We haven't looked at that big monument," remarked Tom, pointing in the direction of the soldiers' memorial.

When we reached it we found this inscription:

> SACRED TO THE MEMORY OF
> THOSE BRAVE AND GOOD MEN WHO DIED
> WHILST IMPRISONED IN THIS CITY, FOR THEIR DEVOTION TO THE
> CAUSE OF AMERICAN INDEPENDENCE.

"Whenever I think of this fitting remembrance of unknown heroes," said the professor, "I can not help picturing to myself the sufferings of those unfortunates who died in the sugar houses and on the terrible prison ships. For some reason the design has never been completed, the original intention having been to place the marble figure of a Continental soldier above the inscription. Do you notice, by the way, that the monument is directly opposite Pine Street? It was so placed, it is said, to prevent the city from cutting a street through the churchyard.

"There is a newer memorial that also honors the heroes of the Revolution," continued our guide. "It was erected April 25, 1900, in the Dutch Collegiate Church at Fifth Avenue and Forty-eighth Street by the Daughters of the Revolution. Its text is as follows:

IN HONOR OF THE
OFFICERS, SOLDIERS AND SAILORS
WHO SERVED
IN THE WAR OF INDEPENDENCE
AGAINST
GREAT BRITAIN,
1775–1783.

ERECTED BY THE
DAUGHTERS OF THE REVOLUTION
OF THE STATE OF NEW YORK.

We spent some more time looking at the well-kept graves around us, and ere we left, the professor read to us the following lines:

"Where the pulse of Wall Street beats,
  Where the money changers go;
Where along the noisy streets
  Runs the life tide, to and fro—
Busy life of old Broadway,
  With its restless human sea—
Here I stop and muse to-day,
  By the graves of Trinity.

"Those beneath these quiet stones
  One unending Sabbath keep,
And the great wheels jar their bones,
  But they may not mar their sleep.
And they murmur not at all,
  Morning, noon, and night-time pass,
Rain and sun, and snow-flake fall,
  Careless footsteps tread the grass.

"Childish fingers press the graves,
  But these peaceful sleepers lie,
(What a worry dying saves!)
  Quiet under every sky.
Twittering bird and whispering elm!
  Bird and dead man, each care free—
Here's long peace to both of them,
  Citizens of Trinity!"

CHAPTER XII

Sauntering out of Trinity's grounds and joining the busy throng that hurries daily past the old graveyard, we walked down Broadway, and halted a moment at Exchange Place to admire the bronze figure of Wolfe, who saved New York from the French; and that of Clinton, who built its great canal.

On the west side of Broadway, at No. 55, there is a narrow passage between the high buildings. It was known long ago as Tin Pot Alley, and a modern terra-cotta tablet recalls the fact to those who pass it in our day.

"Curious name, isn't it?" commented Tom.

"Yes," replied the professor, "the English had a queer way of designating some of their streets. Marketfield, which the Produce Exchange almost entirely covers, was known as Petticoat Lane, because it contained the residences of some of the people of fashion; Nassau Street was originally referred to as 'The Streete that leads by the Pye Woman's'; Whitehall was called Shop Street; William, the Glassmaker's Street; Fulton, Partition Street; and Duane, Barley Street."

"Why, here's an old cannon," remarked George,

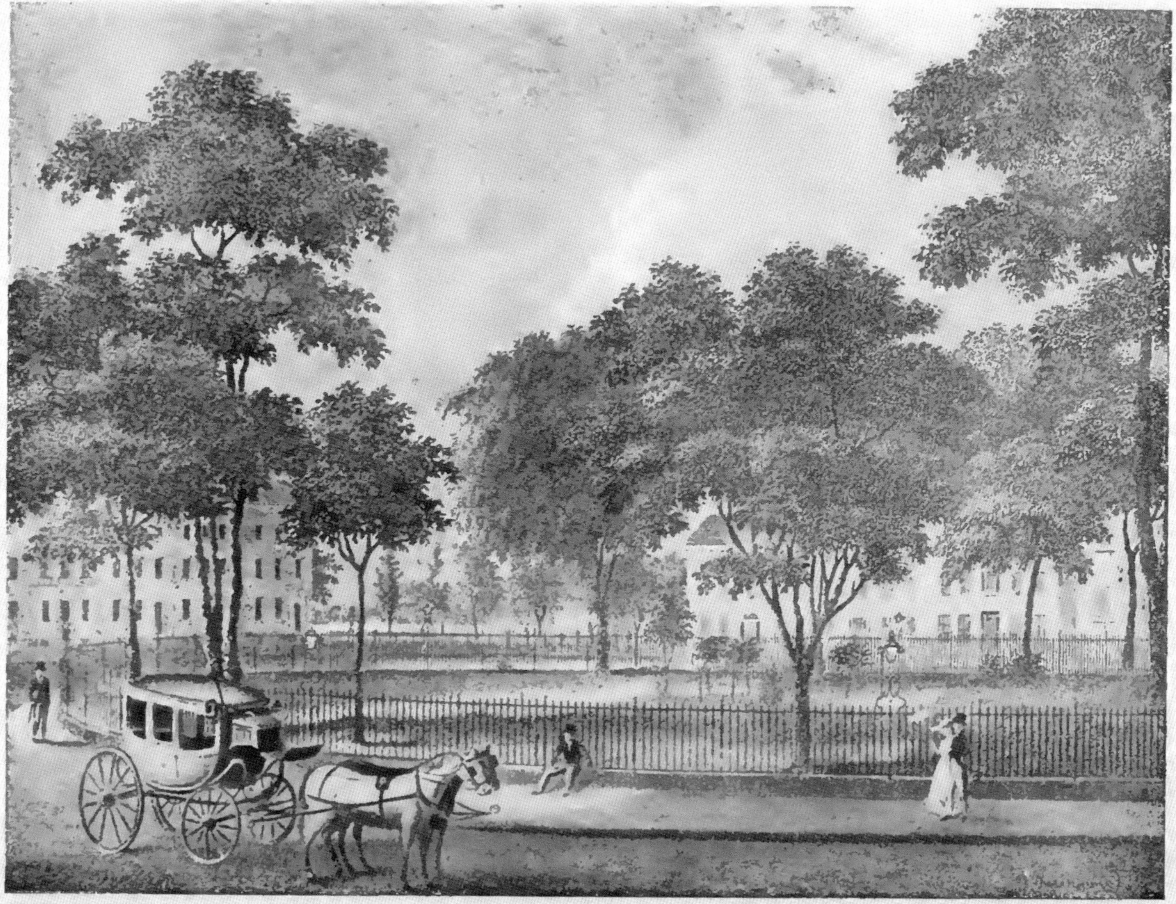

Bowling Green, 1830. From an old engraving.

pointing to one that serves as a post in front of No. 55 Broadway.

"A Revolutionary relic," explained the professor.

Opposite Bowling Green we cast a parting look at the old steamship buildings which, since our first visit, had been sold to the Government to make room for a new Customhouse.

Then we entered Battery Park, which, as the professor reminded us, was almost entirely made land, filled in over the shallow and rocky ground that was once swept by the tide.

"In the early part of the present century," he continued, "many fine mansions occupied State Street, Battery Place, Whitehall Street, Bowling Green, and the lower end of Broadway. A reminiscence of those days is that old-fashioned but still elegant house over yonder on State Street, which bears, as you see, the sign of a Roman Catholic mission. For many years Battery Park was a fashionable promenade, and presented a gay scene on pleasant afternoons.

"But here we are at the Aquarium, originally called Castle Clinton, in honor of Mayor De Witt Clinton. It was one of the fortifications erected in 1812, and still shows, as you perceive, the old port holes, where once fierce cannons peered out. After a time it was changed to a place of amusement, and then became known as Castle Garden. Here Lafayette was tendered an enthusiastic reception in 1824. Ten years later, when news came of his death, a memorial service was held in the same place. Here President Jackson was received in 1832, here Webster delivered some of his great speeches, and here in 1845 President Tyler was entertained. In 1851

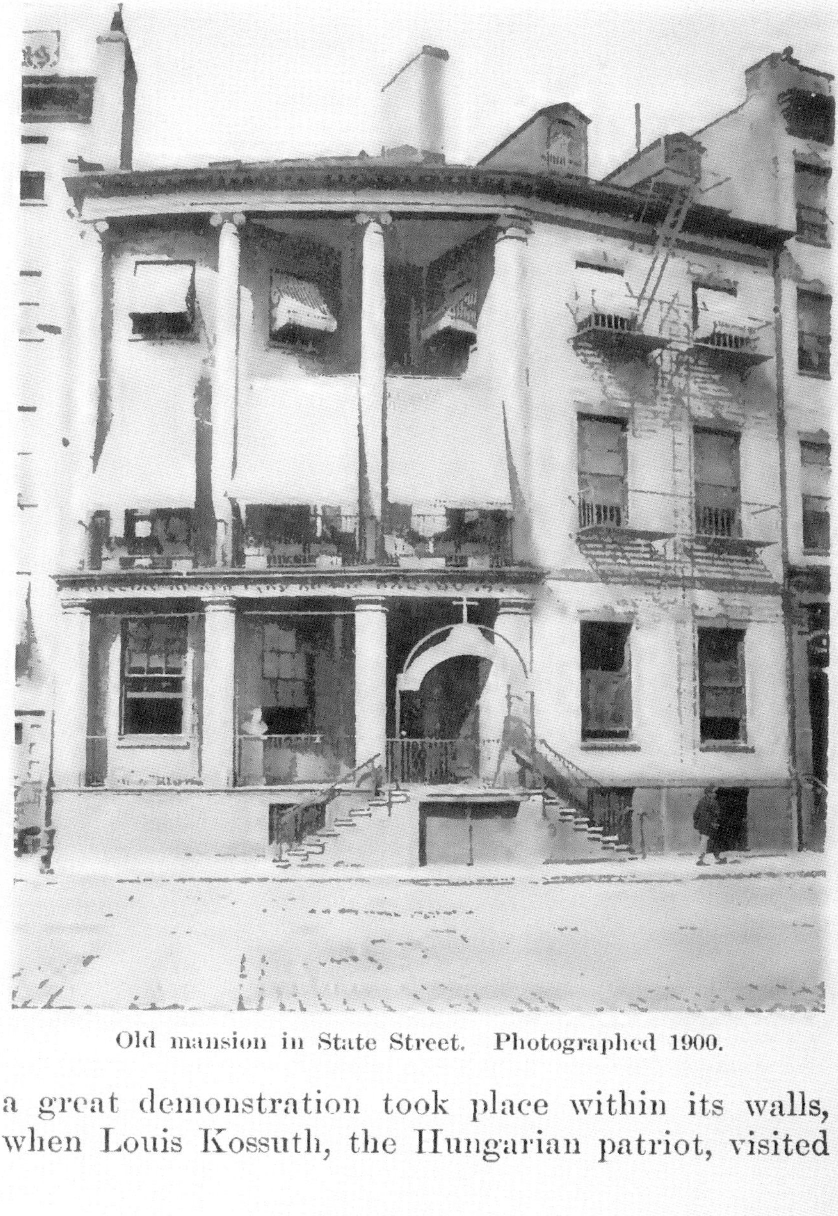

Old mansion in State Street. Photographed 1900.

a great demonstration took place within its walls, when Louis Kossuth, the Hungarian patriot, visited these shores. Later an Italian opera was heard here, and Jenny Lind, the 'Swedish Nightingale,' made her first American appearance under its roof. In 1855 all was changed, and it became a United States immigrant depot, which purpose it served until 1891, when it was turned over to the city, and was gradually made ready for its present purpose."

We spent a pleasant half hour within its walls and then paused near the water's edge to admire Bartholdi's Statue of Liberty.

"Of course," said the professor, "you know that yonder remarkable emblem was the gift of the French Republic, and was intended to express the cordial feeling existing between itself and our own republic. How this symbol of freedom and friendship would gladden the heart of Lafayette could he return now to see it! The forearm was sent to America in 1876, and was shown at the Centennial Exhibition in Philadelphia. Then it reposed in Madison Square until 1886, when the completed figure was placed upon its pedestal. It is interesting to know that the tip of the torch is three hundred and six feet above the water level, and that forty people can comfortably stand in Liberty's head. It is safe to say that no other harbor in the world has so striking, so significant, and so beautiful a symbol to greet the returning citizen or welcome the new arrival.

"Here is a sonnet written by Emma Lazarus, of New York," said the professor, consulting his little book, "that contains some beautiful thoughts regarding Liberty Statue:

"'Not like the brazen giant of Greek fame,
With conquering limbs astride from land to land;
Here at our sea-washed, sunset gates shall stand
A mighty woman with a torch, whose flame

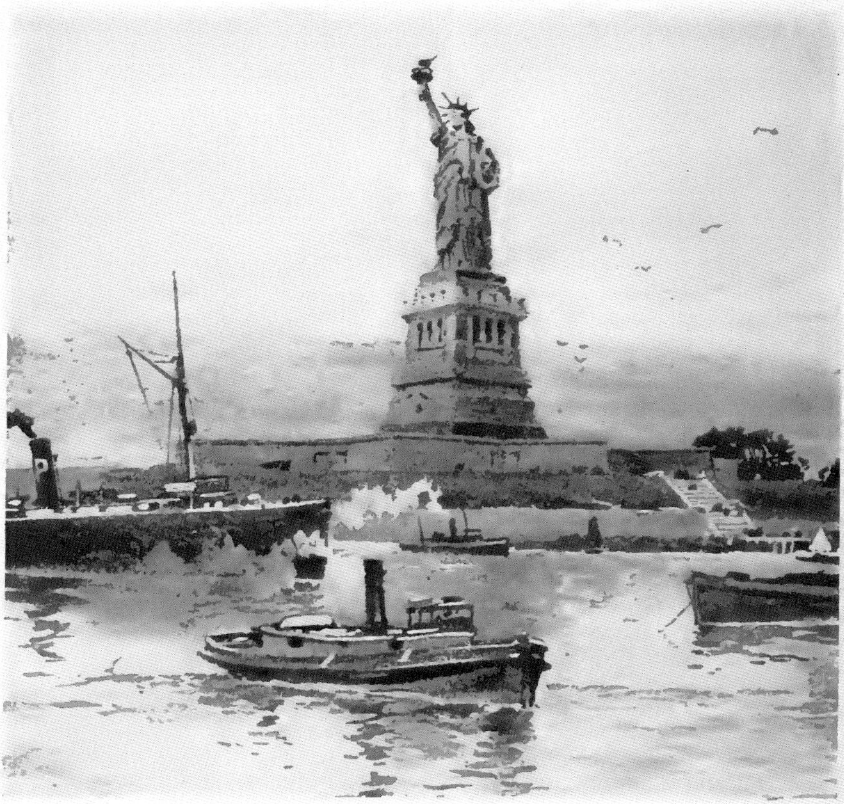

Statue of Liberty.

Is the imprisoned lightning, and her name
Mother of Exiles. From her beacon hand
Glows world-wide welcome; her mild eyes command
The air-bridged harbor that twin cities frame.
"Keep, ancient lands, your storied pomp!" cries she
With silent lips. "Give me your tired, your poor,
Your huddled masses yearning to breathe free,
The wretched refuse of your teeming shore.

Send these, the homeless, tempest-tost, to me;
I lift my lamp beside the golden door!"'

"It is perhaps hardly fair, after looking at this great figure of Liberty, to turn to a small statue, but Captain Ericsson, I think, will not suffer. It has been said that no greater engineer ever lived. He was born in Sweden in 1803, and came here in 1839. A list of one hundred important inventions is the record Ericsson has left behind him, more than one for every one of his eighty-six years of life. The best known, of course, is the Monitor—that wonderful machine that saved the Union. He offered his plan to the Government, and, like Fulton, was laughed at by those who ought to have known better. Fortunately, some few listened, understood, and won him the opportunity to serve, without pay of any kind, the country he had learned to love.

"Note the four plates that show his principal works—the Monitor, the Steam Fire Engine, the Rotary Gun Carriage, and the Princeton, the pioneer ship of our steam marine."

"And here is a tablet," said George, reading the inscription:

THE CITY OF NEW YORK
ERECTS THIS STATUE TO THE
MEMORY OF A CITIZEN WHOSE
GENIUS HAS CONTRIBUTED
TO THE GREATNESS OF THE
REPUBLIC AND TO THE
PROGRESS OF THE WORLD.
APRIL 26, 1893.

Leaving Battery Park and entering Broadway, which we were never tired of following, with its interesting landmarks and its busy modern life, we noticed, at the entrance of No. 19, two fine stone lions, and learned that this was once the residence of Daniel Webster.

Our next stopping place was the corner of Pearl and Broad Streets.

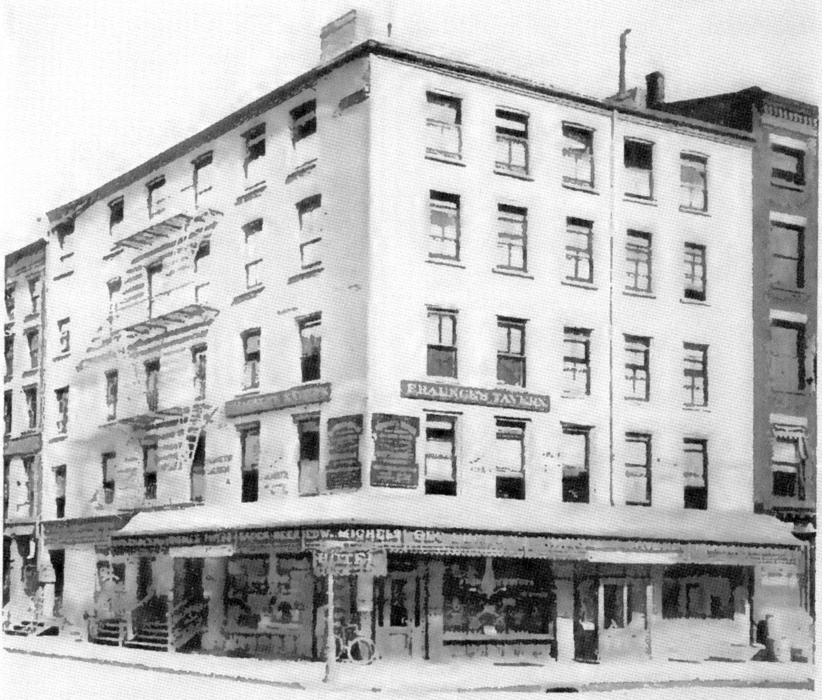

Fraunces's Tavern. From a recent photograph.

"Do you see that building?" said the professor, pointing to the southeast corner; "that is a genuine old-timer."

"Fraunces's Tavern," read Emily, glancing at the words painted in big letters above a restaurant. "'The Oldest Landmark in the City; Washington Long Room.'"

"What does it mean?" asked Tom.

"It was a famous tavern, erected in 1730, and there, somewhat altered, it still stands, being, without doubt, one of the oldest buildings in the city. Taverns, in the time of colonial New York, were popular meeting places, and many important and interesting gatherings took place in their 'long rooms,' as they were called. Before we go let us look at the tablet on the Broad Street side."

We found it easily, and George as usual read the inscription:

FRAUNCES TAVERN—TO THIS BUILDING
GENERAL GEORGE WASHINGTON
CAME EVACUATION DAY, NOV. 25, 1783,
AND ON THURSDAY, DEC. 4TH
FOLLOWING, HERE TOOK LEAVE OF THE PRINCIPAL
OFFICERS OF THE ARMY YET IN SERVICE.
ERECTED BY THE SONS OF THE REVOLUTION.

"Can we see the Long Room?" asked Emily.

"Certainly," responded the professor, leading us up a short flight of steps to a very modern eating room. A pleasant-looking lady greeted our guide, as if she knew his errand, and showed us a round mahogany table, a cupboard, and some old bricks, all of which she said were relics of Fraunces's Tavern. The pictures and inscriptions hanging on the walls, referring to historical events, immediately attracted our attention, and gave the place an interesting air.

At Exchange Place we paused and looked up the steep incline of this narrow lane.

"In 1825," said the professor, "a fine building known as the Merchants' Exchange was erected here at the corner of Broad Street and Exchange Place, but before this time business men used to meet here; and a law was passed in the early days forbidding boys to coast down this hill during certain hours, so as not to upset merchants who gathered daily in this neighborhood."

We had a good laugh at the picture suggested by the probable results of such coasting expeditions, and then turned our steps toward Wall Street, and paused, to use Stedman's words—

> "Just where the Treasury's marble front
> Looks over Wall Street's mingled nations;
> Where Jews and Gentiles most are wont
> To throng for trade and last quotations;
> Where, hour by hour, the rates of gold
> Outrival, in the ears of people
> The quarter-chimes, serenely tolled,
> From Trinity's undaunted steeple."

Before us was the splendid statue of Washington, and the following inscription:

> ON THIS SITE IN FEDERAL HALL
> APRIL 30, 1789,
> GEORGE WASHINGTON
> TOOK THE OATH AS THE FIRST PRESIDENT
> OF THE UNITED STATES
> OF AMERICA.

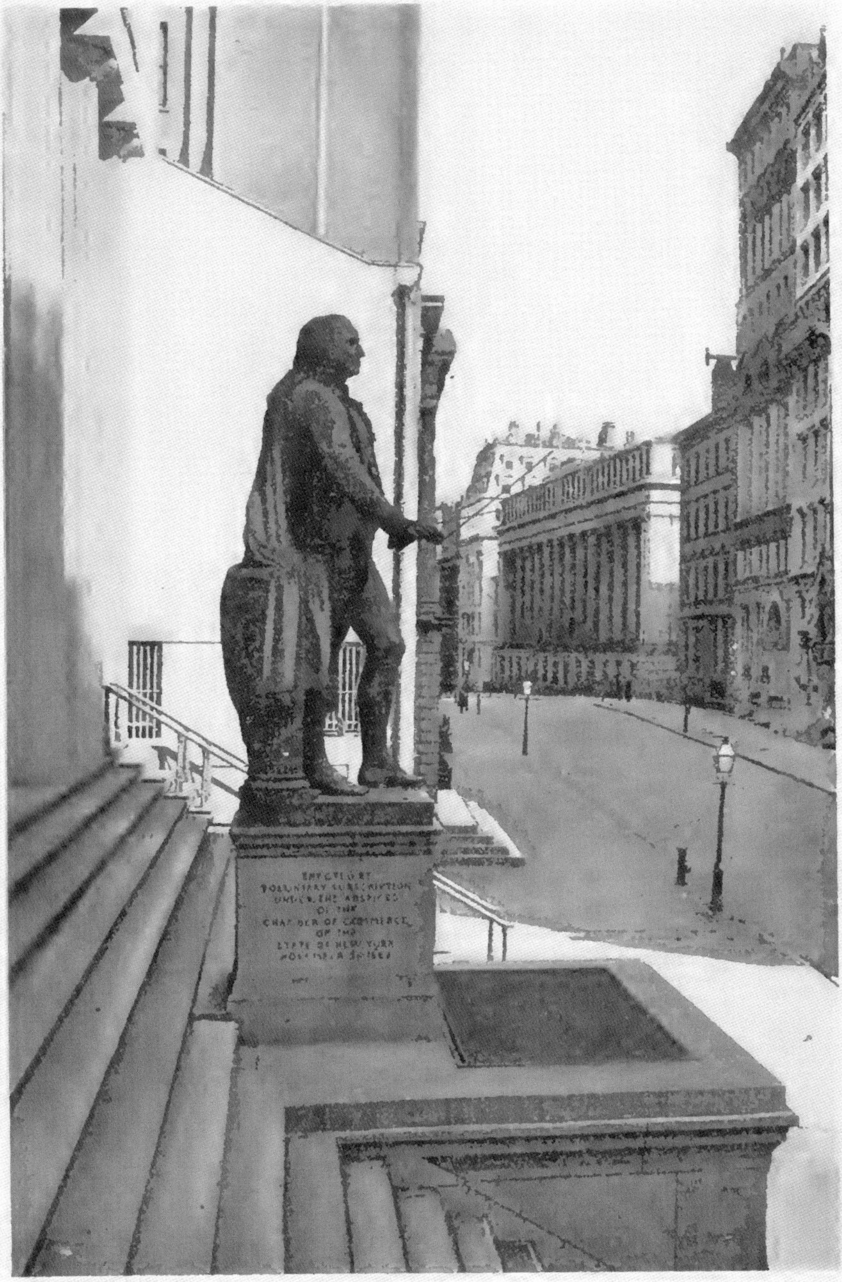

Statue of Washington, Subtreasury Building. Customhouse beyond. From a recent photograph.

"This is sacred ground," said the professor; "it is the precious spot where the union of the States was officially cemented by inaugurating the first President. From that moment the glorious career of the United States began, and, as I trust you will always remember, the ceremony that meant so much in our history, took place right here in New York.

"The whole neighborhood is interesting. As you know, this site was once occupied by Federal Hall; then it served as the location of the Customhouse; and now it is the Subtreasury. Next to it is the Assay Office, and on the next block, where you see those twelve single-stone granite columns, is the present Customhouse (formerly a Merchants' Exchange), which is soon to have a new home where the old Dutch fort used to be.

"Many important meetings have been held in this vicinity. On that awful day in April, 1865, when news reached New York that the great, good, and gentle Lincoln had been struck down by an assassin, throngs of excited men filled Wall Street. At noon a sort of mass meeting was organized, and from these steps of the Subtreasury solemn and eloquent speeches were delivered. Among those who spoke was James A. Garfield, who, little dreaming what the future had in store for him, sixteen years later met a similar fate.

"On November 25, 1883, the hundredth anniversary of the evacuation of the city by the British was celebrated on a grand scale. It was on this occasion that this statue of Washington was erected. It was unveiled by Governor Cleveland, accepted on behalf of the United States by President Arthur, after which an oration was delivered by George William Curtis."

"I know of another statue of Washington in Riverside Park," remarked Emily.

"Yes, near Eighty-eighth Street. That is a copy of a well-known statue in Richmond, designed by Houdon, a celebrated French sculptor, who was a friend of Franklin and of Washington. It may be news to you that the Riverside bronze was a gift of the children of the public schools of this city.

"You have probably noticed," continued the professor, pointing to Washington's form above us, "that there is a sec-

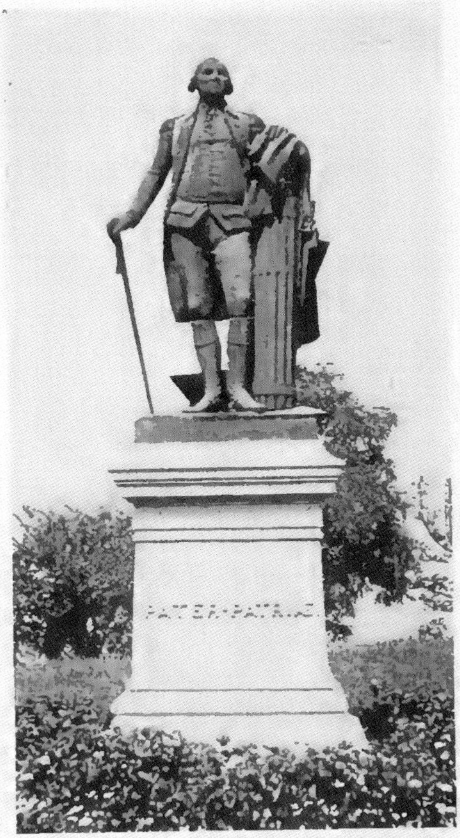

Statue of Washington, Eighty-ninth Street and Riverside Drive. Photographed 1900. It bears this inscription:

A TRIBUTE
FROM
THE PUPILS
OF THE
PUBLIC SCHOOLS
OF
THE CITY OF NEW YORK

ond inscription here, stating that the statue was erected by voluntary subscriptions under the auspices of the Chamber of Commerce. That commercial body is a very old institution. It was organized in 1770, and its early meetings were in Fraunces's Tavern. The most prominent men of the city joined it, but, owing to the Revolution, little was accomplished during its first years. It kept alive, however, and to-day it comprises a fine body of men who help to secure good laws, seek to amend bad ones, aid communities all over the world who suffer from floods, fire, or famine, and originate and lead many a worthy public and patriotic movement. Their rooms are near by, and are well worth a visit."

In the Mutual Life Building, which occupies the site of the old Dutch Church, and the old Post Office, we found the spacious quarters of the Chamber of Commerce, and saw its magnificent collection of portrait paintings, representing more than one hundred men of note. We were particularly interested in the well-known full-length picture of Hamilton, by Trumbull; and in the group, called "Planning the First Ocean Cable," by Huntington, in which the forms of Cyrus W. Field, Peter Cooper, and Samuel F. B. Morse are specially noticeable.

"In 1889, the Federal Union having reached its hundredth birthday, the people of New York made up their minds to celebrate the event in a manner befitting the remarkable growth and the wonderful prosperity of the country, as well as the eminent success of our form of government. One feature of this celebration was a reproduction, as nearly as possible, of Washington's journey to New York in 1789. President Harrison left the capital by train early on April 29th, and reaching Elizabethport boarded a dispatch boat that brought him opposite Wall Street, in the East River. Thence a barge, rowed by twelve pilots, conveyed him to the landing place, where the governor and the mayor received him and escorted him to the City Hall, to take part in a reception. The next day he attended service at St. Paul's, just as Washington had done a hundred years before. In the afternoon, on a large platform erected in front of old Federal Hall, the President sat in a chair used by Washington, and, surrounded by a notable gathering of distinguished men, listened to an ode entitled 'The Vow of Washington,' written by John G. Whittier, and to an oration delivered by Chauncey M. Depew.

"Parades, illuminations, banquets, speeches, music, and other forms of rejoicing made up the programme of a three days' jubilee, a memento of which remains in the shape of the noble marble arch in Washington Square. Thus the second century of the republic was begun.

"Three years later the four hundredth anniversary of the discovery of America was fittingly observed by New York in a celebration that began October 8th and ended October 12th, with the unveiling of the beautiful Columbus Column at Eighth Avenue and Fifty-ninth Street, a gift to the city by its Italian citizens.

"But we have been wandering," remarked the professor; "let us return to Washington and the

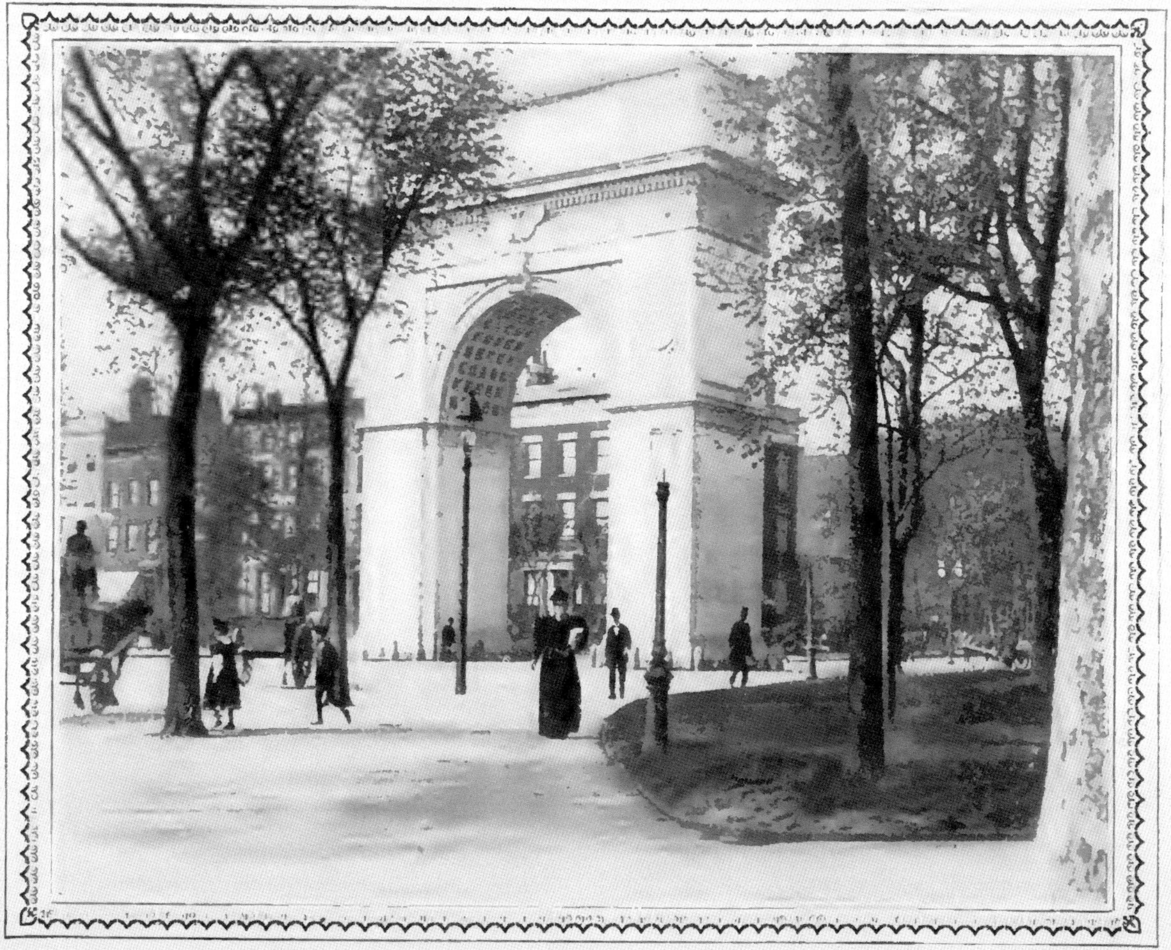

Washington Arch. From a recent photograph.

year 1789. Do you remember where his New York house was located?"

"In Cherry Street," answered George.

"Correct. I presume you have never taken a look at that street, which was once an aristocratic neighborhood and is historically interesting. We can go there now."

As we were passing through William Street between John and Fulton, the professor informed us that Washington Irving was born there.

"A few months before the British evacuated New York, in April, 1783, he opened his eyes upon a world that was to bring him fame and honor. Naturally enough, his mother named him after the most popular man of the day. Six years later, a Scotch maid servant, having young Washington in charge, saw the President and followed him into a shop. Presenting the lad to the great man, she said excitedly, 'Please, your Honor, here's a bairn was named after you.' The grave Virginian, so the story goes, placed his hand on the boy's head and gave him his blessing, little dreaming that he was doing a gracious act to his future biographer."

"Was he born over there?" asked Emily, pointing to two old houses on the east side of the street.

"No; his birthplace was pulled down some time ago. It is quite possible, though, that the two residences across the way were here in Irving's boyhood days; in fact, some people claim that they are the oldest houses in the city."

"Why is this called William Street?" asked George.

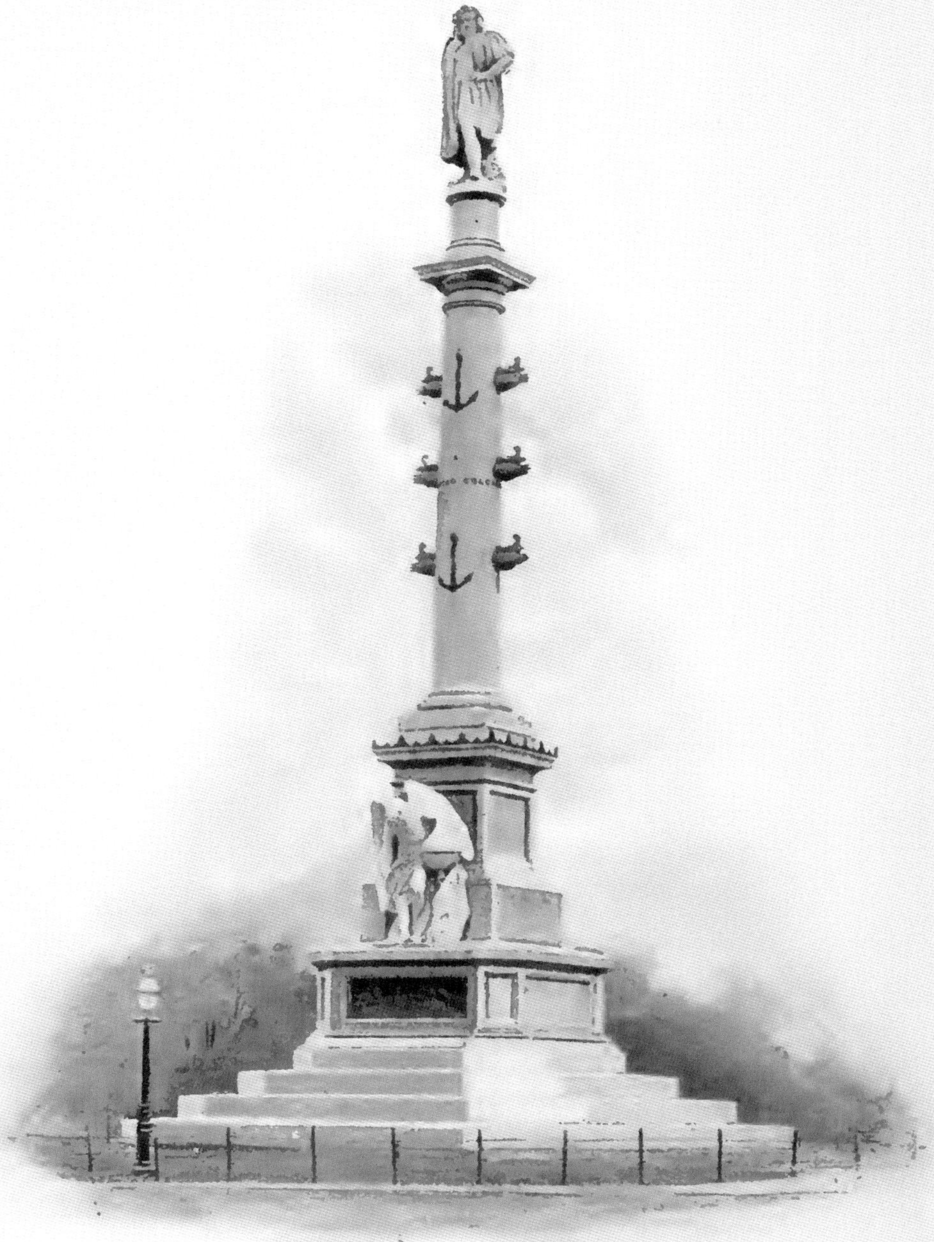

Columbus Column, Fifty-ninth Street and Eighth Avenue.
From a recent photograph.

"After William Beekman, in whose honor Beekman Street was likewise named. He owned a large tract of land in this neighborhood, a portion of which was a swamp. The leather trade now occupies this section, which is still known as The Swamp."

Reaching the bridge, we walked eastward and soon reached the junction of Jacob and Frankfort Streets.

"We are now on ground that used to belong to Leisler," explained the professor. "Jacob was his first name, and Frankfort the city of his birth, both of which are here perpetuated."

Our next halting place was the pier of the bridge at Cherry Street, where we found a new tablet containing this inscription:

THE FIRST
PRESIDENTIAL MANSION
NO. 1 CHERRY ST.,
OCCUPIED BY
GEORGE WASHINGTON
FROM APRIL 23, 1789,
TO FEBRUARY 23, 1790.
ERECTED BY THE MARY WASHINGTON COLONIAL CHAPTER
DAUGHTERS OF THE AMERICAN REVOLUTION.

We took a peep down Cherry Street, but its appearance did not tempt us to linger, and we proceeded to Rose Street, where at the corner of Duane the modern Rhinelander Building stands on the site of the old Rhinelander sugar house.

"Here is a curious reminiscence of the time when

the British held New York during the Revolution," said the professor, pointing to a small barred window to the left of the entrance. "That is a relic of the original sugar house. Through those rusty iron bars many a poor suffering patriot soldier looked out and sighed for freedom or perhaps for death.

"We are not far from another old prison that I promised to show you," continued the professor; "the old Provost, now the Hall of Records, the contents of which, by the way, are soon to be transferred to a fine new building."

Reaching City Hall Park, we entered the structure where once the wicked provost marshal Cunningham ruled with brutal sway. We examined the dark dungeons in the cellar, and then visited the upper floor, sarcastically called Congress Hall, where Ethan Allen and other distinguished prisoners were kept. There are many interesting and valuable maps stored here at present, and a vast collection of real-estate records, the earliest in the full, round handwriting of the Dutch.

"Whose statue is that?" asked Emily, as we emerged from the Hall of Records and faced Printing House Square and its great newspaper buildings, where the pen and the press perform their mighty functions.

"That is Benjamin Franklin, who, as you know, began life as a printer, and so is in appropriate surroundings here; and just beyond, in front of the Tribune Building, is the figure of Horace Greeley. Some day, no doubt, the other pioneer newspaper founders will be similarly honored.

"You remember, no doubt," continued the professor, "that this is the old Common where the liberty-pole struggles took place, and where the people met to discuss the actions that affected their rights. And now, after more than a hundred years, it is still the meeting ground of the citizens' representatives, where laws are made and the city's interests are guarded."

Following our guide we mounted the broad flight of steps that leads to the entrance of the City Hall, and began our tour of the building by visiting the governor's room, the scene of many state occasions. Here we found a number of interesting objects: the desks of Washington, Adams, and Jefferson, and some of the original furniture used in old Federal Hall, on which is carved the national coat of arms; portraits of many distinguished patriots, including Washington, Hamilton, and most of the Governors of New York; also a painting of Peter Stuyvesant, and off in one corner the little twig that once formed a portion of his famous pear tree.

"Can we see where they make the laws?" asked Emily.

"Certainly," answered the professor; "every citizen has a right to come here and see what those who represent him are doing—it ought, in fact, to be called Citizens' Hall. There are two kinds of representatives: councilmen, or members of the upper house, elected for four years; and aldermen, or members of the lower house, elected for two years. There are twenty-eight councilmen and sixty aldermen, each councilman, therefore, representing a larger district than that of an alderman.

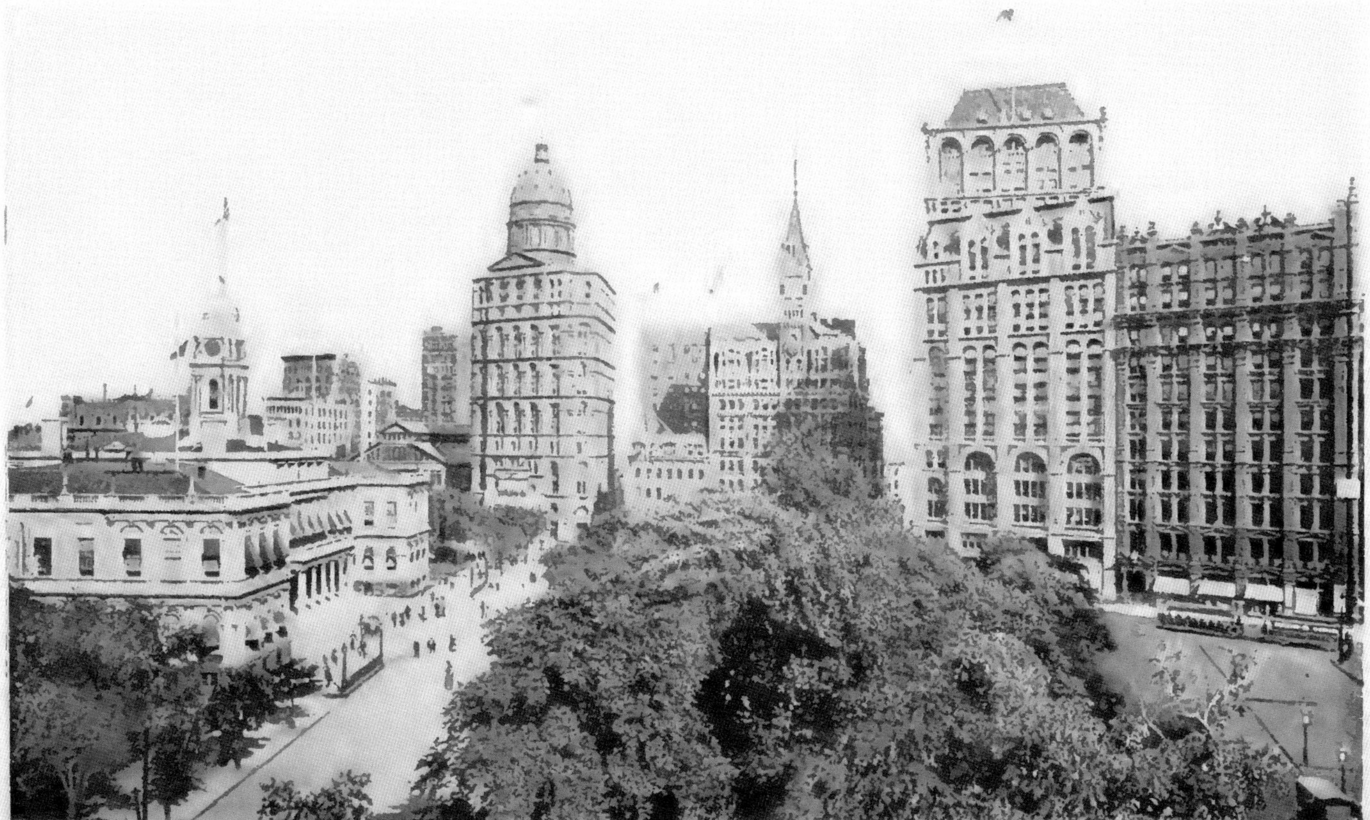

City Hall and Printing House Square. From a recent photograph.

"Properly speaking, the measures passed by the two houses are called ordinances or resolutions. According to their character, they require the votes of a majority, three quarters, four fifths, or of all the members of both houses. Then they are submitted to the mayor, who has ten days in which to approve or veto. In case he does not desire to do either, he can allow ten days to pass, and then the bill becomes effective. Even after his veto a measure may be put in operation if the two houses pass it again by a vote of two thirds, or of five sixths in case the expenditure of money is involved.

"As you can see, the mayor has great power. It is his province, furthermore, to see that ordinances are executed. He also has the right to appoint a number of important officials, and to remove them.

"You now know about the legislative and the executive branches; the third is the judicial, composed of civil justices, city magistrates, and coroners, why apply the law, see that justice is done, that rights are respected, and law-breakers punished.

"But this is not all that the city undertakes to do. It protects us against bodily violence by furnishing the Police Department; against fire, by providing the Fire Department; against disease, by giving us the Health Department; it educates us in its public schools, and lays out for our pleasure public parks and recreation piers. To keep this vast machinery going, and to raise the necessary funds, in the shape of taxes, necessitates other departments, of which you will learn as you grow older."

Having had this explanation we visited the Council Chamber and the Aldermen's Room, both of which are impressive, and contain interesting portrait paintings. We also inspected the mayor's office, the City Library, and finally the Marriage Room, which is the smallest and simplest of all.

Emerging from the building and descending the steps, we turned our attention to a tablet differing from all the others we had seen, in that it was sunk into the pavement. We knew, from accounts we had read, that it referred to the Underground Railway, and we were particularly interested in it because it commemorated an undertaking of our own time, the progress of which we were eagerly watching from day to day. The inscription is as follows:

AT THIS PLACE, 24TH MARCH, 1900,
HON. ROBERT A. VAN WYCK
MADE THE FIRST EXCAVATION FOR THE
UNDERGROUND RAILWAY.

RAPID TRANSIT COMMISSION.

A. E. ORR, PRESIDENT.	CHARLES STEWART SMITH,
JOHN H. STARIN,	MORRIS K. JESUP,
WOODBURY LANGDON,	R. A. VAN WYCK, MAYOR.
GEORGE L. RIVES.	BIRD S. COLER, CONTROLLER.

WILLIAM BARCLAY PARSONS,
CHIEF ENGINEER.

CONTRACTORS.
JOHN B. McDONALD.
RAPID TRANSIT SUBWAY CONSTRUCTION COMPANY.
AUGUST BELMONT,
PRESIDENT.

"And so ends the story," remarked the professor.

The young people began to express their thanks, but the professor interrupted their little speeches by saying: "You have thanked me long ago. The appreciation you have shown was a very satisfactory reward for the trouble I have taken. I was aware from the beginning that you were proud of your city and loved it, and now that you know its landmarks and their history, I feel certain that it has a deeper hold on your affections than before. You understand, too, what the city owes you; remember, likewise, what you owe the city. See to it, when the time comes, that you do your duty, help to select and to elect the right kind of officials, and devote some time and make some individual effort to render the city better, wiser, happier, healthier, and more beautiful as you grow up with it."

ORIGIN OF STREET NAMES

Abingdon Square owes its name to the Earl of Abingdon, who married one of the daughters of Sir Peter Warren, the founder of Greenwich. (See Greenwich Street.)

Allen Street perpetuates the name and fame of Captain William Henry Allen, one of the heroes of the War of 1812. He was only twenty-nine when he died, but left behind him a brilliant record.

Ann Street.—Owners of land frequently bestowed on paths that were cut through their property the first names of their wives.

Audubon Avenue recalls the name of the celebrated ornithologist, John James Audubon.

Bank Street owes its title to a fever epidemic that broke out in New York in 1822, when many people hurriedly left town. A row of hastily erected buildings, principally used by banks, was then built in the vicinity of the present thoroughfare.

Barclay Street, cut through church property, perpetuates the name of the Rev. Henry Barclay, the second rector of Trinity Church.

Battery Place is a reminder of the fact that in 1693 a platform was erected in this vicinity to serve as a battery. In 1753 this was enlarged.

Bayard Street preserves the name of Nicholas Bayard, nephew of Peter Stuyvesant, who played an important part in the early history of the city, especially during the Leisler troubles. He filled the position of mayor and occupied other official posts. The Bayard farm lay between Canal and Bleecker Streets and between Macdougal Street and the Bowery.

Beach Street, a corruption of Bache Street, was named in honor of Paul Bache, a son-in-law of Anthony Lispenard. (See Lispenard Street.)

Beaver Street was a very appropriate name for a thoroughfare in old New York, especially as it happened to be a fur district. The beaver played an important part in New Amsterdam's early history. Van der Donk, one of the first to write a description of the colony, devoted special attention to "the wonderful character and habits of the beavers."

Beekman Street is a part of the old Beekman farm, and honors the name of William Beekman, who came to New Netherland with Peter Stuyvesant and soon became prominent. The Beekman farm extended about a block north and south of the present Beekman Street, and from Nassau Street over to the East River. (See William Street.)

Benson Street recalls the name of Judge Egbert Benson, the first President of the New York Historical Society.

Bethune Street honors the name of the Bethune family, noteworthy philanthropists, whose work was of special significance in connection with the improvement of the Five Points.

Bleecker Street recalls the name of the Bleecker family, and especially of Anthony Bleecker, who for many years was active and prominent in the literary world.

Bowery, in Dutch, means a farm. From Stuyvesant's *Bouwerie*, in the neighborhood of Third Avenue and Thirteenth Street to the city there was a path naturally called Bowery Lane. This was afterward named Bowery Road, and finally The Bowery.

Bowling Green owes its name to the fact that in 1732 it was leased as a bowling green to three citizens who lived in the neighborhood.

Bridge Street locates a bridge that at one time crossed the Broad Street ditch.

Broad Street was originally a ditch or inlet, known as the *Breede Graft*, or Broad Canal.

Broome Street was named after John Broome, Lieutenant-Governor of New York State in 1804, and a prominent member of many commercial and charitable institutions.

Canal Street was originally a real canal—forty feet wide, with a promenade and trees on each side of it. It carried the water from the old Collect Pond to the Hudson River. A stone bridge crossed it at Broadway, and this is now below the pavement of that busy thoroughfare.

Cedar Street and other streets bearing the names of trees suggest the wooded character of Manhattan Island during its early period.

Centre Street indicates its location midway between the

Hudson and East Rivers. Another explanation attributes the name to the fact that the street marks a path through the center of the old Collect Pond.

Chambers Street owes its name to John Chambers, a prominent lawyer and one of the officers of Trinity Church.

Charlton Street directs attention to Dr. John Charlton, an English surgeon, who came to New York with the British army, but liked the city well enough to settle here, becoming President of the Medical Society.

Chatham Square, as well as Pitt Street, perpetuates the name of America's devoted and eloquent friend, William Pitt, Earl of Chatham.

Chelsea Square owes its name to Thomas Clarke, a veteran of the French and Indian War, who bought some land on the bank of the Hudson shortly after the Revolution, built a residence there, and called it Chelsea, after quiet Chelsea, near London, where there is a hospital for old soldiers.

Cherry Street was originally part of a cherry farm.

Church Street was cut through property belonging to Trinity Church.

Chrystie Street was named after John Chrystie, a brave and skillful New York officer who gave up his life in the War of 1812.

Claremont was so called by Michael Hogan, a native of County Clare, Ireland, who once owned the property and named it in honor of his native place.

Clarkson Street preserves the memory of Matthew Clarkson, a vestryman of Trinity Church, who was well known because of his charities and public works.

Cliff Street formed at one time part of the property of Dirck van Clyff.

Clinton Street recalls the names of James, George, and De Witt Clinton, whose records in war and in peace are deserving of the highest honors at the hands of the State that gave them birth.

Coenties Slip, commonly called "Quinchy's Slip," is a corruption of Coentje, as Conraet ten Eijck, who owned land in the neighborhood, was familiarly known.

Corlears Street brings to mind Jacobus van Corlear, who offered the use of his house for school purposes to Governor Stuyvesant, and Anthony van Corlear, the trumpeter, who, it is alleged, gave Spuyten Duyvil its name when he boasted he could swim across its troubled waters.

Cortlandt Street is a portion of a large tract of land that belonged to Oloff Stevenson Cortlandt, the first of that family to settle in America.

Crosby Street was named in honor of William Bedlow Crosby, who inherited the greatest portion of the Seventh Ward. He was connected with many charitable societies, and devoted much of his time to works of benevolence.

Delancey Street recalls the name of Lieutenant-Governor James De Lancey, the original builder and owner of the house that afterward became Fraunces's Tavern, and the donor to the city of its first town clock. The De Lancey family played an important part in New York's history during a long period. The De Lancey farm, covering about one hundred and twenty blocks of our present city, extended from Division Street to Stanton, and from the Bowery to the East River.

De Peyster Street honors Johannes and Abraham de Peyster, both of whom were prominent and wealthy citizens in the early days of the city. (See the statue of Abraham de Peyster in Bowling Green.)

Desbrosses Street commemorates the official career of Elias Desbrosses, who occupied the positions of alderman, President of the Chamber of Commerce, and warden of Trinity Church.

Division Street derives its name from the fact that it divided the two great farms of James De Lancey and Henry Rutgers.

Duane Street owes its name to James Duane, New York's first mayor after the Revolution.

Exchange Place was the site of a merchants' exchange.

Eldridge Street is a reminder of Lieutenant Joseph C. Eldridge, who lost his life in the War of 1812.

Ferry Street was the road that led to the first ferry from New York to Brooklyn.

Fletcher Street was named in honor of Governor Benjamin Fletcher, during whose term (1692–'98) printing was introduced into the colony.

Fulton Street was named after Robert Fulton, and is the only memorial on Manhattan Island to preserve the memory of him who helped so much toward its development.

Frankfort Street was so called by Jacob Leisler, after his birthplace in Germany. His estate covered the section through which the street was cut.

Franklin Street and *Franklin Square*, it is hardly necessary to say, perpetuate the name of Benjamin Franklin.

Gansevoort Street was named after Brigadier-General Peter

Gansevoort, who rendered important service in checking Burgoyne, for which he received a vote of thanks from Congress.

Goerck Street and *Mangin Street* were named after the two surveyors who laid out that section of the city about the year 1803.

Gouverneur Street recalls the Gouverneur family, which was prominent during Leisler's time. A later member of the family, Isaac Gouverneur, owned a house which, previous to the great fire of 1835, was one of the wonders of the town.

Gramercy Park was originally a hill, the shape of which was like a hooked knife, called in Dutch a *Krom-messje*, which gradnally was corrupted into the present English title.

Great Jones Street belonged to the estate of Chief-Justice David Jones, who flourished during the latter part of the eighteenth century.

Greeley Square was named after Horace Greeley, founder, and for many years editor, of the New York Tribune.

Greene Street honors the memory of General Nathanael Greene, whose intellectual qualities, it has been remarked, "were precisely those that have won distinction for the foremost strategists of modern times."

Greenwich Street was the road that led to Greenwich, a name bestowed by Admiral Sir Peter Warren to a mansion he built in the section which afterward took the name of the admiral's house. The admiral was an Englishman who acquired great wealth from prizes he captured at sea. Warren Street was named after him by the Trinity corporation, of which he was an officer.

Hanover Square was named in honor of King George, who was of the house of Hanover.

Henry Street honors the name of Henry Rutgers, a prominent citizen and landowner of early New York who donated a site for the Third Presbyterian Church. His farm adjoined that of the De Lancey family, from which it was separated by Division Street, extending from that line to the East River and from Catharine to Montgomery Street. (See Rutgers Street.)

Hester Street was so called by Barnet Rynders in honor of his wife Hester Rynders, daughter of Jacob Leisler.

Jacob Street, according to some authorities, owes its name to Jacobus Roosevelt, who owned property in the neighborhood, while others believe that it was named in honor of Jacob Leisler.

Leonard Street formed a part of the property of Anthony Lispenard. Three streets were cut through his land, to which he gave the names of his three sons, Leonard, Anthony, and

Thomas. Anthony Street was subsequently changed to Worth Street, in recognition of the military triumphs of Major-General Worth. (See the Worth Monument, Madison Square.)

Lewis Street honors the name of Morgan Lewis, a stanch patriot who fought through the Revolutionary War and later became Chief Justice and then Governor.

Liberty Street was originally called Crown Street, the name being changed after the Revolution, when all references to royalty were suppressed.

Lispenard Street was named after Anthony Lispenard, to whom belonged the Lispenard meadows, a swampy district stretching along the present Canal Street from the North River to Centre Street, and down Broadway in a long, narrow loop as far as Duane Street.

Lorillard Place preserves the name of Jacob Lorillard, a prominent vestryman of Trinity Church.

Ludlow Street recalls the name of Gabriel Ludlow, clerk of the House of Assembly and one of the original vestrymen of Trinity Church.

Macdougal Street was named after Alexander Macdougal, a noted "Son of Liberty," who was arrested in 1770, on a charge of seditious libel, for which he was imprisoned in the Debtors' Prison (present Register's Office), thus becoming the first martyr in the patriot cause.

Maiden Lane is the old Dutch *Maagde Paatje*, or Maiden's Path, a very ancient path laid out by Nature along a rippling stream shaded by overhanging trees. Here, beyond the limits of the town, the maidens and their swains found a romantic spot to wander up and down.

Mangin Street. (See Goerck Street.)

Marketfield Street was the street that led to the market field, which purpose Bowling Green originally served.

Mercer Street recalls the name of Brigadier-General Hugh Mercer, who advised the night march on Princeton, and who, in rallying his men on that occasion, received his death-blow. He occupied a high place in the esteem of Washington, and was deeply mourned by the nation.

Minetta Street derives its name from a Dutch word meaning "the little one"—that is, the little creek to distinguish it from a large creek not far away. The former creek, which originated in the marshy ground in the neighborhood of Washington Square, still flows under the pavements of modern New York.

Montgomery Street honors the memory of Brigadier-General

Richard Montgomery, whose last words before attempting to storm Quebec (December 31, 1775) were, "Men of New York, you will not fear to follow where your general leads!" (See monument, St. Paul's Church.)

Moore Street commemorates the name of Colonel John Moore, a prominent merchant and official. Another explanation attributes its name to the fact that vessels were "moored" in the vicinity.

Morris Street suggests the well-known name of Gouverneur Morris, who, besides occupying many important public positions, was one of the street commissioners appointed in 1807 to lay out the new streets, which resulted in a city of rigid straight lines and right angles.

Morton Street honors the name of John Morton, a well-known merchant of old New York, who advanced large sums to the Continental Congress.

Mott Street was named after a successful butcher, Joseph Mott.

Murray Hill took its name from the Murray mansion. It was here that the mother of Lindley Murray, the grammarian, entertained the British generals, so the story goes, while Putnam and his tired forces made their escape from the lower point of the island to Harlem.

Murray Street brings to mind the name of John Murray, Jr., who was one of the original thirteen trustees of the New York Free School Society, which in 1806 began its first session in an apartment in Bancker (now Madison) Street with forty pupils.

Nassau Street honors the name of the Prince of Orange and Nassau.

New Street was the first street opened by the English after taking possession of New Amsterdam.

Pearl Street, the oldest street of New Amsterdam, was so called because of the pearl shells found along its path.

Pell Street was named after a prominent butcher, John Pell.

Pitt Street. (See Chatham Square.)

Perry Street honors the memory of Oliver Hazard Perry, the hero of Lake Erie.

Platt Street was named after Jacob S. Platt, a highly successful merchant.

Rector Street, being originally church property, naturally owes its name to that fact.

Ridge Street was an actual ridge along the top of a hill on

James De Lancey's property. The slope from Ridge Street to the river still exists.

Roosevelt Street recalls the name of Isaac and of his son Nicholas J. Roosevelt. The former was a member of one of the celebrated committees of One Hundred to guard the safety of New York previous to the Revolution. Later on he became President of the Bank of New York. Nicholas was an inventor whose work in connection with steamboat machinery was valuable. A later member of the family, James Henry, the philanthropist, founded Roosevelt Hospital in 1871. A tablet affixed to one of the walls bears this inscription:

> TO THE MEMORY OF
> JAMES HENRY ROOSEVELT,
> A TRUE SON OF NEW YORK,
> THE GENEROUS FOUNDER OF THIS HOSPITAL,
> A MAN UPRIGHT IN HIS AIMS, SIMPLE IN HIS LIFE,
> AND SUBLIME IN HIS BENEFACTION.

Rutgers Street is a part of what was once Rutgers farm, an attractive neighborhood crossed by a shady path known as "Love Lane." A second "Love Lane" was a feature of Greenwich village. (See Henry Street.)

Rutherford Street recalls the name of Colonel John Rutherford, who was one of the committee that planned the present system of avenues and streets.

Sheriff Street was so named in honor of Colonel Marinus Willett, the famous "Son of Liberty" who subsequently filled the office of sheriff. Willett Street also commemorates his patriotic record.

Spring Street owes its name to the discovery of a spring in that neighborhood about the year 1800, when Aaron Burr's Manhattan Banking and Water-supply Company began to furnish the city with drinkable water.

Stone Street was the first street in New Amsterdam to be paved with stone, which achievement created a great sensation.

Sullivan Street honors the name of Brigadier-General John Sullivan, one of the most active officers of the Revolutionary War, who received the thanks of Washington for his services in Westchester. In Rhode Island he fought what Lafayette pronounced to be the best-contested battle of the war.

Thomas Street. (See Leonard Street.)

Tompkins Street suggests the name of Daniel D. Tompkins, Governor of New York from 1807 to 1817 and Vice-President of the United States from 1817 to 1825.

Tinpot Alley is a curious corruption of *Tuyn Paat*, meaning Garden Lane.

Tryon Row recalls the name of Sir William Tryon, the last of the English Governors of New York.

Vandam Street honors the name of Rip Van Dam, of Dutch descent, who in the year 1731 occupied the important post of Governor *pro tem.* while for a time there was no English official to fill the executive office. He was a great merchant and a prominent ship-builder.

Varick Street was cut through the property of Colonel Richard Varick, a Revolutionary patriot, who afterward became Mayor of New York.

Vesey Street honors the name of the Rev. W. Vesey, Trinity's first clergyman. He preached his first sermon in Trinity Church February 6, 1697.

Wall Street owes its name to the wall of palisades that originally marked its path.

Warren Street. (See Greenwich Street.)

Water Street was so named because it consisted of land that in the early days of the city was literally under water.

Watts Street preserves the memory of John Watts, the last City Recorder under English rule. He was one of the assemblymen that protested against England's right to billet soldiers on the citizens of New York. In after years he founded the Leake and Watts Orphan Asylum. His monument is a prominent feature of Trinity churchyard.

Waverly Place received its name in response to a petition from residents of the neighborhood, who were great admirers of Sir Walter Scott.

Whitehall Street was the thoroughfare that led to Peter Stuyvesant's town house. Whether it was so named because of its white walls, or because English governors who occupied it subsequently were reminded of London's Whitehall, is a question.

Willett Street. (See Sheriff Street.)

William Street, like Beekman Street, perpetuates the name of William Beekman. South William Street was originally called Mill Street, and here the first Jewish synagogue was erected.

Wooster Street recalls the name of General David Wooster, a dashing officer of the Revolutionary War, who fell while gallantly leading a charge against the British at Ridgefield, Conn.

Worth Street. (See Leonard Street.)

BIBLIOGRAPHY

NOTE.—The Dutch records of New York for a long time were almost entirely neglected. At first they were kept in this city, but when, in 1798, Albany became the seat of government, they were transferred to the office of the Secretary of State, excepting those that referred specifically to New Amsterdam. The latter were left in our City Hall.

In 1814 the New York Historical Society (organised in 1804), anxious to preserve and render accessible the State's early records, presented a memorial to the Legislature, the result of which was a translation by Dr. F. A. van der Kemp, in twenty-six volumes, since known as the Albany Records.

These records made plain the fact that much material relating to the earliest Dutch period was missing. Again the Historical Society appealed to the Legislature, but not until 1839 was action taken. In that year a sum of money was appropriated, and in 1841 John Romeyn Brodhead, *attaché* of the American legation at The Hague, was appointed agent to examine the archives of Holland, England, and France, and obtain copies of all papers referring to New York's history.

Unfortunately, twenty years before, a whole batch of important records of the West India Company of Holland had been sold as waste paper. Still, Brodhead succeeded in finding many valuable documents, the copies of which filled eighty volumes, which are now in the office of the Secretary of State.

In 1849 certain of these papers were translated and issued by the State in four large volumes. This publication, known as the Documentary History of the State of New York, was the work of Dr. E. B. O'Callaghan.

In 1853 it was decided to publish all the papers. Dr. O'Callaghan was again employed, and completed his undertaking in eleven volumes, entitling the publication Documents Relative to the Colonial History of the State of New York, procured in Holland, England, and France by John Romeyn Brodhead, Esq.

Subsequently some of the West India Company's scattered

papers came to light. A few stray documents were unearthed in 1851, and several years later another batch was found containing documents relating to New Netherland and to the recapture of New York by the Dutch. In 1889, James Grant Wilson, editor of The Memorial History of the City of New York, discovered among the papers of an old Dutch family the original deed describing the purchase of Manhattan Island from the Indians for the value of sixty guilders.

In the meantime the records referring specifically to New Amsterdam had remained in the City Hall in New York. Early in the century an unsatisfactory translation had been made of one volume, and thus the work rested until 1848, when Dr. O'Callaghan, before taking hold of the State's collection already mentioned, completed the task. These translations, consisting of six volumes, remained, however, for nearly half a century next to the original records, unprinted and almost unknown. A few years ago Berthold Fernow, translator and editor of some of the colonial documents of the State, having been appointed to edit the manuscript volumes, revised the entire material, and the city published it, in 1897, in seven volumes, under the title of The Records of New Amsterdam from 1653 to 1674.

HISTORIES

History of New York from the First Discovery to the Year 1732, by William Smith. (With a continuation to the year 1814.) Published originally in London, 1793.

Called by its author, who was Chief Justice of the Province of New York, a narrative rather than a history. Furnishes evidence of the imperfect condition of the Dutch records at the time, but is interesting as New York's first history.

History of New York during the Revolutionary War and of the Leading Events in the Other Colonies at that Period, by Thomas Jones. Written between the years 1783–'88. Viewed from a loyalist standpoint.

"There can be no greater error than to suppose that the loyalists, as a whole, were willing to submit quietly to the exactions of the mother country and her invasions of their rights and liberties as English subjects. As Americans they felt those grievances and were indignant, . . . but they wished to fight the battle for those rights and liberties . . . with the powerful weapons which the Constitution of England gave to them as to other Englishmen."

New York Historical Society's Collections. First Series, 5 vols., 1809–'29. Second Series, 4 vols., 1841–'59. Proceedings, 7 vols., 1843–'49. Collections, 24 vols., 1868–'92. (For a complete list of titles of the Society's publications, see R. R. Bowker's Publications of Societies.)

History of the State of New York, by John V. N. Yates and Joseph W. Moulton, 1824.

The Natural, Statistical, and Civil History of the State of New York, by James Macauley, 1829, 3 vols.

A History of New York for Schools, by William Dunlap, 1835, 2 vols.

History of the New Netherlands, Province of New York and State of New York, to the Adoption of the Federal Constitution, by William Dunlap, 1839, 2 vols.

Manuals of the Corporation of the City of New York (known generally as Valentine's Manuals), 1841 to 1866 and 1868 to 1870. No issue in 1867. (See Historical Index to the Manuals.)

The History of Political Parties in the State of New York, by Jabez D. Hammond, 1847, 3 vols.

History of New Netherland or New York under the Dutch Rule, by E. B. O'Callaghan, from 1492 to 1664. Published in 1845 and 1848. 2 vols.

The Documentary History of the State of New York, by E. B. O'Callaghan, 1850, 4 vols.

History of the State of New York, by John Romeyn Brodhead, 1853 and 1871, 2 vols. (Period covered, 1609–'91.)

"Descended from an English officer who helped his king to conquer Dutch New Netherland, as well as from a colonial Hollander who stood up manfully for his Republican Fatherland, I feel no partiality in telling the history of the greatest European plantation in America."—*Author's Preface.*

Documents Relative to the Colonial History of the State of New York, procured in Holland, England, and France by John Romeyn Brodhead. Edited by E. B. O'Callaghan, 1856, 11 vols.

History of the City of New York, by David T. Valentine, 1853.

Illustrates the different paths pursued in extending the habitations of the town, and notes "the circumstances which operated to establish the lines of the early thoroughfares and the laying out of the plan of that part of the city originally settled." Includes names and many biographical facts of the earliest inhabitants.

New York City during the American Revolution, being a Collection of Original Papers from the Manuscripts in the Possession of the Mercantile Library Association of New York City, 1861.

The Earliest Churches of New York and its Vicinity, by Gabriel P. Disosway, 1865.

History of the City of New York, by Mary L. Booth, 1867, 2 vols.

"Especial care has been taken to collect the incidents of the Revolution, in which the city bore so prominent a part. . . . In this the writer begs leave to acknowledge the kindness of several distinguished citizens, lineal descendants of our oldest families, who have furnished valuable documents and information."—*Author's Preface.*

Civil List and Forms of Government of the Colony and State of New York, by S. C. Hutchins, 1868.

Battle of Long Island, by Thomas W. Field (Long Island Historical Society Memoirs, vol. ii), 1869.

History of New York City, by William L. Stone, 1872.

The author had special advantages in having access to unpublished manuscripts of his father consisting of conversations with such prominent men as Aaron Burr, Chancellor Livingston, John Jay, Robert Morris, Nicholas Bayard, and others. The book also contains several contributions of special value: The Narration of the Grand Erie Canal Celebration; An Account of the Federal Procession in Honor of the Adoption of the Federal Constitution in 1788; and Washington's Reception and Inaugural Ball in 1789, all by the author's father; and Reminiscences of New York City, by Gulian C. Verplanck. In 1872 these publications had already become very rare.

History of the City of New York, by Mrs. Martha J. Lamb, 1877, 2 vols. (See History of the City of New York, by Mrs. Burton Harrison.)

A comprehensive work, full of interesting details and much genealogical information.

The Campaign of 1776 around New York and Brooklyn, by Henry P. Johnston (Long Island Historical Society Memoirs, vol. iii), 1878.

Harlem, Its Origin and Early Annals, prefaced by Home Scenes in the Fatherlands, by James Riker, 1881.

History of New York City, embracing an Outline Sketch of Events from 1609 to 1830 and a Full Account of its Development from 1830 to 1884, by Benson J. Lossing, 1884, 2 vols.

"A brief history of the city from the date of its foundation until 1830, when the impetus which produced its most marvelous development began to be powerfully felt. This work is essentially a *social* history."—*Author's Preface.*

Colonial New York; Philip Schuyler and his Family, by George W. Schuyler, 1885, 2 vols.

A family history containing much general information.

New York; the Planting and Growth of the Empire State, by Ellis H. Roberts (American Commonwealth Series), 1887–'89, 2 vols.

New York in the Revolution (New York State Archives, vol. i), by Berthold Fernow, 1887. (Contains list of officers of the New York line, the navy, etc.)

The Empire State, a Compendious History of the Commonwealth of New York, by Benson J. Lossing, 1888.

The Story of New York (Story of the States Series), by Elbridge S. Brooks, 1888.

New York City and Vicinity during the War of 1812–'15, by R. S. Guernsey, 1889 and 1895, 2 vols.

Old New York, a Journal relating to the History and Antiquities of New York City, edited by W. W. Pasko, 1890–'91, 2 vols.

New York in the War of the Rebellion, compiled by Frederick Phisterer, 1890.

The Memorial History of the City of New York, edited by James Grant Wilson, 1892, 4 vols.

"A single, complete, and exhaustive work."

Greater New York: Writings and Addresses by Andrew H. Green, 1893.

The Story of the City of New York (Great Cities of the Republic Series), by Charles Burr Todd, 1895.

New York (Historic Towns Series), by Theodore Roosevelt, 1895.

A sketch of the workings of the town's social, commercial, and political life, at successive periods, and of the causes that changed a little Dutch hamlet into a huge American city. Also, an outline of the steps by which the city obtained a free political life, giving prominence to the remarkable and ever-varying conditions caused by the many race elements that have repeatedly changed the character of the population.

History of the City of New York, by Mrs. Burton Harrison (forming an additional chapter to Mrs. Martha J. Lamb's History of the City of New York), 1896.

The Records of New Amsterdam from 1653 to 1674, edited by Berthold Fernow, 1897, 7 vols.

The American Metropolis from Knickerbocker Days to the Present Time, by Frank Moss, 1897, 3 vols.

"A reminiscent, observant, reflective journey on historical lines."

The Battle of Harlem Heights, September 16, 1776, by Henry P. Johnston, 1897.

This work brings together in convenient form for local reference all the authorities, shows that the battle was fought from the *west* and not the *east* of Morningside Heights, and introduces new details.

New York in the Revolution as Colony and State, by James A. Roberts, Comptroller, 1898.

Contains a list of 43,645 men who enlisted from New York State and served in the Revolutionary War.

Historic New York (Half Moon papers), edited by Maud Wilder Goodwin, Alice Carrington Royce, and Ruth Putnam, 1898, 2 vols.

Greater New York, Its Government, Financial Institutions, Transportation Facilities and Chronology. Maps. The Evening Post Publishing Company, 1898.

Historic Towns of the Middle States, edited by Lyman P. Powell (New York City by Joseph B. Gilder), 1899.

A Brief History of the City of New York, by Charles B. Todd, 1899.

The Dutch and Quaker Colonies of America, by John Fiske, 1899, 2 vols.

Historical Index to the Manuals of the Corporation of the City of New York (Valentine's Manuals), 1841 to 1870, 2,325 references, 1900.

The New Metropolis. Memorable Events of Three Centuries (1600–1900). From the Island of Mana-ha-ta to Greater New York at the Close of the Nineteenth Century. D. Appleton and Company, 1 vol., and portfolios.

History of New York State, by William Reed Prentice, 1900.

DESCRIPTIVE AND REMINISCENT WORKS

Anthology of New Netherland, or Translations from the Early Dutch Poets of New York, by Henry C. Murphy, 1865.

A Brief Description of New York, formerly called New Netherlands, by Daniel Denton.

Written in 1670, this was the first printed description in English of the country now forming New York and New Jersey. Reprinted in Gowan's Bibliotheca Americana, vol. i.

Journal of a Voyage to New York and a Tour in Several of the American Colonies in 1679–'80, by Jasper Dankers and Peter Sluyter, translated by Henry C. Murphy (Long Island Historical Society Memoirs), 1867.

A Description of the Province and City of New York, with Plans of the City and Several Forts as they existed in the Year 1695, by the Rev. John Miller, 1843.

Private Journal kept by Madam Knight of a Journey from Boston to New York in the Year 1704, 1825.

Memoirs of an American Lady, with Sketches of Manners and Scenes in America as they existed Previous to the Revolution, by Mrs. Anne Grant, first published in 1808; republished in 1876.

Poems relating to the American Revolution, by Philip Freneau (written at the time), 1865.

Prison Ship Martyr; Captain Jabez Fitch's Diary. A Narrative of the Treatment with which the American Prisoners were used who were taken by the British and Hessian Troops on Long Island, York Island, etc., 1776.

Forty Years' Residence in America, Fifty Years' Reminiscences of New York (including Tales of the Sugar-House Prison in Liberty Street, the Yellow Fever from 1798 to 1822, and Anecdotes of the Revolution), and Laurie Todd, by Grant Thorburn, 1834, 1845, and 1852, 3 vols.

The Pictorial Field Book of the Revolution, by Benson J. Lossing, 1855, 2 vols.

The City of New York in the Year of Washington's Inauguration, 1789, by Thomas E. V. Smith, 1889.

The First American; his Homes and his Households, by Leila Herbert, 1900 (chapter ii, In New York).

Old New York, or Reminiscences of the Past Sixty Years, a Discourse delivered before the New York Historical Society, November 17, 1857, by John W. Francis, 1866.

The Pictorial Field Book of the War of 1812, by Benson J. Lossing, 1869.

Reminiscences of an Octogenarian of the City of New York (1816–'60), by Charles H. Haswell, 1896.

The Picture of New York and Stranger's Guide to the Commercial Metropolis, by Andrew T. Goodrich, 1828.

The Diary of Philip Hone, 1828–'51, edited by Bayard Tuckerman, 1889, 2 vols.

Historic Tales of Olden Time concerning the Early Settlement and Advancement of New York City and State, by John F. Watson, 1832.

The Old Merchants of New York City, by J. L. Scoville, 1862, 5 vols.

The Market Book, a History of the Public Markets in the City of New York from its First Settlement to the Present Time, by Thomas F. Devoe, 1862.

Old New York from the Battery to Bloomingdale, etchings by Eliza Greatorex, text by M. Despard, 1875.

Last Days of Knickerbocker Life in New York, by Abram C. Dayton, 1882.

A Tour Around New York, by Felix Oldboy (John Flavel Mines), 1893.

In Old New York, by Thomas A. Janvier, 1894.

Colonial Days in Old New York, by Alice Morse Earle, 1896.

Some Colonial Homesteads and their Stories, by Marion Harland (Jumel Mansion, p. 276), 1897.

Home Life in Colonial Days, by Alice Morse Earle, 1898.

The Goede Vrow of Mana-ha-ta, 1609–1760, by Mrs. John King Van Rensselaer, 1898.

Nooks and Corners of New York, by Charles Hemstreet, 1899.

Stage Coach and Tavern Days, by Alice Morse Earle, 1900.

Early New York Houses, with Historical Genealogical Notes, by W. S. Pelletreau, 1900.

BIOGRAPHIES

John Jacob Astor, by Freeman Hunt (Lives of American Merchants), 1858; by James Parton (Famous Americans of Recent Times), 1867.

John James Audubon, by Samuel Smiles, 1860; by his Widow, 1869.

James Gordon Bennett, by James Parton (Famous Americans of Recent Times), 1867.

William Cullen Bryant, by A. J. Symington, 1880; by Parke Godwin, 1883, 2 vols.; by John Bigelow (American Men of Letters Series), 1890. Also Bryant and his Friends, by James Grant Wilson, 1886.

Aaron Burr, by Samuel L. Knapp, 1835; by James Parton, 1858; by H. C. Mervin (Beacon Biographies), 1899.

De Witt Clinton, by J. Renwick, 1840; by William W. Campbell, 1849.

Public Papers of George Clinton, First Governor of New York, 1777–'95, 1801–'04. With an Introduction by Hugh Hastings, State Historian. Published by the State of New York, 1899, 3 vols. Also article by W. L. Stone (Magazine of American History, vol. iii, 329).

James Fenimore Cooper, by Thomas P. Lounsbury (American Men of Letters Series), 1884; by Susan Fenimore Cooper (Atlantic Monthly, vol. lix, 199; vol. lx, 474); by W. B. S. Clymer (Beacon Biographies), 1900.

Peter Cooper, by Lloyd Bryce (North American Review, vol. clii, 410).

Dongan, the Great Colonial Governor, by P. F. Dealy (Magazine of American History, vol. viii, 106).

Robert Fulton, by James Renwick (Sparks's Biographies), 1838; by Thomas W. Knox, 1886; by Robert H. Thurston (Makers of America Series), 1891.

Horace Greeley, by James Parton, 1869; by L. V. Reavis, 1872; by L. D. Ingersoll, 1874; by Francis Nicoll Zabriskie, 1890.

Nathan Hale, by I. W. Stuart, 1856. The Two Spies (Hale and André), by Benson J. Lossing, 1866.

Alexander Hamilton, by his son, John C. Hamilton, 1834, 2 vols.; by John T. Morse, Jr., 1876, 2 vols.; by George Shea, 1879; by Henry Cabot Lodge (American Statesmen Series), 1882; by William Graham Sumner (Makers of America Series), 1890.

Henry Hudson, by Henry R. Cleveland (Sparks's Biographies), 1838; by John Meredith Read, Jr., 1866.

Washington Irving, by his nephew, Pierre M. Irving, 1863, 4 vols.; by Charles Dudley Warner (American Men of Letters Series), 1884. (See also Bryant and his Friends, by James Grant Wilson, 1886.)

John Jay, by his son, William Jay, 1833, 2 vols.; by William Whitelock, 1887; by George Pellew (American Statesmen Series), 1890.

John Lamb, by Isaac Q. Leake, 1850.

Jacob Leisler, by Charles F. Hoffman (Sparks's Biographies, second series), 1844.

Richard Montgomery, by John Armstrong (Sparks's Biographies), 1834; by Major-General George W. Cullum (Magazine of American History, vol. ii, 273).

Gouverneur Morris, by Jared Sparks, 1832, 3 vols.; by Theodore Roosevelt (American Statesmen Series), 1888.

Samuel F. B. Morse, by Samuel I. Prime, 1875.

William Smith, the Historian, by Maturin L. Delafield (Magazine of American History, vol. vi, 418).

Peter Stuyvesant, by John S. C. Abbott, 1873; by Bayard Tuckerman (Makers of America Series), 1893.

Public Papers of Daniel D. Tompkins, Governor of New York, 1807–'17, with an Introduction by Hugh Hastings, State Historian. Published by the State of New York, 1898.

Cornelius Vanderbilt, by James Parton (Famous Americans of Recent Times), 1867.

George Washington, by John Marshall (compiled under the inspection of Bushrod Washington from original papers bequeathed to the latter by his deceased relative), 1832, 2 vols.; by Washington Irving, 1855, 5 vols.; by Paul Leicester Ford, 1896; by Worthington Chauncey Ford, 1900, 2 vols.

Marinus Willett, a Narrative of the Military Actions of, by his son, William M. Willett, 1831.

Thomas Willett, First Mayor of New York, by Dr. Charles W. Parsons (Magazine of American History, vol. xvii, 233).

Appletons' Cyclopædia of American Biography, edited by James Grant Wilson and John Fiske, 1887, 6 vols.

Encyclopædia of Contemporary Biography of New York, 1878, 6 vols.

The National Cyclopædia of American Biography, 1898–'99, 9 vols.

The following references, arranged in chronological order, dealing with the city's condition at different periods of its development, may also prove useful:

New York in 1664, Harper's Magazine, ix, 452; xxv, 308.

New York in 1664–'68, Valentine's Manual, 1863, 623.

New York in 1700, Valentine's Manual, 1854, 555.

New York in 1737, Valentine's Manual, 1870, 900.

New York in 1748, Valentine's Manual, 1858, 526; 1869, 837.
New York in 1750, Valentine's Manual, 1858, 527.
New York in 1753, Valentine's Manual, 1869, 755.
New York in 1756, Pasko's Old New York, ii, 36.
New York in 1757, Pasko's Old New York, ii, 166.
New York in 1770, Historical Magazine, v, 244; xxi, 31.
New York in 1772, Magazine of American History, ii, 748; xxiii, 412.
New York in 1776, Valentine's Manual, 1862, 652; Historical Magazine, xiv, 305.
New York in 1777–'83, Valentine's Manual, 1863, 634.
New York in 1783–'89, Magazine of American History, xxix, 305.
New York in 1786, Historical Magazine, xii, 279.
New York in 1788, Historical Magazine, xv, 183.
New York during the Inauguration of Washington, Century Magazine, xv, 850; Harper's Magazine, lxxviii, 671.
New York in 1805, Pasko's Old New York, i, 157.
New York in 1806, Valentine's Manual, 1868, 828.
New York in 1806–'7, Valentine's Manual, 1857, 417; 1858, 606.
New York in 1807, Valentine's Manual, 1859, 564.
New York in 1807–'8, Valentine's Manual, 1870, 847.
New York in 1808–'21, Valentine's Manual, 1864, 847.
New York in 1809, Magazine of American History, iii, 689.
New York in 1857, Valentine's Manual, 1857, 415, 440.

FICTION

A History of New York from the Beginning of the World to the End of the Dutch Dynasty. By Diedrich Knickerbocker (Washington Irving), 1809.
First of the Knickerbockers, a Tale of 1673. Introduces Peter Stuyvesant and Governor Lovelace. By P. H. Myer, 1848.
Anneke, a Story of New Amsterdam, by Elizabeth W. Champney.
Patroon Van Volkenberg, a Tale of Old Manhattan in the Year 1686. By Henry Thew Stephen, 1900.
In Leisler's Times, an Historical Story of Knickerbocker New York (1690). By E. S. Brooks, 1886.
The Begum's Daughter. Leisler's time. Introduces Leisler, Bayard, Philipse, and Van Courtlandt. By Edwin Lassetter Bynner, 1890.
Old New York, or Democracy in 1689, a Tragedy in Five Acts.

Introduces Leisler, Milburn, Slaughter, Schuyler, Livingston, and other prominent men of the day. By Mrs. E. Oakes Smith, 1853.

Beyond the City Gates. Time, 1700. Introduces Lord Bellomont, and deals with the buccaneer period. By Augusta Campbell Watson, 1897.

The Water Witch, a story of the methods employed to smuggle goods into New York in Cornbury's time (1702–'08), showing the latter's corrupt methods. By J. Fenimore Cooper, 1874.

Free to Serve. Life and Fashions of Old New York. Introducing Governor Cornbury (1702–'08), who had a curious habit of dressing in women's clothes. By E. Rayner, 1897.

In Old New York. Time of Governor Cosby (1732–'36) and Zenger. By Wilson Barrett and Elwyn Barron, 1900.

The Dutchman's Fireside. Time of the French and Indian War. By James K. Paulding, 1868.

A Soldier of Manhattan. Time of the French and Indian War. Introduces the Earl of Loudon, General Abercrombie, and General Wolfe. Depicts New York fashions. By Joseph A. Altsheler, 1897.

Satanstoe, a picture of social customs and a description of prominent places of New York in the year 1750. By J. Fenimore Cooper.

Chainbearer. This work is in a certain sense a sequel to Satanstoe. It deals with the Antirent Agitation. By J. Fenimore Cooper, 1859.

A Bow of Orange Ribbon. New York during the Stamp Act Troubles, introducing patriot Marinus Willett. By Amelia E. Barr, 1886.

Philip Winwood, a Sketch of the Domestic History of an American Captain in the War of Independence, Embracing Events that occurred between and during the Years 1763 and 1786 in New York and London. By Robert Neilson Stephens, 1900.

For King or Country, a Story of the American Revolution. Scene, New York in 1775. Describes the Sugarhouse Prison and introduces Washington and Howe. By James Barnes, 1896.

Three Colonial Boys, a Story of the Times of 1776. By Everett T. Tomlinson, 1895.

In the Hands of the Redcoats, a Story of the Jersey Prisonship. by Everett T. Tomlinson, 1900.

Wolfert's Roost, a story of Revolutionary times, dealing with the debatable or neutral ground that lay between the British, who held New York, and the Americans in the Highlands, and was harried by friend and foe alike. By Washington Irving, 1865.

The Spy, a story of the neutral territory. Time, 1780. By J. Fenimore Cooper.

The Fortune of War. A graphic picture of New York during the Revolution, describing persons and events connected with the period when the city was in the possession of the British. By Elizabeth N. Barrow, 1900.

A Colonial Free Lance. Time, 1778. Introduces Sir Henry Clinton. By Chauncey C. Hotchkiss, 1897.

The Continental Dragoon, a Romance of the Philipse Manor House in 1778, describing experiences in the Neutral Territory. By Robert Neilson Stephens, 1898.

The Maid of Maiden Lane, a Sequel to the Bow of Orange Ribbon. Time, directly after the Revolution. Introduces Washington and Lady Washington. By Amelia E. Barr, 1900.

Trinity Bells. Time, 1798. A Story of Algerian Piracy and Ransom. By Amelia E. Barr, 1899.

Story of a New York House. Time, 1807. Reference to the building of the present City Hall. By H. C. Bunner, 1887.

A Romance of Old New York. Introduces Aaron Burr. By Edgar Fawcett, 1897.

A Little Colonial Dame. By Mrs. A. C. Sage.

A Little Girl in Old New York. Time, 1843. By Amanda Douglas, 1896.

The Battle of New York. Draft Riots of 1863. By W. O. Stoddard, 1892.

An Original Belle. Draft Riots of 1863. By E. P. Roe, 1885.

A New York Family. Tweed ring exposure. By Edgar Fawcett, 1891.

The Honorable Peter Stirling. Modern political life. By Paul Leicester Ford, 1897.

INDEX

Abingdon Square, 213.
Andros, Sir Edmund, 48.
Apthorpe House, 113.
Astor, John Jacob, 169.
Audubon, John J., 129.

Battery Park, 13; Battery, 57.
Beekman House, 113.
Bellomont, Lord, 60, 62.
Bennett, James Gordon, 193.
Blockhouses, 178, 180, 183.
Board of Education, new hall of, 175.
Boston, punishment of, 92.
Bowling Green, 1, 13; view of, in 1830, 234.
Bradford, William, 56; tablets, 76, 77; tombstone, 229.
Broad Street, view of, 20.
Broadway, 8; view of, 1831, 188.
Brooklyn Bridge, 206.
Burr, Aaron, 111, 158, 160.

Cable, laying of, 197.
Cabot, 11.
Canada, capture of, 70.
Canal-boat village, 74, 185.
Canal, Erie, 182.
Castle Garden, 235.
Central Park, laying out of, 197.
Chamber of Commerce, 246.
Chelsea Square, 211.
Christmas, 40.
Churches, early, 56, 101.
Cincinnati, Society of the, 163.
City Hall, first, 16, 17; second, 58; present, 175, 253, 254.
Clinton, De Witt, 172; statue of, 233.
Collect Pond, 36, 164, 219.
Columbia University, tablet, 120; view of library, 122; inscription, 123.
Columbus Column, 250.
Common, 82, 88, 89, 253.
Constitutional Convention, 146.
Constitution, centennial anniversary of the adoption of, 246.
Continental Congress, 103.
Cooper, Peter, 172, 197, 198.
Cooper Union, view of, 171.
Cornbury, 69.
Cosby, William, 67.
Croton Aqueduct, 190.
Crystal Palace, 196.
Cunningham, 118, 135, 136.

Dana, Charles A., 194, 195.
Daughters of the American Revolution, 88.
Declaration of Independence, tablet; 97, 98, 104.
Defenses, 1776, 104, 105; 1812, 176.
Defenses, McGowan's Pass, 113.

De Peyster, Abraham, statue of, 78.
Discovery of America, four hundredth anniversary of, 247.
Dongan charter, 48.
Dongan, Thomas, 48.
Dutch: amusements, holidays, 40, 41; characteristics of, 5; flag, 12; ways, 20.

East India Company, 4.
East River, 10.
English governors, character of, 69.
English right to take New Amsterdam, 42.
Epidemics, 186.
Ericsson, Captain, 239.
Erie Canal, 182.
Evacuation by the British, 140; centennial anniversary, 244.
Exchange Court, statues: Hudson, Stuyvesant, 21; Wolfe, Clinton, 233.

Federalists, 146.
Field, Cyrus W., 197.
Fire Department, 205, 207.
Fires: 1776, 117; 1778, 117; 1835, 189; tablet, 190.
Fletcher, Benjamin, 52.
Flour bolting, 47.
Forts: Amsterdam, 11, 12, 79; George, 70, 141; Clinton, 177–179, 181; Fish, 177, 179; Laight, 182; Tryon, 135; Washington, 133, 134.
Fraunces's Tavern, 143, 144; view of, 240; tablet, 241.
French and Indian War, 69.
Freneau, Philip, 137.
Fulton, Robert, 163.

Gas, introduction of, 187.
George III, 71, 89–91, 98, 99, 102.
Golden Hill, battle of, 85; tablet, 87.
Gomez, Stephen, 4.
Gramercy Park, 217; tablet, 218.
Grant's Tomb, 201.
Greater New York, 208, 209.
Greeley, Horace, 192, 252.
Green, Andrew H., 208.
Greenwich village, 6, 187, 213.

Hale, Nathan, 117; statue of, 119.
Hall of Records, 89, 252.
Hamilton, Alexander, 89, 96, 107, 111, 146, 160–162, 227.
Hamilton, Andrew, 68.
Hamilton Grange, 124; view of, 126; trees, 127.
Harlem, 44.
Harlem Heights, battle of, 114; view of battle ground, 116; tablet, 120.
Hearts of Oak, 95.
Herald, the New York, 193.
Holland Society, 9.
Howe, General, 104.
Hudson, Henry, 3; statue of, 21.
Hudson Park, view of, 216.

Indians, 5, 6, 32, 38, 52.
Ingoldsby, Richard, 50.
Inscriptions: Library, Columbia University, 123; Hamilton's tomb, 229; Pitt's statue, 90; Revolutionary prisoners, Trinity churchyard, 230; Washington's inauguration, 242; statue of Washington, Riverside, 245.
Irving, Washington, 249.

James II, 49.
Jay, John, 102, 146, 147.
Jeannette Park, 75.
Jersey prison ship, 137, 138.

Jewish burial grounds, old, 39, 218.
Jumel Mansion, 130 ; tablet, 133.

Kidd, Captain William, 61.
Kieft, William, 23.
King George, statue of, 89 ; tablet, 98 ; destruction of statue, 89.
King's College, 71.
Kingsley, William C., 206.
Kip's Bay skirmish, 110.
Knowlton, Colonel Thomas, 114 ; tablets, 120, 128.
Knox, General, 106.

Lee, Charles, 106.
Leisler, Jacob, 50 ; execution of, 51.
Leitch, Andrew, 114 ; tablets, 120, 128.
Lexington, battle of, news received in New York, 92.
Liberty Boys, 92, 96.
Liberty of the press, 67.
Liberty-pole troubles, 84 ; tablet, 88.
Livingston, Robert R., 97, 152, 165, 223.
Long Island, battle of, 107.
Lovelace, Francis, 44.

McGowan, Andrew, patriotic act of, 112.
McGowan's Pass, 112, 140, 177.
Mall, the, 72.
Manetta Creek, 6.
Manhattan Island, discovery of, 4 ; origin of name, 5 ; shape of, 7 ; sale of, 12.
Maps : 1642, 35 ; 1664, 43 ; 1695, 53 ; 1728, 66 ; 1814, 177.
Milestones, 30, 31, 128.
Minuit, Peter, 11, 12, 22.
Montcalm, 69.
Montgomery, General, 223, 224.
Moore, Clement C., 212.
Morse, S. F. B., 195 ; tablet, 196.
Mount St. Vincent, 113.

Negro plots, 64.
New Amsterdam, captured by the English, 27 ; first view of, 27 ; description of, 38.
New-Englanders, 18.
New jail, 136.
Newspapers, cheap, 192.
Newspapers, early, 65 ; tablet, 76.
New Year's day, 40, 153.
New York adopts Constitution, 148.
New York Directory, first, 158.
New York during the civil war, 198.
New York Historical Society, 76.
New York, name changed to, 44.
New York, name suggests York, England, 49.
New York, in 1642, 35 ; in 1667, 45 ; captured by the Dutch, 46 ; in 1750–'60, 71, 72 ; in 1790, 156 ; in War of 1812, 176.
New York Society Library, 139.
Nicolls, Captain, 26, 44.
Night watch, 57.
Non-importation agreement, 81 ; tablet, 82.
North River, 10.

Old mansion, State Street, view of, 236.
Osborne, 69.

Paas, 41.
Paine, Thomas, 97.
Parade to aid adoption of the Constitution, 147.
Parks, 219.
Patroons, 22.
Pirates, 59.
Pitt, William, 89 ; inscription, 90, 102.

Point of Rocks, 124; view of, 125.
Population, 1695, 52; character of, 1765, 80.
Postal service begun, 44.
Postman, the first, 29.
Post office, old, tablet, 100; 101.
Printing, 56; tablets, 76, 77.
Prisoners, 135, 230, 231.
Prison ships, 137.
Prison-ship martyrs, burial of, 156.
Protestant Theological Seminary 211; view of, 213.
Public-school system, 173.
Putnam, General, 106, 111.

Railroad, New York to San Francisco, 198.
Raymond, Henry J., 194.
Religious persecution, 64.
Revolution, end of the, 140.
Richmond Hill, 107, 113, 214.
Riots, 202–205.

St. John's Church, 220.
St. Mark's Church, 27.
St. Nicholas day, 41.
St. Paul's inauguration ceremonies, 152; view of, 188, 221.
Schools, 17; view of old school, 173; view of modern school, 174.
Seal, 47.
Seventh Regiment, departure of, 199; tablet, 200.
Slavery, 63.
Sloughter, Henry, 50.
Smuggling, 62.
Sons of Liberty, 78; tablets, 87, 88, 91.
Sons of the Revolution, 87.
Stamp Act, 73, 80, 84.
Statue of George III, destruction of, 98; view of, 99.
Statue of Liberty, 237, 238.
Statue of Pitt, mutilated, 98.
Steamboat, first, 165; view of, 166.
Street Commission, 1807, 176.
Street lighting, 57.
Stuyvesant, Peter, town house, 15; character, 16; last director-general, 23; portrait, 24; country house, 26; tomb, 27; inscription on tomb, 29; pear tree, 31, 33.
Sugar-house prison, 136, 251.
Sullivan, General, 106.
Sun, The New York, 51, 193.

Tablets: *Dutch Period.*—First City Hall, 16; first habitations, 9; Fort Amsterdam, 11; Stuyvesant pear tree, 32; Stuyvesant's tomb, 29.
Early English Period.—First newspaper, 76; first printing-press, 77.
Pre-Revolutionary Period.—Golden Hill, battle of, 87; Liberty-pole conflicts, 88; non-importation agreement, 82; Willett's patriotic act, 93.
Revolutionary Period.—Declaration of Independence, reading of, 97; Fraunces's tavern, 241; Harlem Heights, battle of, 120; Jumel Mansion (Washington's headquarters), 133; Kennedy House (reference to destruction of King George's statue), 98; Knowlton and Leitch, 128; meeting of Washington and Putnam, 112; Middle Dutch Church (used as a Revolutionary prison), 100; Revolutionary soldiers and sailors (Dutch Collegiate Church), 231; Washington's arrival in New York on his way to Boston to take command of the army, 103.

Independence, Early Period.— Washington's first residence, 251.
Modern Period. — Ericsson statue, 239; fire, 1835, 190; graduates of College of the City of New York lost in the civil war 202; Gramercy Park, 218; Hudson Park, 217; Morse, 196; Seventh Regiment, site of organization, 200; underground railway, 256; Washington, centennial anniversary of death of, 222; Washington, centennial anniversary of inauguration of, 221.
Tammany Society, 154.
Tea Party, New York, 90.
Telegraph, invention of the, 195.
Theater in Nassau Street, 72.
Times, The New York, 194.
Tribune, The New York, 194.
Trinity, 8, 56, 72, 225, 226, 228.
Trinity Cemetery, One Hundred and Fifty-third Street, 128.
Tryon, William, 103.

Van Cortlandt family, 19.
Vanderbilt, Cornelius, 167.
Van Rensselaer, Killian, 23.
Van Twiller, Wouter, 23.
Verrazano, John, 4.

Wall and water gate, illustrated, 18.
Wall Street in 1789, 151.
Wampum, 38.
Washington Arch, 248.
Washington, Declaration of Independence read in presence of, 97; arrival in New York, 103; headquarters, Richmond Hill, 107; at Kip's Bay, 110; meets Putnam, 111; battle of Harlem Heights, 120; headquarters in Jumel Mansion, 133; farewell to his officers, Fraunces's Tavern, 144; chosen President, 148; arrival in New York, 148; house in Cherry Street, 149; inauguration, 150; grand reception, 154; moves to 39 Broadway, 154; birthday, 154; first President of Society of the Cincinnati, 163; farewell to his officers, 241; centennial anniversary of inauguration of, 221; centennial anniversary of death of, 222; statues of, 243, 245; view of Cherry Street residence, 251.
Willett, Marinus, tablet, 93; patriotic act, 94.
William and Mary, 50.
Wolfe, 70; statue of, 233.

Zenger, John Peter, 65.

THE END